MW00512635

Raspberry
JUSTICE

MAC BRAND

Chapter 1

"**M**arlowe, I'm so glad to see you," Adam said, getting up from one of the bar seats. "Thanks for coming on such unforgivably short notice. I do however think you'll be fascinated by the discussion."

After for all intents and purposes demanding that I come to this meeting, he better be extremely nice to me. Seriously, who cares about *Candide*? Virtually no one.

No one else was at the bar at Harlech Gate Inn main dining room. Extending his hand to shake hers, Adam welcomed her with the broadest smile. Only a few luncheon diners remained. The hostess was busy clearing some tables. The dining room was basically quiet.

"I'm flattered to have been invited to an Anglesey meeting, Adam. Thank you."

"You've been on our radar for some time now. The society is slow to move on things, so it's taken us several months to invite you. And here you are. We're all thrilled you accepted our invitation."

"How lovely, though I'm not sure I deserve it."

Smooth as silk, isn't he, Marlowe, she asked herself as she smiled her own broadest possible smile. What does that mean, "on our radar." I don't want to be on anybody's radar, well, maybe *Adam's* radar would be good. Not sure I'd have to debate about that one for long. Let's not get ahead of ourselves here. You hardly even know the guy. Sit and stay, Marlowe.

"It's just one o'clock. The others will be here in just a minute. If you'll follow me please we can go the meeting room directly. We can make introductions there."

It was five of one when she had pulled into the parking lot at the historic Harlech Gate Inn. Thankfully she was early. Having just left Wynne Capital with the warm, bathing Tuesday afternoon sunlight hitting her face through her 911 open sunroof, she started to relax, to be relieved of the worry of not being good enough to be included in this highly regarded society. It was one of those gorgeous, brilliantly sunny days in mid-May in the exquisite western suburb of Philadelphia called the Main Line. Of course Marlowe being Marlowe, as she had proceeded out Lancaster Avenue toward Harlech her concerns about Anglesey weren't going to stop just because the sun was out.

If she were right about Anglesey, this was an intellectual, cultured group. She supposed any number of more accomplished people would qualify for an invitation. So why her. Not that she didn't want to go. More puzzling was she'd just gotten the invitation yesterday to attend. Why so quick. And why did Adam follow up with her this morning to confirm she'd be there. It seemed unnecessary. How pressing an issue could Voltaire's novel *Candide* be all these centuries later?

"Who are the others, Adam? Anyone I might know?"

"Well I'm pretty sure you haven't met them. You'll likely know who they are."

"Okay, sounds good, looking forward to it!" Know who they are? Not sure I know anyone at all who's recently or even ever read *Candide*. Am I going to feel embarrassed?

Comfortable with any *Candide* discussion, on her way to Harlech Marlowe's attention had focused on something much more interesting. Adam. He was one of those men who would look as stunning in any one of his dark gray suits as a Penn lacrosse jersey. He could be standing in swirling wind and his movie-star brown hair would be perfect. She was intrigued. She was more than intrigued. When she'd received the invitation, her heart skipped more than a beat. She knew Adam only casually. She definitely liked what she saw. She was definitely happy her ex, Stirling Parker, was in the past.

Wanting one final assurance she looked good for the meeting, she'd taken the time to run into the ladies room just off the foyer. Having been to Harlech before she knew there was a full-length mirror there. Observing her reflection for just a few seconds she believed she looked professional yet elegant in her Yves St. Lauren pewter-gray, pin-stripe suit with her skirt one inch above her knees, parchment-colored silk tank, her pearls, plus her three inch cranberry-colored pumps to go with her cranberry bag. It helped of course that Marlowe was in perfect shape. She wore a size six. Her shoulder-length, gently curled, natural blond hair with abundant red natural highlights fell softly on her shoulders. Wearing light liner and mascara made her green eyes the central part of her classically proportioned, porcelain face. She hoped she wasn't overdressed. Still, suppose the others are wearing jeans and t-shirts.

Adam turned away from the bar area heading toward the back of the dining room.

As Marlowe turned to follow him, the muted TV screen behind the bar caught her attention. The local news was on. In the background behind the reporter she guessed she saw what looked like an enormous mansion. It looked vaguely familiar. The tranquil Duffield Manor possibly. If it were Duffield, it would be an unlikely place for any sort of breaking news. Did the squirrels and chipmunks go on strike? Are the geese chasing the cows around the pasture again? Are the horses picketing for more carrots and softer straw? Still a bit anxious about meeting everyone, Marlowe managed to squeak out a tiny grin at the wild animal mayhem that may be breaking news at Duffield. No time to watch more now though.

Adam appeared to be heading toward what might be a door in the far corner of the dining room. Oddly it was wallpapered over with no moldings. If you hadn't known it was there, you'd never see it. To Marlowe's surprise, Adam pushed on it. It opened. They went through, Marlowe following Adam.

"Wow it's dark in here. Are we going in the right direction, Adam?"

She found herself following him in a dimly lit, unpainted, narrow corridor. In a few steps they came to a steep set of plain pine stairs. Because she was wearing three-inch heels, as skilled as she was in such matters, Marlowe decided she should have a firm grasp on the wooden handrail. She and Adam went down, fortunately for Marlowe, uneventfully.

She assumed they were taking a back staircase down to a meeting room. The old looking solid pine door at the bottom of the stairs was slightly ajar. Adam pushed it all the way open as it scraped along the cracked dirty gray cement floor. What she found was no handsome hallway or finished lower level of meeting rooms. She was in an ancient looking basement. She looked behind her and back up the stairs.

The others weren't there.

Chapter 2

Marlowe peered down the hallway past Adam. Where exactly was she. She knew Harlech Gate Inn was a sprawling building with several additions constructed around the historic inn, said to have been a house dating back to the sixteen hundreds. Many people believed a secret section of the basement was part of the Underground Railroad. Listed on the National Register of Historic Places, the inn had large dark-wood exposed beams, hardwood floors, and antique lighting fixtures upstairs in the public area. Marlowe found herself in definitely a basement, not a hall to some finished area. She figured her suit, pearls and heels might be a tad too much for the basement. She was more surprised than worried.

It was an extended building so eventually they would have to reach the meeting room. She grinned at her immediate notion that the meeting room was going to be in the mechanical room. They'd be sitting on produce crates. So much for the supposedly elite Anglesey Philosophical Society. Marlowe would make it her business to spread the word that members never spoke about their society because they were embarrassed. They knew people assumed they were this aloof group. They should have been called the Orange Crate Society with discussions focused on the basest reality shows' characters.

Adam slowed a little and turned his shoulders around to talk to Marlowe as he kept walking.

"Our meeting room is down this corridor, apologies for the lack of nice finishes down here. I'll show you to our private room, then go back to collect the others. They're chatting about how they want to handle the discussion of *Candide*. I'll only be gone a few minutes. Okay?"

How to *handle* the *Candide* discussion? I know I'm trying to be a somewhat cultured lady. This is, well, ridiculous. From Adam?

She searched his face for signs of something which might be inappropriate or even troublesome. It seemed like something wasn't right being down in a basement for a meeting.

"Ah, of course," she answered without betraying her uneasiness.

She didn't know why except she stayed four or five steps behind him as she followed Adam down the hallway, then into a narrower hallway. All the while she was thinking, he brings me to a dusty, tired, old basement, and wants to take me, he says, to a special room without some of the rest of the group. Not seeing anything which even looked like it might be an entry into any kind of real, proper meeting room, she fleetingly asked herself what she'd she gotten herself into. Though not really troubled, she wasn't exactly unconcerned either.

They passed by tidily stacked boxes of food, kitchen supplies, battered used kitchen equipment. Not finished, Adam led her through a maze of what looked like centuries-old passageways with dim, bare-bulb lighting. Roughhewn floor joists above of the restaurant plus a warren of old pipes and wires were not more than seven feet overhead. It occurred to Marlowe the one bright point in the trip through the passageways was there was absolutely no evidence of rodents. Considering everything else, that was a small comfort to Marlowe. Seeing no cobwebs either was icing on the cake.

At the end of the last passageway Adam halted at a glossy paneled door made of timeworn mahogany. The massive door, affixed to the frame with long, fancy-strap-iron hinges, had a heavy iron handle secured by an old brass lock. The surrounding wall hadn't been cleaned in years. The door looked like it belonged in some twelfth-century castle rather than in the basement of an old Bryn Mawr inn. She viewed it with equal parts shock and curiosity. Adam unlocked and opened the door. Stepping inside he flipped a switch to turn lights on. He motioned for Marlowe to enter.

With the modest of smiles she moved timidly to just inside the doorway. The early stages of a frown signaling her concern, she asked in a stronger than normal voice, "What is this place, Adam?"

Finding herself about to be alone in a striking thirty foot wide octagonal room she noticed all the walls were solid, no windows. No door other than the massive entry door.

With a quick smile, slightly cocking his head apparently at the question, he said, "It's the Anglesey meeting room."

"It is?" she said, her voice rising, not moving her head, without any fake smile, she looked from the room back to Adam.

"Please come in, Marlowe. I'll be back in about ten minutes. Please make yourself comfortable."

He left pulling the door closed behind him. Marlowe listened for the sound of Adam leaving or what might be a lock turning. All she got was total silence. It was just her and the room. She wondered why he'd closed the door.

"Holy cow, this is a whole other thing," she whispered to herself as she began looking around. The intricately patterned, coffered ceiling was constructed of what she judged might be dark old walnut. The walnut paneled wainscoting was similarly detailed. Above it was muted gold-colored moiré wallpaper. A pair of heavy looking, ornate sconces on each of the eight walls provided the light. An oil portrait hung on each wall with the exception of the walls with the door and the opposite wall. Four of the portraits were of men, two were of women. Marlowe studied each one. In their forties or fifties the portrait subjects were dressed in clothing in a style centuries old; their expressions were serious, not grim. Though she knew little about art, she judged the paintings as well as the frames to be extremely old. It appeared the portraits had been done at various times because while generally similar in look, the paint and the artistry of each was different as were the sizes and frames.

On the wall opposite the door was an ancient looking, obviously hand-drawn map in a simple gilt frame. Unlike the portraits it was covered with glass. Marlowe walked over to get a better look. It was dated in script, 1319, in the lower left corner.

"1319? That can't be," Marlowe mumbled as she examined it more closely.

It appeared to be a map of what looked vaguely like Wales, where she had visited with her parents when she was about seven. Questioning why a fourteenth century map was on the wall, not in some museum, her attention then focused on the carpeting. She was fascinated to see the one-foot high script "A's" woven in golden thread into a maroon plush wool carpet. "'A' for Anglesey...." she muttered.

Having strolled around looking from wall to wall examining the portraits and sconces, Marlowe began to concentrate on the obviously heavy, antique, octagonal, dark wooden table. Eight well-appointed, opulent, comfortable-looking black leather chairs were positioned precisely around it. Marlowe used both hands to pull one out. She guardedly sat in silence on the edge to await Adam's return.

Her self-doubts rolled right in to fill the time gap. Marlowe with her country past, had concerns she would not fit in on the Main Line, or she would always be seen as an outsider. Hers was neither a moneyed nor a privileged background. The only part of Marlowe's childhood she assumed might have been similar to that of the girls on the Main Line was the influence of her older brother. She was fully aware Skip managed to give her the skills which carried over for her to become a successful business woman, despite growing up in their little one-horse town.

Setting aside her self-doubts, refocusing on the Anglesey meeting room, her gaze rose to the ceiling, then the moiré, the A's in the carpeting, the fancy chairs, the map, the portraits, the seriousness of purpose of the room. It seemed so surreal. Beyond odd.

It was as if she were suddenly thrust into an assembly in some dominant, commanding, medieval castle. The lords exhibited solemn expressions, stood stiff with purpose, as though the decision were about to be rendered to send legions of knights forth on a three-year campaign against the rest of Europe. Tapping her feet in step with the knights, Marlowe started to imagine the thumping, steady cadence of detachments of men, spears forward, moving toward war.

Looking around the room she graduated from thinking the room was important, almost reverential to thinking it was way too much, over the top. She began to look at it as possibly the insane, absurd trappings of perhaps a lunatic fringe society. Nevertheless, her hands slightly nervously shaking, she swiftly saw the irony of her situation. She was in the exact room she wanted to be in. Yet she was questioning the core of the society she had been energized by such a short time ago. Feeling the pressure to gather herself together before Adam came back, she suddenly heard a woman's pleasant voice saying hello outside the door.

With one last tap she rose from her chair.

Chapter 3

Marlowe was privately embarrassed by her ruminations of a few moments earlier. She watched as the door opened. An attractive middle aged woman carrying an ornate silver tray of small pastries and a full crystal pitcher entered. Adam and three other people followed her in.

Though she had never met him, Marlowe recognized one of the men as Jack Danett, the inn's owner. Marlowe grinned, a mixture of a friendliness augmented by relief that in fact she hadn't been deposited in a dungeon.

She took a step forward to greet Adam's associates.

"Welcome, Marlowe. I'm Angela, Jack Danett's wife. I hope you'll enjoy some home-made goodies and iced tea during your meeting."

"How lovely, thank you, Angela."

Marlowe spoke warmly as if none of the notions of the last ten minutes had entered her mind. One thing she hadn't considered at any length was how many Anglesey members might be present. If pushed she'd have guessed at least ten. Marlowe, it turned out, was one of only five people at the meeting. She didn't know if that was good or bad.

She quickly noted with the exception of Adam the others were casually dressed. While she'd had no idea whom she would meet, she'd anticipated everyone would be dressed appropriately as a professional. She was mildly disappointed. That didn't last long. Quick introductions having been made, Adam poured ice tea for everyone in the glasses Angela had laid out on the table. Franny Barrett took the seat on Marlowe's right. She introduced herself as she passed the tray of pastries to the others who had also sat down.

"My name is Franny Barrett. Such a pleasure to meet you." Marlowe did a quick double take—she was taken by surprise. She was not expecting Franny Barrett to be at an Anglesey meeting. She didn't recognize her right away though she'd seen her in photographs. She was dressed in tight jeans, a white T-shirt, an off-white blazer and two-inch strappy, white summer wedges. She knew Franny was a highly regarded professor of nineteenth-century English literature at Adlington University in the nearby town of Wayne.

After Franny, Malik Beresford, sitting at Marlowe's left, welcomed Marlowe. Franny added he owned a string of apartment buildings from Washington DC to Toronto. Marlowe knew Jack Danett owned Harlech as well as three other local high-end restaurants.

Franny looked at Adam.

"Adam, I've never known you to be shy. I know you only met Marlowe briefly in the past, please tell her a bit about yourself."

Looking handsome in his navy business suit, gold and navy tie with a white button-down shirt Adam said, "I think Marlowe knows I'm a partner in the real estate law area with Hatherwood, LLP at One Liberty Place in Center City. I went to Penn undergrad and law school. That's about it."

At about six feet three, Adam was trim. She learned later he worked out at the fitness center, additionally played squash at Penleigh Creek Country Club in Gladwyne. As a real estate attorney, known to be brilliant, strong willed, capable, yet relaxed. At about thirty five years old, he'd never married. His squared jaw and steel blue eyes didn't hurt either, nor did his easy, slightly crooked little grin showing perfect white teeth. She'd seen him to say hi to a couple of times since a concert months ago. She wanted to know more. That was one reason she accepted the Anglesey invitation without hesitation. Anglesey itself was important. However, in her heart of hearts, Marlowe acknowledged just maybe it came in second.

Leaning forward toward Adam, her shoulder-length curly brown hair getting in her eyes, Franny sat grinning.

"Add to that you're consistently named in the Best Lawyers in America, are on boards of various major nonprofits both in Center City as well as here on the Main Line."

At this point Adam was shifting his weight around in his chair. With a hint of an ever so slightly crooked smile, he was blushing as the others including Marlowe laughed at his discomfort.

Adam's cell vibrated. He looked at the number as though he were expecting a specific call. He turned away from the table to pick up. Turning back he said, looking at the other members, "What happened has been confirmed."

With Adam back, Franny turned in her chair to face her guest, "Before we begin, Marlowe, by way of further introduction, will you tell us a few things about yourself so we may get to know you better?"

"Certainly, Franny. As I'm sure you know, I'm a money manager at Wynne Capital. I grew up in the tiny town of Somerbury in upper Bucks County, went to Yale undergrad and grad school. From there I went directly to Wynne. I'm on the Board of Directors of Chandler House, Donegal Library, and I'm the Vice President of my club, Somerset Tennis and Squash Club."

"Marlowe, we're delighted to have you here as our guest for our discussion today. Though you're a guest, we have a serious request of you before we commence. This society was started many years ago. From the beginning we discussed all manner of topics, many of them philosophical. Any we discussed in terms of situations ongoing in real life at those times were treated properly. We always wanted our talks to be honest as well as private so we could openly talk without fear of any repercussions. We ask you to respect this. Remember our discussion here today must remain confidential, not to be discussed with anyone."

As Marlowe sat there looking at Franny she peripherally became aware the others were looking at her intently. She was now astounded. Fine, *Candide* could be considered by some to be a novel about controversial philosophical positions, even though it was written centuries ago. What's the big deal so we have to talk about it clandestinely. What possible action could ever come after reading it.

Marlowe's eyes shifted almost involuntarily to one of portraits hanging on the wall across from her. As she stared at it, it crossed her mind that he, those in the other portraits, as well as the people in the room right now, had been having meetings like this for a long time. What had they talked about. What action might they have felt the need to take. Did the public know? Did anyone know what they did? Was it illegal? Did they care if it were?

Why meet down here in this hidden room which is apparently always locked? The members were open to discussing anything, including, it dawned on Marlowe, things that were illegal or at least inappropriate. It was a huge leap from discussing general fiction themes or characterization. Rock and a hard place. She wanted to be in that Anglesey room. Did she.

Ideas were darting around in her mind like a ping pong ball being shaken inside a beach ball. What should she do.

"That is agreeable, Franny," Marlowe agreed.

"Excellent," Franny said, nodding a smile back at Marlowe.

Marlowe had no idea what was going on. Was all this about a discussion of a 1700s novel? What was Anglesey really. What did they do? She decided to keep a clear head to closely follow the *Candide* discussion, which she assumed they would get to next.

"It's presumed each of us has read the book or consulted any other critical essays or books we knew might be helpful. We won't discuss the plot, setting, point of view, or characterization *per se*. Let's start right in on what Voltaire's message to his reader is. Who wants to open the discussion?"

Malik was the first to speak. The rumors she'd heard were the members of the Anglesey Philosophical Society were truly brilliant, Magna Cum Laude people. Malik's commentary confirmed that, as did Jack Danett's. Who knew a real estate tycoon, moreover a restaurant owner, were capable of making these sorts of analyses about a literary work. She expected Adam to be equally brilliant. He didn't disappoint her. Last was Franny, who drew on her vast knowledge of English and European literature to add additional nuances. Though no longer nervous, Marlowe started to worry a little over what remained for her to say. They'd covered the salient points with dazzling detail.

Having completed her comments, Franny turned to Marlowe. "Your thoughts?"

Marlowe relaxed. She sat back as though she were teaching a college class about Voltaire. She herself had handled many such essay questions in a European lit class at Yale.

15

She began, "Throughout the novel, having seen many occurrences of horrible things happening to people, Candide decides to live quietly by literally cultivating his garden." Looking at each of the others in turn, she continued, "Simply stated the garden is a metaphor for life. As the story progresses it becomes clear the theme is we are to live not only to our own benefit, also to that of our neighbor, Voltaire's 'garden.' If someone or a group of people are in difficulty, depending on the specific circumstances, we are obligated to help them."

"Well said, terrific summary, Marlowe," Jack said.

Glancing at the other members then turning back to Marlowe, Franny continued, "Saying it a bit differently, adding just a touch more, on occasion we have to right wrongs to help society when it finds itself incapable for whatever reason of effectively doing what is necessary."

Malik and Jack looked at each other nodding their heads. Although they were obviously pleased with her response about *Candide*, Marlowe again swiftly became aware of a subtle yet pointed change in the mood. She had no understanding of what was transpiring. It was almost as if something had been settled, maybe her opinions were not exactly accepted, more they were approved. There was something else though. It seemed to Marlowe that their reaction was too quietly intense to be merely an agreement that she was qualified to be a member of their society. It seemed there was something more.

Adam asked, "Marlowe, what do you think specifically about—"

Suddenly there was noise behind Adam.

Angela burst through the door. Through her considerable flowing tears, she was barely able to blurt out, "Duffield Manor! The police raided it. The animals!"

Adam was on his feet. "Angela, are you okay? What are you saying? Who told you this?"

"Some details have just come on the news though unconfirmed. They're saying they found animals torn apart. They are either dead or in critical condition," she choked out. "There isn't any more information than that."

Running to her husband, "Jack, Duffield is only twenty minutes away from here—what's happened? Oh my God!" Angela hunched over, fully distraught.

"Are you sure they said Duffield Manor?" Adam asked.

"Yes, they said it several times."

"*What?* That can't possibly be," Marlowe said getting to her feet, stunned, not understanding. Her mouth formed an "O."

A deep frown now etched between her eyes. She stared at Angela in disbelief. It was all she could do to stop herself from firing questions at Angela. She wanted more details. She wanted them right then. She knew she wasn't going to get them. As far as she was concerned the meeting was over. She was leaving.

She hastily went around the table to Adam. Grimacing, looking up at his face, she put a hand on his shoulder. "Adam, thank you for inviting me to the meeting. I'm going."

She bolted toward the door and was gone, her three inch heels thundering down the hall.

Chapter 4

Marlowe slid into her 911. She threw it into first gear, flooring it out of the parking lot heading for Duffield. Her heart was pounding. The few remaining people in the lot looked aghast at how fast this woman was going. She was immediately on the phone to her friend, Ashanti.

"Ashanti. Duffield!"

"I figured you'd call. I heard about it on the radio. I remember you've been there before, right?"

Upon hearing her best friend's voice Marlowe's emotion began to show itself. Her voice was shaky, breaking, even though she was trying to keep her composure.

"The horses! I told you about the ones the Federsons have. They rescued those horses. What happened to them? Oh my God, Ashanti I love those horses! Who could possibly hurt them?"

Tears started washing down her face. She was leaning forward into the steering wheel certain it would make the car go faster to Duffield.

"Easy, Marlowe, we don't know what happened yet," Ashanti soothed. "Maybe nothing really happened. You know how these reporters get sometimes. They get carried away. Still, I agree, let's go. I just finished my last appointment and still have hospital scrubs on.

I'm on my way. Maybe we can help if something did happen. I knew you'd be upset and want to go. I'm not far away."

"Yes, please go, Ashanti. I'll meet you there. If something happened there the police might not let us in. I don't care, I *have* to go!"

Knowing Ashanti was going to be with her, Marlowe was able to collect herself. Her best friend was one of those women who are classically beautiful, flawless skin, eyes exuding friendliness as well as concern for whomever she is talking to. Marlowe adored her. On rare occasion, she felt the need to confer with her about private subjects. Just knowing she was going to be at Duffield, Marlowe moved quickly from fear to determination to get there to find out what was happening.

The Federsons had about ten rescued horses on their property plus numerous dogs as well as other animals. She'd had the honor of spending time with the horses whenever she attended the various charity galas at the mansion. Some of the charity events were for the local Main Line Animal Shelter, where Marlowe was a member. Outrage was beginning to boil up inside Marlowe.

She knew each of these horses had been rescued by the animal shelter from terrible circumstances. Ginger and Roy Federson took them all in. They hired two young men to care for just the horses. What could have possibly happened to them? It didn't compute. If something did happen, she was not just going to look away. Somebody had to do something about it.

The thought of any animals being hurt reeled in her memory of her Strider's suffering before she rescued him. If she needed any strong encouragement to go to Duffield it was something that had happened with her dog. Soon after she had adopted him from the Greater Philadelphia Animal Shelter she reprimanded him for pulling over the kitchen wastebasket. Strider had dropped his head, cowering, apparently realizing he had sorely disappointed the master of what he dearly hoped was his forever home. His ragged tail was down. He was totally still. His ashamed look had cut Marlowe to the quick. After all of this time she still remembered it. She had helped Strider. Now she needed to help these poor animals. Her next notion was something happening to them at Duffield was a preposterous notion.

Ashanti called back. "Marlowe, how was the meeting?"

"Let's talk about it later. I can tell you it was captivating, in some ways weird, at the same time."

Marlowe called Sol. "Sol, I didn't get a chance to tell you this morning. Yesterday I received an invitation to a meeting today from Anglesey. I just wanted to check in."

"You didn't go, did you?"

"I did. All I can tell you is that at first there was a peculiar conversation. Then we talked about a book. That was it."

"We should talk more about this when you have time, Marlowe. You shouldn't go to another meeting. Please listen to me. You know I have your best interests at heart. I'm not feeling well, pain in my chest. I'm on the way to my cardiologist again. Let's speak later."

Marlowe started to anticipate what she might see when she got to Duffield. She'd been at the Federsons for several galas. She loved the property. Located at the end of a private cul de sac, Duffield was one of the splendid 1880's stone country mansions. It was replete with three-story turrets, literally tons of limestone, arched windows with intricate leaded glass, stunning, high pitched terra cotta roofs, a myriad of intricately designed pillars, an immense porte cochere the size of a four-car garage, with oversized oak front doors to boot. It was constructed of what Marlowe deemed majestic things. It was a treasure.

Indeed, so were the owners. They were widely considered to be some of the loveliest, generous people on the Main Line. Roy was the sole heir of the Federson fortune made in a railroad-engine repair business, long since merged into a large public company. She'd met the owners at the Conservancy gala. Ginger and Marlowe quickly became friends. Their horses or dogs being hurt at that property made no sense. Was it possible the police had raided the Federson's? It was ridiculous even to contemplate. Nothing in her life prepared her for what she'd heard from Angela at Harlech.

Animals being abused on the Main Line? Impossible. She vaguely knew it went on elsewhere. Marlowe was so engrossed in her Wynne business, she'd heard only scraps about it. Marlowe was from Somerbury a little town in Bucks County, not a big city. Animal fighting was something from her protected background she simply wouldn't be able to grasp. It couldn't be that. Then what?

Adam called, interrupting her ruminations.

"I tried you at your office. They said you weren't there. I saw you pealing out of Harlech like someone was after you. What's going on? Are you okay?"

"I'm okay. I'm going to the house."

"What house?"

"Duffield!"

"Why are you going there, Marlowe?"

"The horses, Adam. The Federsons have rescued horses. Ashanti just said maybe dogs are involved. I have to see about the horses. It can't be dogfighting. I was talking to my friend Nick just last week about everything the shelter is doing. The SPCA has agents who go out when animal abuse complaints come in. Nick said they had basically put an end to all of it. He told me the police are making this dog-fighting stuff up, just trying to get more money to run the adoption center."

"Nick? Nick who?"

"My friend Nick Gavin. It came up in a conversation about a month ago. Why? Do you know him?"

"No. Stop. He said that? At my office now, gotta go."

The line went dead. "Whoa! Did he just hang up on me? He just hung up on me!" Marlowe inadvertently laid off the gas as a deep frown began to appear.

" I knew it…. I might have been good at the meeting, nevertheless not good enough for a guy like Adam."

Chapter 5

If she hadn't known exactly where Duffield was on quiet Deer Hollow Lane, she would've known she was close. Five local news vans were at the beginning of the street, apparently waiting for something.

As she passed them approaching the Federson's she saw a township police car parked along the road at the stone pillars of the open wrought-iron estate entrance gate. The red emergency lights were flashing. A police officer was standing in front of the gatehouse. She was looking in Marlowe's direction.

Marlowe became alarmed. Something was definitely going on. It must be bad. Why all the news vans, why the cop at the gate. All of a sudden Marlowe realized this might be a big deal—she was now assuming the worst, beginning to panic. Should she have come? She was just going to wait for Ashanti.

Marlowe knew the fifteen thousand square foot Duffield mansion sat about a quarter mile back from Deer Hollow presiding graciously over its hundred acres of conserved ground. Acres of open fields, grounds and gardens surrounded the home, barn and separate stables. Marlowe guessed the oversized two-story stone barn for cows and other animals was at least three hundred yards to the left side of the house. The fieldstone stable, home to the horses, stood about a hundred feet to the right of the barn toward the house.

Right in front of the stables was the paddock, an expansive, rectangular, stone walled courtyard. The horses used it for exercise space when they were not out to pasture or in their stalls. The wall of the stables itself comprised the paddock rear wall. Constructed of stone, the other three walls stood about five feet high. A wide wooden gate faced front toward Deer Hollow.

Just then she saw Ashanti's silver BMW coming up behind her. She breathed a sigh of relief as she pulled over to wait for her.

Ashanti pulled up. Marlowe slipped off her heels. She reached across to the passenger seat for the sneaks she kept in her car and quickly put them on. She threw off her suit jacket on top of the heels. Getting quickly out she ran back to Ashanti's driver-side window.

"Ashanti, I'm glad you're here," Marlowe said giving her a quick hug. "Should we see if we can go in? Maybe we should go back. See the police officer? She may wave us away."

"We're here, let's go. Let's leave your car. Get in."

It was then they heard a siren. A Greater Philadelphia Animal Shelter van came up fast behind them, emergency lights also flashing. It passed them without slowing down. At the gate it jammed on the brakes careening around the turn speeding in the driveway.

"Should we still go?" Marlowe asked, getting more agonized.

"Yes, we're going." Ashanti started to drive to the gate. "Did you hear the news update?"

"No. What did they say?"

"The Greater Philadelphia Animal Shelter received a call about eleven this morning. It was about something bad having to do with animals at Duffield. Apparently believing the caller was telling the truth, the shelter Humane Law Enforcement agents called the township police for more guns, more arrest power."

"More guns, Ashanti? Guns, for God's sake?"

"That's what they said. They said the shelter coordinated arriving here at the same time. By the time they got here, no one was here except a housekeeper. That was all the news. Nothing more about what was found or what happened."

Marlowe instantly wondered where the housekeeper, William, was. He didn't live on the estate though he was there daily. Surely he couldn't be a part of whatever took place.

She had no time to think about these things. The officer authoritatively waved fast at them to go through the gates onto the long Duffield driveway.

"Why is she waving us in?" Ashanti asked, shooting Marlowe a hurried look.

"I don't know. Maybe she thinks we're supposed to be here. Let's ask her."

Ashanti stopped at the gatehouse. She leaned out of her window. "Is there some reason you're waving us in? We aren't with the shelter or police."

"I don't care if you're the man in the moon, honey, as long as you aren't the press. They've been told to stay away—off the street. They need all the help they can get in there so I'm telling you to get in there."

"Are you sure—"

"I don't care who you are! Get in there. They need all the hands they can get to help! Don't you park in the way of those Subaru SUVs. They're being used as more ambulances to take these poor animals to

Penn Veterinary and every other vet in the area. Stay out of their way—these are life or death vehicles! Now go in! Help!"

"Help? What do you mean 'help'?" asked Ashanti, her eyes wide, her hands gripping the steering wheel like she was trying to rip it out.

"Get in there you two. Stop jawboning!"

Putting her foot down hard on the accelerator, her face getting red, Ashanti yelled, "Oh my God we're going in!"

Marlowe let out a terrified scream and grabbed her seat belt.

Chapter 6

With an expression of shock and surprise, Marlowe thrust her arms forward as if to stop any vehicle coming toward them.

"Ashanti, look out! The Mill Creek ambulance is coming toward us fast!"

"I see it!"

"Let's get over on the grass. Here comes another one—this one's an animal ambulance! It's from Blooming Ridge Rescue."

"That one's moving too," Ashanti screamed. "Here comes one of those Subarus! What has happened here!"

Marlowe knew the main driveway led directly back from the gatehouse entrance to a cobblestone courtyard in front of the mansion. A secondary driveway turned off left from the main driveway within fifty feet of the entrance gates. The drive normally wound in a pleasing curve to the paddock. Marlowe saw the activity and vehicles were at the paddock area. They made the left turn starting back.

"Wait!" Marlowe cautioned. "The Mill Creek ambulance is coming. Its siren and lights on—they don't do that except for emergencies, human emergencies."

"This must really be bad, Marlowe."

The ambulance and Subaru flew by, one right after the other. They swerved around the gatehouse picking up speed as they went. The policeman energetically waved them through.

"Driveway's clear, let's go!" Marlowe said, trying unsuccessfully to calm down.

Ashanti picked up speed. They approached thirty or more various vehicles parked on the lawn blocking the view of the paddock. They saw rescue vans from all over the area including Clarks Noll Shelter, Notting Hall Animal Sanctuary, Woods Society Rescue. Marlowe's stomach tightened. Her breathing deepened preparing to confront she knew not what. Her eyes raced from left to right and back again taking the whole scene in.

Ashanti stopped her car clear of the emergency vehicles. Marlowe saw the anxiety in her face. She knew the same was on her own as she strained to see where the horses were. They started walking the rest of the way following the voices of men and women directing others around.

They broke into a run as they approached the area on the other side of the vehicles. The paddock was right in front of them. They stopped in their tracks as though they'd just seen they were on the edge of a cliff. Marlowe frantically looked for the horses. She saw none.

They saw at least seventy-five men and women, some in police or ambulance rescue uniforms. Others were in Greater Philadelphia Animal Shelter uniforms including Luca Pasquale, Director of Humane Law Enforcement. Many more were in medical coats that had started out being white. They were red with blood. They saw at least five emergency triage tables. A score of vets and nurses were working feverishly on bleeding animals at emergency operating tables. People were still unloading medical supplies. Still more unloaded empty animal cages from the shelter vans. Some carried animals from the paddock to the line at the triage tables. Others attended to them until a doctor could examine them. After a vet examined them other people carried the smaller animals that might live to cages at the animal ambulances. Larger injured dogs still alive went in the human ambulances and the Subarus.

"It's not the horses, it's dogs as well as other animals! Either way, we shouldn't have come," Marlowe groaned, her voice breaking. "I can't even watch animal programs, documentaries, because they always show animals being killed, animals killing other animals for food. And this? With blood running? O my God!"

Feeling crushed by what she quickly assessed as over three hundred dogs dead or in severe jeopardy, she realized many others had already been taken away.

"What did we expect to gain by coming for God's sake?" Ashanti added, traumatized, her hands holding either side of her head. "What did the policewoman mean they need all the help they can get? What should we do? I'm a neonatologist, I don't know what to do!"

Though the authorities had been on site for a couple of hours, the scene outside the paddock was incomprehensible to Marlowe. She so loved all animals this was crushing her, she could barely function. How could she help, what could she do, she didn't know anything about medicine.

She watched people bringing bodies out of the paddock, putting them down side by side along the paddock wall not forty feet from where she was. She stood staring first at a black pit-bull with its ears gone, the bases bloody. Then two tan pittys both with part of their mouths hanging off the bone. Then a beagle. Then a brindle pitty. Then a boxer mix. Her eyes skipped over more dog bodies to bodies of chickens, chicks, ducks hawks. All covered in blood. All exhibiting a horrendous death.

Marlowe had heard references to fighting at the Philadelphia Animal Shelter. From those scraps she was able to quickly put together what she was seeing for real. She knew some of the dogs she was looking at or were over on the operating tables had attacked each other. They were readied to fight by bait a fight worker had given them before the real fights. The bait was small dogs or birds. They were thrown to the fighting dogs to rile them up, to get their juices flowing for the real fights, for the real show. When she had heard such things discussed at the shelter, she was sure they were exaggerations even though some of the other volunteers said no they were not. Her only role at the shelter was to walk the dogs available for adoption. That's all she did. She didn't know what was really occurring. It was obvious now what she had heard was fact.

The dead were lying in dirty blood, patches of fur and feathers. Some were so mangled they looked like they had been mauled by a pack of hyenas. Others looked like they had been torn to shreds by wolves. Some eyes were still open. Legs of some were up in the air. Some were without a leg, many were without ears or tails. All, whether bird or dog, had great gashes, oozing, open wounds on their bodies.

But no hyenas had been here. There were no wolves.

Chapter 7

"**D**on't just stand there! Get inside the paddock," a man wearing a shelter t-shirt yelled at them. "Go! Some animals are still alive, not for long unless we get the bleeding stopped. Carry them to the triage tables or the vets at the examining tables. Go, you two! The dead ones are out. Move it!"

Another shelter volunteer shouted at them taking towels from a stack at one of the Subarus. "Here, take these towels. Be careful how you handle any of the animals or you'll kill them. This is the most vicious goddamn dogfight I've ever seen. We're going to get the bastard who did this." Trying to contain himself he said, "Go ahead—it won't be easy to see."

"Oh my God!" screamed Marlowe.

Shocked into action she took the towels, running toward the paddock. Ashanti was behind her. She ran into Marlowe when she got to the open paddock gate. Marlowe had come to a sudden, complete halt.

Before them were over fifty animals, torn apart, bleeding, lying in their own blood clearly in utter throbbing agony and trauma. Some were groaning. Some were trying to make noises. Most were lying in total silence. If they still had eyes, and could, some were looking up.

Most were looking defenselessly straight ahead. The biggest dogs, two Great Danes, appeared to be almost dead, their fur slashed and bitten off on numerous places on their bodies. Her anger was rising to the boiling point, her face was red with rage at the atrocity she was witnessing. Her fists were clenched. Then she saw the Danes.

"Ashanti, there are two of us, they're heavy, let's get one of the Danes!"

Both now intent on saving lives, they ran to one of the Danes. Marlowe told Ashanti to put her towel crosswise under the back haunches. Ashanti tucked the towel in. Marlowe gently lifted the back of the black Dane onto the towel. Without a word, the two friends worked as a committed team, their focus now elbowed out their emotions. They used the second towel for the head and the front shoulders and legs. While they were concentrating on the Dane, they heard shelter people carrying other animals out of the paddock. They lifted the Dane as tenderly as they could and carried him out in their makeshift sling.

Each rescuer moved professionally, steadily tending to their victims. It struck Marlowe and frightened her they looked like they knew exactly what they were doing, they'd done it before. Does this mean yes, they have done it before?

In the process of wondering at their composed demeanors and comportment, Marlowe recognized one of the doctors. He wasn't a vet. He was an orthopedic surgeon from Penn whom she knew from Somerset. Marlowe and Ashanti carried the Dane over to him to be next for care.

The doctor read her face of recognition. "I had to come. I feared the worst. I hoped to be able to help."

Marlowe turned to Ashanti. "You are a doctor. You can help here too!"

Ashanti's face contorted in tears. Looking at Marlowe guiltily she said, "I, I can't, Marlowe, I just can't. I'm just a baby doctor."

Turning back toward the paddock, Marlowe said, "Okay. Let's get the other Dane."

"I'm sorry, Marlowe," she said in a tiny voice, trying to wipe away the tears.

Putting her arm around her, Marlowe said, "Forget it—we have plenty we can do here. Let's go."

They turned and ran to get new towels from the shelter van. They saw two vans packed with crates of animals departing to deliver them, she supposed, to veterinary medical hands across the Main Line, just as the officer had said. Two older men were loading a Tails Rescue animal ambulance and another Subaru. The vehicles flew off with their patients. Marlowe saw one of the returning ambulances coming straight from the gates at the road. Ignoring the driveway it was coming at high speed directly across the grass toward the paddock.

Spurred on, Marlowe and Ashanti ran to the paddock. They were able to move the black and white Dane the way they had the previous one. It was harder since this dog was heavier. She seemed unable to try to lift any part of her body to help them.

When they got her over to one of the doctors, he took only one look. "This one's dead. Put her over there," waving them to the side of the paddock where the other bodies were.

Seeing the appalled looks on the women's faces, the doctor sternly ordered, "Get back in. Bring me another one right now."

Looking at Ashanti who started to cry, he demanded, "Don't you dare cry! Our work isn't done here. We have more lives to save. Go!"

They turned to take the dead Dane to the growing number of dead animals. They dashed back into the paddock working silently side by side with the other aid workers. Finally, they gingerly transferred the last live animal in the paddock, a hawk with two broken wings. The ambulances were gone. All were delivering their precious cargo toward help and hopefully sustainable life. Only the last Subaru, which waited for the hawk, remained.

Marlowe and Ashanti, stared at the ground, mentally and physically exhausted, blood on them. They sat down on empty animal cages which miraculously hadn't been needed.

Chapter 8

Being a neonatologist at Eastbury Hospital Ashanti was used to medical situations when she had to react quickly and expertly. What she had seen in the last hours was well beyond anything even close to what she was accustomed to. Marlowe, and probably Ashanti, didn't want to talk about what they had just undertaken. Marlowe was simply drained.

Regardless her eye was caught by a few of the shelter agents taking a break sprawled under an elm tree near the paddock. The Greater Philadelphia Animal Shelter agents were the team of about twelve agents that answered animal abuse complaints. They carried guns and had arrest powers. Marlowe and Ashanti joined them. One of the agents was Chico.

The shelter had a long history of protecting animals from abuse. The agents were trained to respond to complaints of animal cruelty or neglect. They investigated direct physical abuse, animal hoarding, animal fighting, all situations of neglect. Marlowe had the highest respect for the dedication of these agents who worked tirelessly for the wellbeing of animals.

"It's Marlowe, isn't it? Remember me from when you walk some of the dogs at the shelter?"

"Yes, hi, Chico. This is my friend Ashanti."

Marlowe liked Chico because if he was at the shelter when she was there, he was always supportive of her coming to walk the dogs. He had told her once she reminded him of his daughter Margarita back in Mexico. Marlowe told him on more than one occasion it saddened her that her work at Wynne Capital kept her from spending more time at the shelter to help the abuse team. She'd told him her brother Skip had trained her from when she was a little girl to be able to accurately shoot a revolver.

Sitting down on the grass with the agents, Marlowe and Ashanti relaxed.

"I don't know why you two came here today. Chico said. We're sure glad you did. This was the worst we've ever seen. We see a lot on a smaller scale in the city."

Looking at his watch and then at his fellow agents, he said, "Let's go, gang. We need to load the dead ones and take them back to head-quarters. Marlowe—" Chico stopped and turned toward Marlowe and Ashanti.

"Chico?"

"I'd like to say something to you. I hope you don't mind my saying this after all you've seen and done today. You *must* walk the dogs like you do. You must invite your friends to do the same. There are so many animals that don't get adopted. People don't know about that. Those animals which don't get adopted get what people call 'euthanized.'"

"I guess."

"If you'll allow me, let me explain what 'euthanize' means." Chico was looking from Marlowe to Ashanti and back as he spoke. "That word suggests there is something wrong with the animal, that it can't be saved from some injury or sickness or is in great pain."

Ashanti nodded.

"The stark reality is the animals are killed simply because they aren't lucky enough to be adopted, they have no home, literally no place to go. There is just no room for them anywhere at all to live. So they are eliminated, killed. Over a million and a half dogs a year are killed because they just don't fit in."

"What? That can't be." Marlowe was appalled. She had no idea of the enormity of the fate of these innocent animals whose only fault was they had been born.

"That's what I'm telling you, Marlowe. You and your friends need to get to the shelter to walk the dogs as many times as you can. Then the dogs have been exercised and are calm when people come to find a dog to adopt."

Turning again to his guys, he said, "Let's move out."

Marlowe and Ashanti stared at Chico as he walked to one of the shelter vehicles. In quiet grief, the two friends watched two shelter agents performing the heartrending, grisly task of placing the remaining nameless, now unloved, dead animals into the vans. Marlowe's eyes, sadly roving across the scene, were interrupted.

Luca Pasquale was standing at the end of the paddock toward the barn, intently watching something. She followed his gaze. She saw a woman getting out of a black Ford sedan parked near a black Expedition. A man in a dark suit got out of the SUV. They started talking staring over from time to time at the paddock. They were too far away for Marlowe to hear what they were saying. The Expedition looked like the same kind of SUV she'd noticed parked not too far from her house on the private road Chatham Lane in Haverford. She'd seen it just last night. It struck her as a peculiar coincidence.

"Ashanti, look over at the barn. What are the guy in the suit and the woman doing here? They weren't involved in the rescue. Never lifted a finger."

"I've no idea, why?"

"I'll be back, I won't be long," Marlowe said.

She walked over to one of the township police officers who was kneeling down taking photographs of bloody scissors just outside the paddock gate. Marlowe had heard animal fighters docked the ears of fighters so they wouldn't be ripped off during the fight. They were docked on site. No anesthetic. Clip. Clip. Done. She'd also heard the people who went to the fights and left immediately afterward so they wouldn't be caught.

Averting her eyes from the scissors, Marlowe asked, "Pardon me, officer. Do you have any idea who those two are over at the barn?" Marlowe read his nametag. He was Officer Alten.

Rising, the officer said, "Who might you be?"

"Marlowe Evans, sir. When I can I walk the dogs waiting at the shelter to be adopted so they can get some exercise so not be so hyper."

"So you're part of the shelter family. I'm Henry Alten," he said, carefully placing the scissors with his gloved hand in an evidence bag. "My guess is they're FBI, ma'am."

"FBI?" Marlowe asked frowning, startled at his guess.

"Yes, ma'am. I heard they were at another big dogfight out in Lancaster County a couple of months ago too. Why the FBI is here at a local incident is beyond me, can't tell you. The cops got the guy in Lancaster County. Or at least they said they did. I heard they got the guy who ran the fight. The money guy behind him got away. I heard the Lancaster cops don't know who he is. What the FBI may know might be a whole different thing. Something else, Marlowe. The Lancaster cops think the FBI has created a specific team to investigate these fights. That's their only assignment, they're not investigating any other kind of federal crime."

"You think the FBI knows or has some ideas?"

"Let's put it this way. Why is the FBI here at Duffield on a local raid? That's the question. It's local. If this might be part of something larger, something that, say, crossed state lines or involved something else, then maybe the FBI might have an interest. You didn't hear anything from me. The only reason I'm taking the time to talk to you about this is you take your time to volunteer at the shelter. I saw how hard you both worked to save the animals. You two are fine, upstanding citizens. That's why you should know. Understand now, I'm not saying anything I shouldn't be saying as an officer of the law. Rest assured if the FBI is involved, they will get the felon behind this. Nice talking to you. Gotta get back to what I'm examining."

"Thanks so much for talking, Officer Alten."

"Something else." The officer turned back toward Marlowe. "I get the impression you have more than a passing interest in the fight. I get the feeling you want to somehow figure out who's involved. Keep in mind what I'm going to tell you right now. Okay?"

"Okay," Marlowe said, not having any understanding at this point of what the Officer was telling her. She did surmise this was going to be important.

"Don't know for sure, it's a rumor, a little confusing. Some of my buddies think other FBI agents are in town for something having to do with a money laundering case. They are thinking these guys here, if they are in fact FBI, are just about the fight. My buddies don't think there is a connection at all between them, who knows."

"One more thing if you don't mind my asking. Who notified the shelter?" Marlowe wondered if the Federsons even knew what had happened yet.

"I was one of the first responders on the scene this morning. An older man who said his name was William was down at the entrance gates in his truck waiting for us. He said he was the housekeeper. The owners were away. He had had an early call from the stable hands who had come in to take care of the horses. They had found the mayhem. The last thing he got out before he started slumping over holding his heart area was there were many animals at the stables who were hurt. A Mill Creek ambulance was behind me. I guess the medics took him to the hospital. It looks like he was having a heart attack. I've not seen him since."

"So he was not responsible for the fighting. What about the stable hands?"

"No, those two young guys were sitting back at the gatehouse porch crying their guts out when we got here. No, it wasn't them. We sent them home, told them to come back tomorrow. We will take care of the horses for them today. Some of the shelter people knew what to do. The horses have been fed and watered. Those guys didn't even have a car. Their mom had dropped them off. I think one of the Subaru drivers took them home."

Marlowe took a few steps back so the officer had room to work. He obviously knew what he was looking for as well as how to preserve evidence. Since apparently the FBI was involved, as was the Main Line Animal Shelter in addition to the local police, Marlowe questioned who was the lead investigative body. It seemed like the FBI was standing off, yet had an interest. Thanking the officer, Marlowe went back to Ashanti. Marlowe looked at her watch.

"It's already after five. Let's go. We can't do anything more here."

Marlowe didn't want to add more sadness to what Ashanti already felt. She decided to keep the conversation with Officer Alten to herself. There was the question about the FBI. Why were they here. Was the FBI at her house? That didn't make any sense. On the other hand, was it just a coincidence? Marlowe was slowly getting an understanding of what kind of people were running these fights.

They slowly walked toward the car. Ashanti put her hand on Marlowe's arm then stopped.

"Marlowe? I've got to tell you many of these animals transported alive out of here today will die from their wounds, despite the medical care they'll receive. The others… the others will undergo surgery, be in distress and more pain for weeks as their wounds, we hope, start to heal. It isn't over for them even though they didn't die this day in that paddock. It isn't over by a long shot. Their agonizing suffering will continue."

"I know…. I know you're right." Marlowe agreed softly.

She reached to hug Ashanti. They both broke down, beginning to sob.

After a couple of minutes Marlowe quietly said, "We should go."

Unsuccessfully choking back the tears when she got in her own car, Marlowe turned the key. Giving a small wave to Ashanti as she drove by, Marlowe sat with the motor running. Her only real reference to animals was when she was a child living with her parents and brother Skip in a tiny own, Somerbury. Her dad got her a donkey and later a horse. It was her responsibility to take care of them. She learned how to do that and loved them both to pieces, the memory of which brought a small smile to her sad face.

Putting her car slowly in first gear, Marlowe's smile faded.

"*That's* what animals are all about, damn it, that's how they are treated. So *what are you going to do about it*, Marlowe?"

All tears were gone.

Chapter 9

The following morning Marlowe arrived early at Wynne. Several colleagues had gathered in the front hall talking about Duffield. In the uneventful towns of the Main Line events like the Duffield incident were basically unheard of. Marlowe wanted to hurry by. She forced herself to linger to listen to see if she could hear anything new, anything that might be a clue as to who was involved.

It wasn't long before she was struggling not to replay the events of the day before in her mind. She wasn't successful. The Danes and all the others sadly paraded themselves in front of her.

Just the mere sight of people talking about what she'd seen brought tears to her eyes. Trying to wipe them away, she reminded herself, I have a job to do at Wynne Capital. She had client portfolios needing attention especially after taking the entire afternoon off the day before. On the drive over from her home on Chatham Lane Marlowe had heard reports showing stock futures were down substantially. She expected the market to dive on the opening at 9:30. That wasn't her only concern.

She was scheduled to give a small seminar at the office at 11:30. She needed time to prepare her presentation for the three women—early forties, wealthy, married—who she hoped would establish as new clients. Her new client of a few months, Judge Gwyn Llewellyn, had recommended to one of her friends to speak with Marlowe to see if she might be the one to review their holdings including estate planning. . Marlowe was looking forward to the opportunity to interact with three prospects. Everyone knew Judge Llewellyn was wealthy. Marlowe hoped her friends would be too. She'd been especially careful to wear her nicest navy suit, a white jewel-neckline blouse, Parker's gift of a single strand of pearls, small pearl earrings, and low navy pumps. Marlowe's guess was these women would be looking at each detail. She wanted to portray herself as exactly what she was: a professional woman who welcomed the opportunity to manage their money properly.

By eleven twenty Marlowe had taken care of emails and phone calls. She was ready to walk to the conference room to meet the ladies.

Despite being a small firm Wynne had spared no expense when it came to the appearance of its offices. Located in a two-story, historic brick building registered on the National Register of Historic Places, the exterior was flawlessly maintained. The entire interior had been gutted then redesigned to provide every advisor with a spacious private office. The conference rooms on the first and second floors were stunning. They looked more like boardrooms with their taupe, detailed cornice and baseboard moldings, the wallpaper of *fleurs-de-lis* in various shades of darker green, additionally eight plush executive chairs covered in oatmeal-colored fabric.

Earlier that morning Marlowe's assistant Maria had set out white linen napkins with a bold "W" stitched in blue on one of the corners. The ladies had arrived at Wynne early. Maria had greeted and shown them to the conference room. They were now already seated around the oval cherry conference table. Maria had made coffee. She was just setting out a cut-glass serving plate of small, delectable-looking maple Danish pastries she had picked up from the Bakery House in Bryn Mawr on her way into the office. Maria stayed in the room for the meeting in case she was needed for anything including opening potential new Wynne accounts for Marlowe.

It was exactly eleven thirty when Marlowe entered the conference room. She introduced herself to each woman, Jayla Wallace, Brianna Barrington, and Helene Greycott.

Marlowe put on her broadest smile. "I'd like to welcome you to Wynne Capital. Thank you for coming. You've met my assistant, Maria Alvarez, who is responsible for these delectable looking which she promises are no-calorie treats! My remarks to you won't be long and will take the form of what I think is an amusing, illustrative anecdote." What she wasn't saying was that she knew she had to work hard to get their money to manage. That meant using "Josephine."

The ladies each took out notebooks and pens, ready to write down what would hopefully be words of wisdom that could be helpful to them. Ready to listen, they sat back a little in their chairs sipping their coffee.

"First a question," Marlowe said looking at each of the women.

The ladies noticeably stiffened.

"None of you has more than sixty percent of your net worth hidden under your mattress, do you?"

Helene's posture went from relaxed to ramrod straight. She frowned. Her mouth hung down in disbelief that Marlowe would ask such a question. Marlowe could no longer keep her grin in check. She started giggling. Finally getting the joke the ladies broke out in relieved laughter.

Taking her seat, Marlowe was laughing right along with them. She'd learned in the early going it was much better for her to sit instead of stand when she conducted an education seminar. Nor did she use charts or industry vocabulary. She felt communication was more effective as well as productive if everyone were seated, She also used normal, plainspoken, everyday language.

"Okay, now that we've broken the ice for all of us, the little story I'm going to tell you is about a fictitious woman, Allison, who lives in Pennsylvania, who believed she was meticulous in organizing, including managing, her financial affairs. Let's put ourselves in her shoes to see what happens to her."

Marlowe leaned forward in her chair. "Stay with me!"

"Suppose Allison (you) and her husband have two children, no will. You die, dad gets the kids. Bad, but okay, at least the kids are safe. Suppose you die. What's more, dad dies too at the same time. Who gets the kids? Good question."

"The future of your children lies in the hands of? The *state*."

Marlowe leans forward, the early stages of a frown appearing.

"Yikes! It could be that that sister-in-law, Josephine, whom you can't stand for a million reasons, may end up with the kids! Holy cow! What are you supposed to do? You need a will containing estate planning."

"Let's add insult to injury with another situation. Your husband, in addition to being flat-out gorgeous, has been able to build a sizeable retirement plan at the office. You know, a 401(k) and a profit sharing plan. He's only forty-three years old, so he hasn't gotten around to making a will for you both. After all, he's busy and he's young. You'll have time to address that later. In his retirement plan he's made prudent investment selections—he's *so* clever! Now he has over a half million dollars in his plan. You're named in the plan as the primary beneficiary. Poor thing, your husband dies."

Marlowe leans back a little, her frown now apparent.

"In a timely way, you get the retirement money, roll it into a Roll-over IRA and name Jason, your sixteen-year-old-son, and Janie, your fifteen-year-old daughter, the primary beneficiaries. Jason and Janie are well adjusted and mature in addition to being top students. You've taken the time to explain to them if something were to happen they should call your financial advisor who will take care of the investments for them. So you're all set for your kids. Life is organized. Nice job."

Marlowe pauses for about fifteen seconds.

"Nope. Not even close, ladies."

"You've gone to Center City to shop for a dress for your first date since your husband died. You've found an incredible Ralph Lauren ever-so-slightly sexy dress. Yes, the dress is from Needless Mark-up. It was on sale. Just four hundred fifty dollars. What a bargain! It will be a special night. The dress is without a doubt a must-have. You start crossing the street with your dress in the shopping bag. You're so happy about the prospect of having a social life again you don't see the enormous SEPTA bus coming right at you. The driver's on his cell phone. Yup. The kids have lost their mom too."

The ladies are each beginning to look sad for the so unfortunate Allison and her dead husband. And what will happen to the kids is a big concern.

"Remember who could end up with your kids? You took care of the retirement money. You never did get around to the estate planning and new will. Who gets them? Correct. *Aunt Josephine. That's bad*! Could it be worse?"

Jayla speaks up, "This is terrible, even if it's fiction!"

"Yup, it could be worse, Jayla, I'm sorry to say. Ready?"

"Jason and Janie are still minor children. Guess who has control over the money they get as beneficiaries of your Rollover IRA? Guess who can make a single withdrawal of half million? You got it. *Aunt J!* The half million ought to be used for the kids, but Josephine is Josephine. We know what that means. Well, the rest is too depressing to think about!"

The women were looking from one to another. Marlowe could tell each one was thinking about her own circumstances. She stayed quiet. In the gap Marlowe felt almost ashamed she was enjoying telling the Aunt J story. She felt like she'd abandoned the animals at Duffield. She caught herself just in time to avert a breakdown right there in the seminar.

Marlowe remained silent while waiting for the women's attention to be back on her.

There was a heavy knock on the conference room door.

Chapter 10

In the next second the door opened.

A woman who looked like she was in total anguish walked in. Marlowe stared in disbelief as she saw the woman, dressed in old jeans and farm shirt. It was the owner of the Duffield mansion, her friend Ginger Federson.

"Oh God, Marlowe, they didn't tell me you were here with other people, I assumed you were in here by yourself—I'm so embarrassed."

Jayla was on her feet going over to Ginger. "Ginger, you're back from Florida! We all heard. Are you okay?"

Neither Brianna nor Helene knew Ginger though they knew the ongoing news about the fight. They joined Marlowe and Maria in getting up to go over to Ginger. Feeling the love from these five women opened the tear floodgates. Maria took her arm helping her sit down. One by one the others moved their chairs around the table to be closer to Ginger.

"It was simply awful," Marlowe said.

"I know you were there, Marlowe, which is why I had to come see you. I'm so sorry for interrupting you all."

"There's nothing more important than you being here, Ginger. What can we do to help you? Jayla said.

Turning from Jayla, Ginger said, "Marlowe, forgive me for walking in. They said you were in here. I need to—"

"Nonsense, Ginger," Jayla said. "A quick introduction to you of Brianna and Helene. Now ladies, let's leave right now. Marlowe and Ginger need to talk. Marlowe, we don't need to hear any more, I'm sure we all will be transferring our accounts over to you."

"If I may be of assistance, please let me know," Maria offered.

"Many thanks, Maria," Jayla said.

The three women got up, leaving their chairs where they were and left with Maria. Marlowe reached out for Ginger who was again trying to gather herself.

"I'm so sorry, Ginger," Marlowe said. "This is so awful, I don't know what to say."

"Marlowe, I'm so distraught about this, I have nightmares every night. Roy is even worse. He thinks it's somehow his fault. I know you were at the house, I can't thank you for being there, helping as you did. The police didn't go into detail about each thing they are working on. They did say you along with a doctor friend worked until all the animals that were still alive were transported out. I can't imagine what it must have been like. When the police called us last night we came up from Florida. We couldn't get a flight until early this morning. By the time we got to the house the boys taking care of the horses had been there I guess… I guess they cleaned up."

"How is William?"

"He had a heart attack. He's resting comfortably at Eastbury."

"At least that's good."

Ginger's eyes were wet. She was no longer crying. She looked like she knew she had to calm down for some reason.

"There's something I want to tell you. William said while we were away in the last month or so he saw a couple of cars come in the driveway, drive around, then go out again. He said it happened a few times. While we're away he comes to the house to clean during weekdays. You know Deer Hollow Road isn't well traveled so unless there is a guest coming or a delivery, few people would be on the road. I can't imagine anyone would think of driving in. It's so quiet there half the time the entrance gate isn't even closed.

"At the time William said he didn't think anything of it. Now since all of this happened, he thinks there may be some connection. Roy agrees with him. The only thing William could remember was the cars were big, looked like newer models. He remembered one of them was a Mercedes except he didn't remember the color.

"So many people have Mercedes around here. It could have been almost anyone. He didn't see who was driving. Marlowe, you deal with wealthy people all the time here. If you could keep your ear to the ground you might hear of something that could help the police. This is why I had to come see you right away."

"Well, I do end up hearing a lot of things in my job. You're right, whoever was at the incident at your house would have had money. I'll listen, Ginger. If I hear anything at all, I'll call the police right away."

"And Marlowe, I have a second thing to be embarrassed about."

"I cannot imagine that, Ginger, I seriously cannot."

"Well, it's about money. Roy and I have been talking about moving our various accounts to you for months and we just haven't done it. We are doing it now. Your assistant Maria was here today. I'll call her for the forms."

"Many thanks for that, Ginger. We'll talk with the accounts come in."

What Marlowe didn't say was she was thinking about Duffield all the time, about the dogs and animals that were so savagely killed. She didn't know how yet, regardless she was going to find out who the perpetrator was. Then make sure he was prosecuted to the fullest extent of the law.

Maybe more than that.

Chapter 11

Ginger opened the door to leave. Marlowe saw Jayla sitting in a chair right down the hall. She got up, hugged Ginger as they passed each other then walked over to Marlowe who was still standing in the conference room doorway.

"Jayla, can you give me one minute in the conference room, I need to make a quick call. Be right out."

Marlowe went back into the room. She had no call to make, even so as Ginger was leaving, Marlowe had the beginning of an idea about Duffield. She sat down to think clearly about it, her elbows on the table, her head supported by her hands. She remembered what Ginger had said. The cars William saw. Deer Hollow Lane was a cul de sac. No one would be on the road just passing by. At the turn onto Deer Hollow there was a sign saying it was a cul de sac, no through traffic. Yet apparently more than once a car or cars were not only on the road, they entered the Duffield grounds, freely driving around. They could have just nosed into the driveway, backed out, then left the way they came if they had been lost. A lot of people knew the Federsons spent much of the winter in Florida, so no one in the cars would have been there to visit.

Marlowe stood up quickly, pushing her chair into the wall, her arms akimbo. She'd figured something out. The organizer had already identified Duffield as the location for the fight. They needed to find out when the stable hands and William left for the day. That's why they were there. That had to be it. This was the first clue to finding out what happened. Maybe it meant the perpetrator was local. She'd have to work from that perspective. Marlowe calmed herself down then opened the door for Jayla to come in.

They sat down at the conference table.

"That was rough, Marlowe, are you okay? I didn't know you were there. Poor Ginger, it's all just so awful, awful beyond words. Do you have a couple of minutes to talk to me? You probably have other appointments so I can make an appointment to come back to see you if that's better."

"I think I'm good, honestly, at managing money. I'm not knowledgeable about detective work. I'm planning on speaking with Gwyn. She's put a lot of people away so can probably coach me about how to recognize clues. I know this sounds crazy, my biggest love is for animals, it's just the way I was raised. Right now it's my major focus."

"I understand what you are saying, Marlowe. This is something you need to do. It was clear to Jayla Marlowe was completely serious. Remember if you find you need my help, including Brianna and Helene's, we will be honored to do what we can."

"Thank you and the girls for your confidence in me regarding the animals, the dog fight. I will not let the animals or you down."

Marlowe and Jayla shook hands as though they were consummating a business deal.

"To be honest I'd much rather have you come in the room, have coffee with me. I don't want to go back to my office to just sit there reliving what happened at Ginger's. It's not something I can forget. Please come in, Jayla."

Having freshened her mug, Jayla said, "I just wanted to let you know everyone loved what you said. Maria will be opening a number of new accounts for you. You're knowledgeable to the extent you can take a step back to convey your point in humorous stories we can enjoy as well as learn from. You obviously have a command of investments too. The three of us talked after we left the conference room. We all think you're the one to help us get on our financial track. I also wanted to say, you may remember you were recommended to us by Gwyn Llewellyn. She said you were terrific. She was certainly right. All four of us are in the same garden club so we all have time to talk about things while getting our hands dirty."

"Nothing like dirty hands to get a good conversation going! Tell me more about your garden club, Jayla, it sounds like a really good group. I need all the help I can get in the gardening department. I've tried to plant a few things outside my house. They looked really good, at the outset."

Marlowe explained with her elbows out with her hands extended up, "it wasn't long before one by one they knew I had no idea what I was doing so just resigned themselves to an inevitable short life."

"Oh Marlowe, there you go again! You're just too funny! You're such a find, I'm so glad Gwyn recommended you. We're going to be working together."

The two women sat there looking at each other with big grins on their faces.

"About the club, The Odyssey Garden Club is an outstanding group of ladies. We meet each month at a member's home. We have such fabulous, interesting discussions about all manner of plants, shrubs, trees, landscaping in general. We're planning something too. You should think about coming with us! We're going to the charming country of Wales. Gwyn has an ancestral home on the coast. We're invited to join her for two weeks to see the gardens there."

"I must say I'm definitely jealous. I love England and Wales. After the U.S. they're my favorite countries. Where's Gwyn's home?"

"It's on the island of Anglesey. It's a little, well not too little, island off the northwest coast of Wales. A charming place I understand."

Marlowe couldn't believe her ears. Anglesey. The Anglesey Philosophical Society. The map of Wales in the meeting room. What a coincidence. While Gwyn had become a client a couple of months ago, Marlowe didn't know much about her background.

"You know her family came over here much before the Mayflower passengers, though few people know. She's a profoundly incredible woman given all she's done in her life in addition to her years as a judge."

Finishing their coffee, as Jayla was about to leave she explained it was only a few months ago when Gwyn had retired from the bench. She now focused on maintaining the grounds of her property. looking after her horses and dog.

"She's an expert on trees, especially oaks. She has all types of oaks on her property. Some are young as oaks go. Some are much older. One is said to be four hundred years old. Gwyn adds to them from time to time. As you might imagine, she has full time gardeners."

"Gwyn is truly one of the most foremost women in the Philadelphia are. Everything I hear about her is first class. By the way, thank you for stopping by the office to chat about your investments."

"Well, I must say, at this point, yes the investments. More than that now, Marlowe. We girls know you are serious about everything you do. That includes Duffield. Just know we three who were here today, plus of course Gwyn, are right behind you. As you do more investigation on this you may need money. We don't know for what yet, at any rate we want to be extremely clear about this."

"I don't know what direction this will take or whether I will need any money at all."

"Whatever you need, you will get with one phone call."

Chapter 12

On the way back to her office Marlowe stopped by Maria's desk.

"I'd never heard that little Josephine story before," Maria said. "Good work! On a different subject, Sol called. He needs to talk to you. By the way, Earl is here to pick me up for lunch. Do you have time to meet him?"

"Sure, it's about time I meet your boyfriend of two years, Maria! From everything you've said this guy is a keeper. Let's do it!"

Maria and Marlowe went to the Wynne foyer where Earl was waiting for Maria. Marlowe noticed right away Earl was dressed in fashionable Brooks Brothers type clothes and a quick glance outside showed a top-of-the-line Mercedes double-parked. When Maria went over to Earl he gave her what could be called an aggressive kiss on the mouth. It took place in no more than ten seconds. Marlowe was taken aback by his lack of etiquette. As anyone would have seen by the elegant, expensive looking décor of the foyer, Wynne Capital Management was a very professional place. Comportment would always be the best whether there were clients in the offices or not. Maybe it was his clothes, his manners, or lack thereof, or the double-parked car. Marlowe had some reservations about him.

After meeting Earl, Marlowe went back to her desk and called Sol. "You should be wary of them, Marlowe. I urge you not to go to any meeting."

"The meeting was yesterday and I did go." Remembering she was bound to keep the meeting confidential, she said nothing further.

"Oh. I know you can't tell me what you talked about. Are you going to go to another meeting?"

"I haven't been invited to go again."

"If you're invited, don't go. I know I sound like a broken record. It may not be what you think it is. I know you're busy, talk to you later, Marlowe."

She valued, further, respected Sol's opinions. He'd been a client from the beginning, back when Marlowe had few files in her file cabinet. She'd seen him reading the *Wall Street Journal* one day in a café named Dillon's. Eager to get a client, Marlowe struck up a conversation.

"I see you're reading the *Journal*. Any recommendations on financial company buys?" So began their years long friendship.

Marlowe didn't know if she would be invited back for a second meeting, or more importantly, whether she would want to go after what was discussed at Harlech. She needed to dig deeper to find out who they really were and what, if anything, they did.

Marlowe's mahogany desk was positioned such that she could look out the two large windows that overlooked the professionally designed Wynne grounds. However her eyes were unfocused, seeing nothing. While surprised, moreover delighted, by what she judged as the potential amount of assets coming to her to manage from the Jayla ladies, Marlowe's ruminations turned briefly to why Gwyn had strongly recommended her. It was all to the good. The reason didn't really matter. Her focus changed to her monitor. Nothing special was going on there with the stock market. Typically the commentators on CNBC were just talking for the zillionth time about the direction interest rates might go.

She left.

Chapter 13

After a good night's sleep then the morning's work on two portfolio reports completed, Marlowe was feeling much better. Another thing she knew would make her feel better was the drive to Gwyn's house. She was going to take her time to smell the roses along the way. She had some time before she had to leave.

She was going to put it to good use by researching the Anglesey Philosophical Society. She didn't know why still she had an intuition that Anglesey might in one way or another hold some clues to Duffield. It made no sense to her, nonetheless, there was a little something nagging at her. How might they pivot from a dusty novel to the Duffield stable.

One of her favorite sites was Wikipedia. Nothing came up. "Philosophical Society" was too broad. She typed in "Anglesey," which she knew could be a dead-end. It was. It said nothing about anything even approaching the society. Google was next. Nothing having to do with the Anglesey society however of course lots about Anglesey. While she found it all interesting, none of it helped her. She tried another idea.

She'd spoken a few months ago about investments to the Board of the local historical association because it was thinking about establishing a foundation to help preservation efforts in the township. She called Harry Donohoe, the Board Chair. Harry owned a real estate title company. Because it was spring, a lot of settlements would be taking place so he would be busy. She took a chance. To her surprise he picked up right away.

"Harry, this is Marlowe, so sorry to call you on what I'm sure is a busy day for you. I have a quick question for you."

"Shoot, kid!"

"You are obviously knowledgeable about township as well as general local history. Do you know anything about the Anglesey Philosophical Society?"

"Every now and then I've heard the name. Occasionally someone will ask me about it. I'll give you the same answer I give them. Other than people asking me about it, I've no idea at all what it is or if it even exists."

Shocked he knew nothing, who they were, who the members were, she persisted.

"You've probably checked with your buddies on the Board, right?"

"Right. Wish I could help, Marlowe. I'm glad you called. After listening to you we think we're going to start a small endowment fund. We'll be coming to you for a donation. You're probably sorry you called, aren't you!"

"Not at all, always happy to contribute to the historical society. Thanks, Harry."

Marlowe's quick conclusion was there was no information she could find on the net, nor anything from the local experts. Yet the Society obviously existed. It had to be just local. It was now clear to Marlowe the only way she was going to find out about it was to ask people. The problem was, as she now knew from the meeting, no member was going to talk to her even casually about it.

However, as luck would have it, an opportunity had presented itself the day before. Not that she contemplated it would really be fruitful. On the other hand when she was at Somerset the prior day she happened to run into one of the freely acknowledged intellects there. Marlowe had nothing to lose when she saw Harvard Ph.D. Becky Stanfield right outside the locker room.

"Hey, Becky" Marlowe said, trying to be as cordial as possible with a nice smile, also a wave.

"Marlowe, hi, playing some tennis, not at Wynne this afternoon?" Becky had asked, seeing Marlowe in her tennis clothes.

"Just beating up the backboard. The creep won. Wouldn't you think I'd get tired of the same result all the time?"

Marlowe was grinning, enjoying her own comments. "Odd question for you, Becky. Do you know anything about the Anglesey Philosophical Society?"

"Never heard of it," Becky had said, turning to leave the locker room area. "Gotta go."

Marlowe accepted Becky was weird. The fact that she started to practically run out was just one more confirmation of what pretty much everybody judged about her. It had been worth a try. At least for now, she'd run into a brick wall. At least for now she had to move on from Anglesey research. With everything handled at Wynne, she needed to refocus on Duffield.

She was about to get up from her desk to head out to Gwyn's when something popped into her mind, something, given everything occurring at the Anglesey meeting, she'd just forgotten. "Julie Hudson."

That was the name Adam had said when he left the meeting to answer a short call about her. At the time Marlowe deemed it was rude of Adam to take a phone call during a meeting. The others seemed to know what it was about. They appeared not to mind in the least. When she searched she found "Julie Hudson" to be a common name.

Marlowe rapidly ran down the Julie Hudson entries. Nothing seemed important enough for Adam to have taken the call. Then her eye was caught by a recent search headline, "Major corporation employee murdered. Left in an alley in Seattle." The article from a newspaper was short. It suggested the woman was supposedly the daughter of a Philadelphia area resident. Marlowe stared at entry. Maybe, possibly there could be some local connection. Even so, why take the call right then? Why not call back later. "Julie Hudson" was another dead end for Marlowe.

When she got in her car heading for Gwyn's, Marlowe opened the sunroof, she also put the windows down a couple of inches to breathe in the spring air. For the first time that spring it was warm and the sun was out with only a few clouds in the sky. It was a perfect day to take an unhurried, relaxed drive to Gwyn's. Marlowe needed to take just a casual drive to Gwyn's.

Though having lived on the Main Line since college, Marlowe continued to marvel at the pretty historic towns like Haverford, Gladwyne, Villanova, as well as Bryn Mawr which were so lovely this time of year. Somerbury was mostly small homes, pastures and cornfields. Here, the air was full of smells of blossoms. A myriad of fresh, vibrant flowers, rhododendron and azaleas were arching their stems in pursuit of the sun as they were beginning to bloom. The manicured grass on the eye-catching, splendid Main Line properties, many of them mansions, was at its most luscious green. Off-leash dog parks were filled with eager, cavorting dogs with their equally enthusiastic owners.

The abundant flocks of Canadian geese were making their rounds to the various placid estate ponds looking for a suitable place to start their families. Marlowe never tired of living in the stunning community she now was fortunate enough to call home.

From her office in Bryn Mawr, going north of Montgomery Avenue, one of the main streets of the Main Line, Marlowe passed gorgeous home after gorgeous home on her way to Gwyn's Snowdon. Each one on a gloriously stunning day like today was worthy of being the subject of a great artist's painting. Each property had manicured, healthy-looking lawns as well as professionally landscaped grounds. Most owners employed landscaping crews to maintain the property from the snow plowing to the mulching with triple ground hardwood premium mulch in April then June. Driving on the private roads was a happy diversion. Some of the largest homes, built in the 1880's to 1920's, were mansions so large private schools, churches or other institutions ultimately bought them. As a result, these dramatic, striking buildings were preserved for next generations to savor.

Marlowe was very much looking forward to seeing Gwyn. In the short time they'd known each other she'd already become a friend. Simply classically beautiful, she was gracious, generous, and elegant. Her dress was always stylish. She had the understated look which emanates from true beauties. The rumor was as a young woman Gwyn fell madly in love. Six months after their wedding her husband died tragically in a private plane crash. Gwyn was three months pregnant. Since then, as far as Marlowe was able to learn, Gwyn had never even dated anyone.

Before she'd met Gwyn, she'd already known the name Judge Llewellyn. Marlowe was pleasantly surprised when Gwyn sought her out. She was a woman who could have anyone managing her fortune, her numerous trusts and foundations. During the first meeting in

Marlowe's office, they discussed a wide variety of topics, some financial, some not. They clearly liked each other. Marlowe was shocked when Gwyn informed her she was transferring all the accounts. Everyone knew the judge was part of an old wealthy family from Wales. Like the Duffield mansion, Gwyn's home, Snowdon, was another historic mansion most people knew about, though few had seen.

Because the pace of their initial conversation in the office was fast, Marlowe had no time to start thinking about why she was getting the assets to manage. Gwyn however took the opportunity to explain it was, of all things, because Marlowe had helped her niece Claudia, whom Marlowe knew from the Main Line Animal Shelter where both were volunteers.

Claudia wanted help investing her 401k at work. Gwyn explained she'd known about Marlowe's growing reputation as a stellar money manager for a while. The fact she would take time to help a young woman whom she really didn't know, who had no other money to invest impressed Gwyn. She explained it demonstrated Marlowe's admirable professional character.

Passing sprawling fields, more rolling hills, more woods, more lovely homes, Marlowe began to unwind. This drive is much better for the psyche than yoga she said to herself. Besides who wants to think about your own breathing all of the time. Marlowe never did get the big deal about breathing in yoga. I mean don't you naturally breathe on your own? Do you really have to concentrate on breathing plus have a coach telling you when to breathe? I mean seriously, what's the big whoop about yoga?

On the other hand, she was quick to reason, a lot of her friends who went to yoga classes did seem a lot more content. They had rounded lives of a husband, kids, maybe a job, nice house, lots of friends, usually a country club membership or two. Marlowe appreciated she had a fascinating job, one of the coolest jobs in the world, and oh yes, a cool car. Who was happier? Who had voids in her life? Marlowe had to admit maybe they were happier. Maybe not as professionally accomplished as she was, maybe that wasn't important. And more than a few of her girlfriends were giving back in some form or another to those less fortunate, whereas Marlowe really was not. "It can't be the yoga for heaven's sake," Marlowe heard herself saying aloud.

When was she going to get that rounded thing going in her life? "Hey, Marlowe," she said to herself, "sure, you're a big deal. Ask anybody and they'll tell you, and they truly mean it. Really, are you? Where's the love of life, of giving back, of giving to you for Pete's sake in the form of a nice, hunky, no, just nice, husband."

Sometimes after these self-imposed interrogations, she figured maybe it was a case of the grass being greener on the other side. In truth, she knew it wasn't the case. One day, she always promised herself, when she had time to truly focus on aiding the less fortunate in some way and finding a husband, she'd do that, and take yoga to boot. Of course, she knew she was delusional because "someday" never seemed to be available.

Finally with a broad smile, she commanded, "Knock it off, Marlowe! Focus on this marvelous day for once, enjoy the drive to Snowdon."

"And oh yeah, *breathe*, Marlowe, *breathe*!!"

Chapter 14

In a great mood, turning down Gwyn's road, Acorn Lane, in Glad-wyne, Marlowe saw the soft rolling hills, fields and pastures on the left. Never having been to Snowden before, she assumed these were part of Gwyn's property because black wrought-iron estate fencing started after she made the turn onto Acorn. Behind the fence were arborvitaes, Leyland cypresses, also cherry laurels planted in natural looking groupings. Perfectly pruned red roses mixed with cotoneasters in front of the fence completed the sense of a property that was loved. Snowdon was one of the most dramatic estates of the Main Line.

She approached the entrance to the mansion. The wrought-iron gates slowly opened. She waved to the attendant in the charming stone gatehouse just inside the grounds. It was magical, enchanting. She leisurely drove along the long, meandering drive. Acres of gardens surrounded the house. Pastures and fields lay beyond the gardens; thick woods were beyond them to the sides and rear of the house. Four dapple-gray horses were grazing contentedly in the pasture to the left of the house. As Marlowe got closer, the horses raised their heads, one whinnied "hello." Marlowe energetically waved back. She was certain Gwyn had requested they welcome her on her way in.

Glancing to the right of the house, she saw a lone stallion feeding on hay in his own pasture. Marlowe slowed, then stopped to look at the animal. He was a thoroughbred, which she recognized because she remembered those crazy Somerbury riding days. The stallion looked exactly like her Red Ribbons. She remembered with fondness when Skip had explained to her a "hand," when it comes to measuring horses, was four inches. Ribbons was fifteen hands three inches high, quite a handful, which she loved. Though her dad had gotten her an old English saddle as well as an old McClellan army saddle, she with her girlhood friend, Teddi, much preferred riding bareback.

Marlowe grinned as she recalled some of the perilous riding adventures they had engaged in. About which they'd never told their parents. After she grew up Marlowe often wondered why they hadn't both been killed on one of those wild, thundering rides down the grass airstrip at IG Agricultural Sales. Having ridden to the far end of the quarter-mile long strip, they would position their horses heading in the direction of their barns located well beyond the other end of the airstrip. When they were ready Teddi would give the "go" sign of her right arm fully extended pointing toward the end of the strip. They each gave their horses their heads by fully slackening the reins. Exhilarated at the idea of going back to their barn and used to the game, both horses instantaneously were in a full-blown gallop with Teddi and Marlowe yelling their heads off in excitement.

It was outrageous fun however incredibly dangerous. They didn't see the danger. At age eight they were experts at staying on their horses. Even if the horses veered sharply, they never fell off, ever. Marlowe was always convinced Red Ribbons knew, though the person on his back was small, he and the package made a fantastic team. He wanted to please that little package. They were great pals.

Now at Snowdon, with the sunroof open, the fresh air flying around in the car, Marlowe was happier than she'd been since before Duffield. Her whole face was aglow with the remembered excitement of the races with Teddi and her horse Dusty and how much fun they had had as kids. They didn't have a care in world then. Marlowe hadn't been riding since she left Somerbury for Yale.

Her deliberations now drifted to her only recent reference of horses for her, the Federson's. She remembered her favorite, a palomino named Honey. In a flash, just that quick, the memory of Honey and the others being safe, even so the massacre of the dogs moved in. Feeling instant tears coming on, Marlowe grabbed for the radio dial to put on a rock station, turning it up loud to drown out her torment. It worked. In a minute, continuing in the gently curving drive toward the house, she breathed in the peacefulness around her and turned the radio off.

Though not familiar with different types of trees, Marlowe's eyes were caught as she finally recognized oak trees were lining the asphalt drive. The design was irregular as though they hadn't been planted at one time to form a symmetric approach to the house. They appeared rather to have been planted over time with some over eighty feet high, others just twenty feet. The driveway culminated by turning directly toward the front of the mansion to a stunning formal courtyard laid in cobblestone edged with three rows of lengthwise running brick. A classically designed white wooden gazebo with intricate moldings with perfectly proportioned pillars sat in the center of the courtyard. Pink dogwoods, white limelight hydrangeas with a pachysandra ground cover surrounded the gazebo, completing the beautiful welcoming courtyard. To Marlowe the view of just the courtyard with the gazebo was more attractive than her entire house on Chatham Lane.

It was just one thirty. Marlowe parked on the edge of the courtyard, picked up her folder of papers needing to be signed, got out of her car to walk to the front doors. She was fascinated by the grandeur of the three-story Elizabethan Manor style house of red brick and limestone. It was easily twenty thousand square feet with eight towering chimneys. A smiling older woman in a gray uniform with white trim opened the door.

"Welcome to Snowdon, Ms. Evans. My name is Missy. Please, won't you come in?"

"Thank you, Missy."

"Hi, Marlowe, glad you could make it!" said Gwyn striding through the enormous dining room on the right. Though dressed simply in khaki Bermuda shorts and a white cotton sleeveless shirt, Gwyn looked elegant, the perfect resident for such a magnificent home.

"Hi, Gwyn, thanks for inviting me to your splendid home."

"Missy, we'll be sitting out on the back terrace."

"Very good, Judge Llewellyn."

"It's such a fantastic day I think the terrace would be nice. It's quite lovely this time of year."

With her eyes wide open glancing first at the living room on the left, then right at the massive staircase with the formal dining room beyond, Marlowe followed Gwyn to the back French doors of the reception hall leading out to the terrace. What she was glimpsing was flawless interior design: ornate molding, casings, polished exquisite antique furniture, Orientals, heavy fabrics, portraits. Every aspect of the rooms appeared to be museum quality fit for a king. Or, in this case, a queen.

Marlowe and Gwyn sat in one of the many rattan armchairs. Putting her folder beside her chair, Marlowe surveyed the formal gardens extending for at least two acres to the back. The landscaping was so extensive as well as exquisitely maintained that sitting on the terrace was like sitting in a quiet corner of nearby Longwood Gardens in Kennett Square. Every planting section was in neat, carefully planned symmetric lines. The lawns were perfectly mowed, hedges neatly clipped. The garden, while formal, had no topiary or statuary. It had a natural look enhanced by a variety of trimmed grass paths. From where they sat at the center of the wide brick terrace the main path leading away from the house led directly to the back of the gardens. Looking down the path, between and past the two flanking, rectangular reflecting pools to the end, Marlowe saw another white gazebo, much like the one in the front only larger, maybe twenty feet in diameter.

Having waited quietly as Marlowe looked over the gardens, Gwyn noticed her looking out at the gazebo.

"I sometimes walk down the path to sit by myself in the gazebo viewing the grounds. It relaxes me. If I've had a difficult day for some reason, it soothes me back to normal. It's a quiet, contemplative spot."

"I can certainly see why you say that. From there you'd have a whole different view of the grounds, one that is quieting, restful. Gwyn, this whole estate is remarkable," Marlowe said looking off to the left beyond the horses where the stables and other outbuildings were.

Missy appeared with a tray of glasses of iced tea, chocolate chip cookies, china dessert plates and napkins. She placed the tray on the rattan table between the chairs. Marlowe took a cookie. It was still warm.

"Wake me later. I'm in heaven, all this in addition to these swoon-inducing, just baked, chocolate chip cookies?"

Taking a taupe linen napkin with a script "S" embroidered on it from Missy, Gwyn said, "Marlowe, surely you don't have that much will power?"

Gwyn promptly picked up three cookies for her plate. Winking at Missy, she continued, "Missy and I have an arrangement worked out.

She won't bake cookies unless a guest is coming over, because if she does, she and I will eat them all. So you should know, Marlowe, I had only one reason to invite you here this afternoon."

"I get it." Marlowe was laughing. "In that case, if I'm being made the scapegoat anyway, I'll take another two."

"Bravo, Marlowe!" Missy and Gwyn were both laughing.

A large white puppy came running around the corner with his tail wagging, his mouth open in a wide, toothy grin.

"Hey, Raspy, I figured you'd show up. Come over here to say hello to Marlowe Evans, the greatest money manager you'll ever meet."

Raspy was on his way to greet this new person sitting with his master when he came to a dead stop in front of the cookie tray.

"Be a good dog, go help Dominic and James. Doggies, which includes you, can't have chocolate," Gwyn said, giving him a pet on his head.

Raspy looked at her, got the message, moved off again heading out as fast as he'd come in.

"He's adorable!"

"He's a three-month old pup. Such a personality! You'd think he was trying out for the circus!"

"I'm utterly enthralled by your estate, Gwyn," Marlowe said, shifting her eyes back to the gardens.

"My family has lived on these grounds for hundreds of years. Over time, we've managed to plant a variety of specimen trees. You may have noticed we've been partial to oak trees from the beginning. It's a family tradition. From time to time I add one or two as needed. Dominic and James, whom you can see way out there, take great care to prepare the ground. They use our backhoe to prepare the ground to receive the trees. They have been with the family their entire lives, as had their parents and grandparents. The same goes for Missy. They've been fully dedicated to the family for a very long time."

"You may not know," Marlowe said, "I'm not from this area. I grew up in a small town in Bucks County. Forgive me for not knowing. How long has your family lived here?"

"A good long time, Marlowe." Reaching for her iced tea, Gwyn went on, "From the beginning we've always lived on these grounds surrounding you. Naturally, not all of the descendants live here, just me. You may have noticed some of the old portraits in the house as you walked through. Other family members disbursed over time to other parts of the country, New York, Boston, Washington, many different places. Of course, the home as well as outbuildings themselves have changed, been replaced many times since the early days. This house was built in 1901. The barn and some of the outbuildings were built in the early 1800's." Gwyn paused to drink her tea.

"How long were you a judge in Philadelphia?"

"Many years. It was not long after I graduated from Penn law school when a position as a judge opened. I was selected. Believe me, I've seen many cases in my courtroom, hundreds of them."

"Maybe I'm naive. Isn't being a judge satisfying in many ways? You get a chance to put some really bad guys in jail."

"I wouldn't argue. However, I'd take exception to it being satisfying. For those cases where I was successful in putting away criminals, I couldn't have been happier. Notwithstanding a fair number got away without conviction, which wasn't the fault of the police. The Philly police force does a tremendous job in trying circumstances. I can't say enough about the officers and detectives—they're highly dedicated men and women. Sometimes it's the sentencing guidelines which aren't stringent enough. Or a defendant is caught, convicted, goes to jail. When he gets out he's up to no good in one fashion or another again. I found such situations exasperating, to be honest, incredibly annoying. To be perfectly honest I wished I had the wherewithal to dish out much tougher penalties to those who got off with some light sentence."

"I do understand your frustration. With the good work you were able to do in your courtroom, why did you retire early?"

"Good question. The short answer is I finally made the decision to leave about three months ago."

"I can appreciate you saw a great deal that didn't go as it rightly should have. It's obviously an incredibly frustrating situation. I'd be less than honest though if I didn't say the courts lost a superstar when you left. All of the newspaper and magazine articles and the TV announcement of your retirement were jam-packed with accolades."

"Thank you. I'm glad you understand."

Reaching for the folder she'd laid on the terrace, Marlowe said, "With all of the beautiful surroundings on top of good conversation, I almost forgot to ask you to sign these. Maria will have me visited by the Securities and Exchange Commission if I don't remember to ask you to execute these forms."

"You're nice to bring them over. We could have done them electronically so as not to cut into your day at Wynne. I did want to talk to you about a couple of things."

Handing Gwyn a pen and the forms from her briefcase, Marlowe watched as Gwyn signed each form at the "sign here" arrows.

Marlowe's official business was completed. What next.

Chapter 15

Handing the forms back, Gwyn asked, "By the way, an entrepreneur you may have met along the way, Nick Gavin. Do you know him? His name came up in a conversation recently."

"Oh my goodness, yes. I've known him ever since I can remember," Marlowe said smiling, always happy to talk about Nick.

"I haven't met him. I'm curious, what kind of a man is he?"

"He's been wonderful to me my entire life. He's been almost a second father. From time to time, he'll call to see how I am. Then there are the occasional parties at Rocking Horse Downs near New Hope, about an hour plus from here. I've always known if I ever needed anything, he'd be there for me." Marlowe loved Nick from the time she'd been a small child. After her mother died Nick called Marlowe every month or so to check in. He wanted to make sure she was okay. He made her promise to let him know if she needed anything.

When she was in her early twenties it had crossed her mind that here was a man who was successful, living a full life. Instead of her frustrating quest to find a husband, maybe the perfect man had been around from the beginning. Maybe Nick was the man she should be with despite his being older. One thing could not have been clearer to her,. He truly loved her. He would always be around to safeguard her.

In the end she concluded Nick was too much older than she was. She never contemplated it further.

"Just curious again, does he ever gamble on anything?"

"You know, I don't know. I do know he and dad had a kind of falling out a long time ago when I was little. It was something to do with money. I have half a memory betting was a part of the argument. I think Nick wanted some money and Dad didn't have it. Either that or he wouldn't give it to him. Something like that. Nick and Dad were poor then. Dad still is. Nick isn't. Anybody who knows him will tell you he's worth millions."

Missy unobtrusively came from the house to refill the iced tea glasses. Gwyn and Marlowe looked at each other mischievously, both with a little smile and a twinkle in their eyes.

"I will if you will, Marlowe!" Gwyn challenged, her hand ready to pluck up a cookie.

"Far be it for me to be an impolite guest," Marlowe said darting in to beat Gwyn for another cookie, coming in second. "Taking a second one as the consolation prize, Gwyn!"

Enjoying more tea with their treats they both moved their chairs so they were looking out over a broader expanse of the estate. Marlowe took her navy suit jacket off and opened the top button of her white silk blouse. She could still see the gazebo. She could also see the horses to the left. Both Gwyn and Marlowe were leaning comfortably back in their chairs on this splendid spring day.

"It really is lovely here," Marlowe said, turning her head toward her client, who was now much more her friend than client. "All of the plantings are lush. The oaks are simply gorgeous, so many different kinds. Have you ever asked Dominic and James to subtly label each of the species, maybe try to date them? Dating might be hard to do though."

"Not at all. I have a written record of them, the species, the date, which family member planted them."

"Astounding! Do you have a record of the other trees planted on the estate?"

"Oh no, just the oaks. Some oaks can live hundreds of years. You may not have noticed the woodwork in the house is oak, all of which came from this property." Turning to face Marlowe more directly, Gwyn asked, "Getting back to Nick for a quick moment, out of curiosity, has he ever talked to you about any of his business associates?"

"No, never. Why?"

"Because the person who mentioned him in conversation told me Nick's daughter was just murdered. I just guessed you might know his business associates."

"His daughter? What daughter?" She snapped to attention, her eyes riveted on Gwyn.

"Julie Hudson."

"I didn't know Nick had a daughter. Well of course, he *did* have a daughter. Years ago Nick said she died. I know he was married. He got divorced after only a few years. You must be mistaken, Gwyn," Marlowe said picking up her iced tea, easing back in her chair. "What happened?" Marlowe asked, trying to softly dig a little deeper into why Gwyn wanted to talk about Nick.

"She was murdered, close range, which means it was personal. They don't know exactly what happened yet.

"You're saying a killer with some specific motive set out to shoot her?"

"That's what it appears to be."

"I don't think the Nick who was part of your conversation with someone else is my Nick." Having listened to Gwyn's story, Marlowe was sure the Nick she was talking about wasn't Nick Gavin. It had to be someone else. She would have known about Julie.

To try to get information about Duffield from Gwyn, Marlowe asked, "By the way, Gwyn, have you learned anything from your contacts about what happened at Duffield?"

Marlowe and Gwyn talked about the news reports. Marlowe told Gwyn she with Ashanti were at the scene. She gave her a general description of what she had seen without getting into the details until she started relating what happened with the second Great Dane.

Gwyn unexpectedly got up from her chair, then sat stiffly down again. Marlowe was startled. She noticed Gwyn's demeanor was beginning to change. She became somber—there was no doubt about it. Marlowe turned fully toward Gwyn reaching out her hand across the tea and cookie table to touch Gwyn's arm. Gwyn was now looking down, frowning. Her muscles had visibly tensed. Her breathing became forced as her face started to wash with pain.

Just then Raspy rounded the corner, trotting over to Gwyn putting his head on her lap requesting pets. Marlowe was surprised to see Raspy having the opposite effect on Gwyn than he should have been having. Gwyn started to get tears in her eyes. She lovingly stroked his white head.

"Raspy is a funny dog with his unusual coloring," Gwyn was able to get out. "See the little reddish spots on his back? His mother was my dog. She died three months ago."

"I'm so sorry, Gwyn. So awful. Was she sick?"

Gwyn's voice was breaking, low and agitated. She shook her head. "I really don't want to talk about this."

Marlowe got up to move a little closer to pet Raspy.

"Gwyn, we can talk about it later if you want to. Let's focus on this big puppy here. It looks to me like he wants to jump up on your lap. I don't think he'll fit he's so big!"

Gwyn's face was getting red. She started to cry. She gently pushed Raspy down. His tail wagging, he lay down in the sun a few feet away.

"Marlowe, I don't know if I can get through telling you this but, but, you must hear it. It's why I wanted to see you today."

"Why you wanted to see me today?"

Gwyn's voice grew louder as though trying to force the words out. "You need to hear it. I told you I left the bench three months ago. Three months ago I took my dog for a run at Crescent Hill Park. About a half hour after we arrived two men called her away. They took her. Just like that. They put her in the cab of their pickup and just left with her. I was frantic. I called the police immediately on my cell. I couldn't see the truck really. It was too far away. I couldn't give them any description of it. She was simply gone!"

"Oh Gwyn, how—"

Gwyn was leaning forward. Her hands were holding either side of her head. "She had a microchip in her. The police found her a week later. She was in Lancaster County at a barn."

"At least you found her! Where is she?"

"Yes, they found her. She'd been killed! In a fight! Gwyn got up quickly in full-blown tears. Her chair crashed over backwards frightening Raspy away. "I'm sorry," she got out, "I can't tell you the rest,

Marlowe! I wanted to, I need to, but I can't. I wanted you here so I could tell you, but now I can't!"

Duffield. Marlowe remembered the police officer said a Lancaster barn. The other dogfighting site. The whole horrifying seen from the Federson paddock instantly forced itself into Marlowe's mind, her own tears coming. She got up moving toward Gwyn to comfort her.

"Was it bad, Gwyn?" she barely got out, not knowing what else to say.

"You've no idea, Marlowe. She was torn up. I saw a photo of her. A hind leg was missing. Her ears and her head and—" With that she was sobbing loudly, "Marlowe, I know you love animals, the Main Line Animal Shelter," she said concentrating on Marlowe's eyes.

"Marlowe I need you to—I need you to help me find out who did this! They need the harshest punishment possible! You agree, don't you?"

She couldn't get anything more out. Gwyn spun around and ran inside the house. Through the open doors Marlowe could see her dashing up the stairs taking them two at a time.

Missy came charging out of the house glaring at Marlowe. "What happened? What's wrong?"

"I don't know exactly," Marlowe stuttered trying to choke back her own tears. "Gwyn was telling me what happened to her dog."

"To *Raspberry*? Oh my lord!" Missy shrieked. "Oh my lord! It was all so terrible, terrible I tell you! She has nightmares every night!" she screamed running into the house.

Missy stopped at the foot of the stairs and shouted at Marlowe, "Why did you ask her about that dog?"

"I didn't ask her. She just started telling me."

"What? Why did she want to tell you that? Why did she bring it up? Why?"

Missy ran up the stairs calling after Gwyn.

Marlowe stood there staring after her in bewilderment, shock, and total sadness.

Chapter 16

Clearly Gwyn was not coming back out. Marlowe picked up her host's overturned chair, then sat back down in her own chair. She hadn't meant to cause her new friend such grief; her eyes filled with tears. She hadn't pressed for any additional information. Gwyn had wanted her to know. She'd said, "I want you to know, I want you to help me." How? Help her with what?

Trying to take a sip of her ice tea , spilling some on her chair, Marlowe pictured Gwyn's dog, Raspberry, and what her friend had started to say about the dog's legs and ears and head. Marlowe felt tears pooling as her mind imagined what had gone on inside the barn. She stood up. She had to get away, to leave Snowdon. She knew she was in no condition to drive. She walked slowly out into the garden area between the twin pools and toward the gazebo. She quickened her pace and ran the last few yards. She sat down heavily on a bench, trying to gather herself.

For a moment her eyes wandered to the gardens. The shrubs, the flowers, the ponds, the walks, the sun, the birds, the sky–it was all so beautiful. That scenic vista vanished in an instant.

The plight of Raspberry rushed madly in to take its place. Forcing its way in after that was the paddock scene from Duffield. To the woman whose only meaningful animal reference was from her child-hood happy times in Somerbury it was devastating.

Everything she'd been trying to escape came crashing down around her and her eyes started to smart. During the time after the fight at the Federson's Marlowe had been in shock, unable to feel the comprehensive enormity of what she'd witnessed and the blood on her hands. It was as though her brain automatically stepped back, protecting her from the pain. It had placed a wall in front of what she'd seen so her guts weren't ripped out. But that was then.

Now, here at Snowdon, the wall had been shot through with a cannon and fell to pieces in minutes leaving Marlowe fully exposed to the scene at the Duffield paddock. In her heart she knew all of the repression was going to end right then. Though her head was spinning she knew she had to confront it all if she were to emotionally heal and become functional, become functional to solve the mystery of who murdered all the animals.

Tears came to soothe her eyes. They would not be soothed. She knew it was coming, the things she'd repressed for years. She'd always had the ability to quickly shift her focus when terrible things presented themselves to her without warning. She knew that defense was gone now. Her face flushed. Her emotions thrust the flush down her neck and into her soul. She finally broke down in sobs. She made no effort to control herself. Her whole body heaved. The pageant of visions, the imagined sounds, it was too harsh, too dreadful to process, one thing after another. Added to that was the cumulative effect brought on by Gwyn's breakdown.

If Gwyn couldn't handle it, how could she, who was nowhere near the resilient, stalwart person Gwyn was. What she saw at the raid at Duffield, what she glimpsed despite trying to avoid and block out at the shelter when she witnessed injured animals brought into the veterinary hospital by the cruelty agents. The look of terror and excruciating agony in the eyes of the animals, some with scars—. All of a sudden, it all set in on her like a suppressed remembrance of the vilest nightmare.

She had repressed the enormity of what she had seen. Now it came relentlessly crushing through into her inner core into the hole which had been festering for the better part of twenty years, put there by her father, a hole which made her feel powerless. Gwyn was powerless to stop Lancaster, and Marlowe's core had already been severely pierced to leave a hole she'd never been able to mend. By his actions her father had made it clear to her she was not worthy, that she was not ever going to be capable of anything. Graduating from Yale, being successful at Wynne, getting the invitation to Anglesey, were not enough. They would never please her father, they wouldn't please him because he wasn't even watching her. She wasn't worth it. Marlowe believed e word of this, that down deep she was powerless, powerless to make any difference in anything. Piled on top of Duffield, Lancaster, Raspberry, there was something else.

Marlowe had trained herself on the few times she watched TV to be careful to be ready to change the channel if a show came on about animals. At any moment on these shows the viewer could see a lion chasing and ripping apart another animal, or some animal being hurt in some way, or even a commercial for an animal shelter showing a poor animal without a home, who wouldn't live if someone didn't adopt him.

The threat of seeing a show on TV or in a book when she turned the page to one of bad things happening to animals was real to Marlowe. While it had been there from her early teens it was driven home with tremendous force when she spent a couple of days in Jackson Hole.

It was a lesson taught by a mother and child.

Chapter 17

A few years ago, on a plane to a client meeting in Jackson Hole, she had turned the page in an oversized book. Without warning, it was staring her in the face. A photograph.

Here at Gwyn's, all of the repressed feelings, images from Duffield then hearing about Raspberry having been torn to shreds alive smashed the gate open for Jackson Hole to march uninvited, implacably into her mind.

It was like lava boiling up from deep in her memories, cascading out, annihilating anything in its path. This was the memory she had not permitted herself to revisit. This time, with everything else bombarding her, the memory presented itself to her for her to watch, moreover, worse, to feel. Buried closer to the surface than she ever believed was what had transpired in that Jackson Hole field.

Marlowe had taken a book about the pioneer movement west of the Mississippi along on the plane when she had gone to review accounts belonging to a wealthy family. She was to meet the clients in the late morning, stay overnight then go back the following morning. She'd planned to rent a car after the meeting to see some of the areas surrounding the town. From her reading she'd learned the pioneers stole the land plus anything on it, attacking, killing both the Indians and the bison in their path. Many early photographs from the time of the westward movement were in the book. One of those photographs haunted her from the moment she'd seen it on the plane. It was indelibly etched into her mind. It was obvious this one particular photo had been taken later in the day after the specific incident had occurred. The photo was of literally *thousands* of dead bison. Those westward moving pioneers had killed them all.

After her client meeting Marlowe had rented a car to drive to a field where she'd been told bison might be grazing. Having never seen a bison Marlowe was excited about the possibility. It was about two o'clock when she got to the field. No one else was around. The dirt road was obviously sparsely traveled. She saw four bison right away and drove to where they were. She got out of the car, even though she knew she shouldn't.

She stood in the short grass of the field, just beside the van. There they were. Four real bison were minding their own business, chomping away on the grass. Two were standing together. Another was a few feet away from them with her calf. Marlowe looked with fascination at each of the bison in turn, studying their brown fur, marveling at their great heavily furred heads, smallish horns, their long tails. These were great beasts, beautiful in their strength and bulk. The calf was of slight build with light tan fur. She guessed he was about six months old. He stayed close to his mother.

She mentally gazed at the photo she'd seen on the plane. The details, the images of blood and fur intermixed with each other, slowly began to appear. It had been a massacre. A quick turn for one so massive and muscular interrupted her images. The mother bison took steps slowly, obviously deliberately, toward her, the calf at her side. She stopped just fifteen feet in front of Marlowe. She faced her dead on.

Marlowe tightened. She knew from her reading, a bison's temperament is often unpredictable. Typically bison are passive, calm unless they perceive something threatening, however slight. Then they can become instantly provoked enough to charge. She'd read despite their heavy physique they are remarkably fast. They can run at more than thirty miles per hour plus use their heads to butt anything, or anyone, in their path. One had to be wary of them. It quickly registered in her mind to make matters worse, the bison had a calf she categorically would protect. Marlowe stood motionless. It was not that she couldn't have moved. She could have slowly, carefully, backed away to get in the car. She swiftly realized she was not going to move because she didn't want to.

Instead of backing away, Marlowe looked directly into the bison's eyes. Still facing the bison, she slowly, almost instinctively, walked sideways not toward the bison though on a parallel to the dirt road. The bison ever so slightly lowered her head following Marlowe's measured movement until Marlowe stopped about ten feet behind the car.

She concentrated on the bison. She was not afraid. She was somehow drawn to her. She wanted to make certain the bison was not needlessly provoked in any way. Marlowe stopped moving. The bison's muscles seemed to tense. Other than the slow turn of its great head following Marlowe's movement, she had no other reaction, not even a blink of her eyes. Having walked now well behind the car, Marlowe half realized she was a good distance away from the door of the car. She looked briefly away from the bison to look at the calf. He had moved up to his mother's head nuzzling in the thick fur on her neck. He was young, oblivious to what might be a true threat to himself, his mother or their two friends eating contentedly at a distance behind him.

Marlowe's eyes moved slowly to see beyond the bison. Houses were in the distance. The main road from Jackson Hole to Yellowstone was a quarter of a mile to the left. To the right was more grassy plain. These bison, this mother of this calf, were living among homes now, stripped of their wild beauty, corralled among cheap housing. It struck Marlowe as a heartbreaking tragedy of their lives compared to those of their ancestors when the herd would not have numbered four. It would have been in the thousands, surrounded by mountains and grassy plains for as far as the eye could see, when they roamed free, unfettered, proud.

The bison was not moving an inch, not flinching, not paying any attention to even her calf at her neck. Then slowly, almost unperceptively, her head with its horns lowered slightly more. The bison looked at Marlowe as they do when they are deciding whether to charge to protect their calf and themselves. The bison's muscles were tightly poised, at the ready at a moment's notice in anticipation of a possible looming disaster about to reveal itself. Marlowe wholly focused her gaze. She stared directly at the buffalo's eyes. The buffalo stared back. Each was intent, engaged.

In the short period of time while this standoff occurred, it registered to Marlowe it was highly unusual for an animal, any animal, to look directly into the eyes of a human, to stay focused not on other parts of the body, just the eyes. For Marlowe, it was as though a tightrope were strung from her eyes to the buffalo's then back again for she looked deep into those large brown eyes. In that moment, looking into the eyes of the mother ready to risk her life to keep her calf, her child, safe from threats of whatever magnitude, in a Coleridgian willing suspension of disbelief, Marlowe drank in and now truly comprehended the enormity of what the mother's forbearers in the photograph had endured.

Marlowe had seen in the photo the results of the mindless slaughter, the bleeding, the calves running without their mothers then being run down by the horses, left to slowly bleed to death in agony, their broken, trampled bodies barely hanging on to the thread of existence hoping for the miracle of life to be pumped back into them, hoping for their mother to magically appear. They were the lucky ones because they died by the end of the day. Others just lay there for another day while the crows and eagles ate them and their live brethren lying writhing in excruciating pain while the birds literally ate their festering life away.

Standing looking straight into the eyes of this bison mother, Marlowe saw through the ages what those white pioneers had done, done because the beasts were in their way, they were inconvenient.

Extrapolating, she saw what men still do, not to bison now, to other animals. How these men torture, maim and kill them for what they call sport or simple inconvenience. These are planned attacks on defenseless animals by men, like Pharaoh, whose hearts are hardened and revel in their blood sports, the persecution of living, breathing beings. Pioneers like these had seen bison calves looking to their mothers for protection even as the calves saw their mothers cut to ribbons before their innocent, doomed eyes.

In the photograph she had seen, Marlowe had heard the silent screaming of bison. The cries were an echo of the slaughter of the day. That silent scream was the same scream emanating from this bison standing before her. Not knowing what might happen, this bison through her dark eyes was pleading for the safety of her child. Marlowe looked directly at the bison before her, drinking in the steadfast gaze. The mother had not moved an inch. Marlowe saw in her eyes unforgiving anguish, outrage, loathing, indignation at what happened all those years ago.

In that moment, Marlowe understood.

While it seemed she had been standing there for hours, she realized all of this probably had occurred in the space of just a few minutes. She continued to gaze into the bison's eyes thinking the bison had somehow sensed Marlowe's epiphany. Then, without warning, the bison blinked and ever so gently raised and cocked her head. Her attitude changed slightly, as though she sensed her message to this one person had been completed and received. She looked at her child and then steadily back at Marlowe. Marlowe saw it.

Marlowe saw the message, saw the desperate pleading to stop it, for once and for all, not for her, but for her calf, as well as her calf's calf, to give all her animal brethren the simple respect they deserved as living beings. Marlowe was certain the bison was making an unwavering appeal, insisting she had neither a voice which could be heard for herself nor for her calf, however Marlowe, if she understood, was willing, did have the voice, so could put a stop to the killing, the torture. This one person standing before the mother could be the voice, salvation of all innocent, blameless animals, so thereby give to them the protected, secure life they by right deserve.

Marlowe stood transfixed. Silently weeping for the slain ancestors of this bison and for all tortured animals she helplessly wondered what the resolution was to this profound entreaty.

She was jolted back to the present when the mother, followed by her calf, turned to join the other two bison.

To Marlowe this renewed image of torture, maiming, mutilation of animals left to bleed in unfathomable pain was something she could never forget. Those long ago scenes of slaughter had passed down the decades to lodge in Marlowe's mind so sharply she could see and feel them herself. Getting back in the car, tears welling up, she reeled with agony at the memory of those godforsaken, barbaric times of the westward-moving settlers.

Whether the tightrope was really there, whether the silent scream from the rugged and majestic bison was really there didn't matter. What mattered was that mother's soul and Marlowe's soul had met in the continuum of life, miraculously connected for a few precious moments. Those moments and that connection were indelibly imprinted in Marlowe's mind. Marlowe remembered thinking, where's the outrage?

Where's the anger, the indignation about the bison of long ago? Where's the rage against animal torturers, killers now? Why isn't this on the cover of *Time*, of the *Wall Street Journal*, even of *Vogue*, for God's sake instead of the fashion trash? Why are people not talking about this? This is the United States of America, why isn't this stopped? People just move on, think about what's for dinner, about where their kids are going to college. Marlowe knew then she couldn't do that. You must find a way. You *must*.

"Remember Jackson Hole, Marlowe."

Chapter 18

Leaning forward on the gazebo bench, Marlowe propped herself up with her arms on her legs. She was staring at the gazebo floor-boards. "Marlowe," she said, "what happened there was six years ago. Remember 'Remember Jackson Hole'? You have to admit you've been successful in one thing in your life." Marlowe chided. "You've been able to run away from the bison."

"You've been able to just move on with your life as though what happened in that field didn't happen, you didn't swear to yourself you would do something about it. Was your old man right, Marlowe? Was he? Are you powerless ineffectual, like he said? Either remain power-less, forget it all and move ahead with your life. Or rise up, do some-thing about it this time. Which is it?"

The afternoon sun had passed lower at Snowdon. Marlowe sat back trying to calmly confront her own accusations, which she knew were true. She'd done nothing. The bright light shone under the gazebo roof was now shining on her face. The tsunami of gloom was leaving her. Finally, after what seemed like hours, she had quieted, her limp head hung low. She was breathing softly. Her eyes were closed. Her legs were stretched out on the flagstone. Her hands were clasped on her lap in what looked like prayer. She was exhausted, almost close to sleep. She began to feel the warmth on her face, which made her feel better. A male cardinal chatted on a forsythia bush nearby. She became aware of a slight sound. A squirrel sitting on the railing on the other side of the gazebo had a morsel in its mouth, patiently trying to expose any food it could get. As she watched the squirrel, a smile found itself creeping across her face.

Guilt was weighing heavily on her, the guilt of being unable to stop Raspberry's killers, the butchers of the bison, the death squad at Duffield, the slaughterers at the barn in Lancaster County. The anger and horror had been quietly building in her like a fine storm. When Gwyn told her about her cherished Raspberry, it all exploded, sending her hopelessly down a spiral into the depths of her own soul to find nothing, no power, no idea how to put a stop to it, nothing.

Though weak from the upheaval, the intense, debilitating emotions were expelled. She was relieved of the visions, at least for now. The little squirrel, through his persistence, showed her though events in the past were so terrible, life was still here. So was purpose. She felt slightly heartened at the doggedness of the tiny animal, intent on his job of finding his afternoon snack. With a new sense of some sort of unnamed promise, she lifted her head, felt the warmth of the sunlight, saw the dapple-grays grazing in their distant pasture. She rose.

Unsteadily Marlowe walked to the edge of the gazebo, down the two steps, back onto the green grass carpet path toward the house. She saw Dominic and James going about the business of their lives, heard the birds, saw the breathtaking array of flowers swaying lightly in the soft breeze. She slowed, turned to stared for no reason at the dapples, her focus gradually diffusing into nothingness. Her eyes were wide though were seeing nothing.

Standing alone, Marlowe deeply exhaled then softly asked, "So what am I going to do?"

Continuing to gaze sightlessly at the horses, Marlowe reflected how she'd been searching for herself, for what she really wanted to do. She didn't want to settle for just being a Financial Advisor. She had to do something meaningful. What could she do about everything she was confronting. She was just one person, a person with a full schedule.

She looked away from the horses and turned to look back toward the gazebo. Her nightmares were now taking on a much more serious nature as she looked at the gazebo, the bison making a hasty trip in front of her. Am I doomed to a life where I do nothing about those horrid things I see going on around me, where animals lose this death battle? Is it the few men who perpetrate these acts on animals, who put their foot up on a bison to pose for a photograph, get caught, get a slap on the wrist. That's it? This is your chance, your chance to sew up the hole you're always talking about once and for all. Right now. You want victories. This is the only victory you will need. If Gwyn wants your help in something having to do with this, do it. This is your focus now, Marlowe. She looked back at the dapples. One was looking at her. She held out her right arm, pointing at him.

"I promise you I will do this."

Looking back at her, the dapple arched his neck, picking his head up, staring back at her. She turned back toward the house and spied Missy in an open second floor window looking out at her. Marlowe gave her a little wave heading back to the terrace.

"I'm sorry, Ms. Evans," she said in a hushed voice at the bottom of the stairs.

"How's Gwyn?"

"She's sleeping comfortably now. She'll feel better in a couple of hours. Don't worry yourself. It wasn't your fault. I don't know why

Judge Llewellyn wanted to tell you about our dear Raspberry. I'm sure she had a reason. I do apologize, Ms. Evans, for my outburst."

"Oh, Missy, no apology necessary," responded Marlowe reaching forward to give her a hug.

Marlowe felt she was now a part of the family at Snowdon. She didn't know how, nevertheless she felt it. Maybe because she had precious little family left, just her treasured brother, Skip, really. Other than him, a father whom she seldom saw, no husband, not even a boyfriend.

Missy opened the front door for Marlowe. "Max will open the gates for you as you approach the end of the driveway. Goodbye, Ms. Evans."

"Take care, Missy, I hope to see you again."

Nodding with a confident smile, Missy replied, "Oh, I think you will, Ms. Evans, I think you will."

Briefly scanning Missy's face, Marlowe tried to read what she meant. She came up empty.

Chapter 19

After the difficult afternoon she'd had at Snowdon, Marlowe wasn't going to go back to her office. She headed home. She decided on the spot to call her brother Skip to see if he could meet her for dinner at Somerset. In addition to Nick, Skip was the rock in her life. She wanted to talk to him about Duffield. She needed to discuss with him what might be her next steps in identifying the fight organizer to bring him to justice.

"Hi Marlowe!"

"Dinner tonight at Somerset?"

"Of course. 7:00?"

"Done. See you then."

Her brother had always looked out for her as a kid. He continued to do so. Marlowe needed that feeling tonight. She wanted to talk to him about the Main Line Animal Shelter. He'd just gotten off the Board of Directors last year. He was likely still connected there. He would know Luca. Since Marlowe was relatively sure the perpetrator was local, the shelter may know who he is, or at least have suspicions. Maybe even Skip might have an idea.

Skip was at the bar when Marlowe arrived at the club. She gave him a big hug, which she found herself holding longer than normal.

It was like when she was a kid, hurt herself doing something and went to Skip for help. Five years Marlowe's senior, Skip would assess her for injuries then hold her until her crying had turned to smiles again. At least for the moment, that's all it took again for Marlowe's spirits to rise.

"How's my big brother doing? I'm sure you haven't been behaving yourself. Spill it, what've you been up to?"

"Frustrating, Marlowe, really frustrating," he said, shaking his head, frowning.

"Why, what's going on?" Marlowe asked, concerned.

"I can't break seventy eight—it's killing me."

"You're bizarre, Skip. A whole lot of people would be glad to have such a golf score."

"Unfortunately I do know this, not much consolation though. What are you drinking? I'm buying."

"Terrific, I'll have a pinot noir. With all of your ill-gotten gains and clubs you belong to you may not remember, Big Stuff, you aren't a member of Somerset."

"I know that, my dear. I remember your club number. I've been signing."

"Did I mention you're pitiable beyond words?"

Getting the bartender's attention, Skip asked, "Jackson, may I please ask for a pinot noir for my beautiful talented little sister here?"

"Of course, Mr. Evans. Another Dewers for you, sir?"

"How kind of you to ask. Yes, thank you."

Skip had on a charcoal gray suit, crisp white shirt, pink tie. He was the kind of man who could get away with the pink tie. Always at weight, Skip had put in a fitness room in his condominium. He used it daily. It seemed to Marlowe that Skip simply had his life in order, his feet firmly on the ground. Things were under control in his life, as they always had been. He was cool, confident, self-effacing. It didn't matter what the subject, Skip had it down pat. She loved him because he was her brother. She also loved him for his strength of character, a trait she suspected may not be the norm in men.

When their table was ready, Marlowe and Skip went into what she knew to be one of the finest dining rooms in the area. After ordering, Marlowe related without details what she and Ashanti had done at Duffield. She also briefly told him what Gwyn had told her about Raspberry. Even in these abbreviated forms, both stories made her visibly upset.

Skip reached across the table to took her hand in both of his. "Marlowe, you need to remember who we were, who you still are. You aren't aware of what's been going on in the world of animal fighting or animal abuse. Unfortunately most people are accustomed to hearing about these things. They are hardened to it. I doubt you read anything other than financial papers, magazines. CNBC is your regular TV. When was the last time you watched the world news?"

Marlowe shrugged.

Skip wasn't letting her off the hook. "How much do you have under management, Marlowe?"

"Including today, a whole lot," she said.

He grinned, feeling better, she grinned back. Skip always had that effect on her. It was particularly comforting to be with Skip tonight.

"A few hundred million or more? You see? This is where your life has been. You've been focused on your job, your clients. Look at you now. While we're on the subject—"

"What subject?"

"Men."

"I don't recall being on such a subject at all, Skip," giving him her version of an evil eye, which included a curled upper lip.

Sitting back like he'd just won a card game, Skip said, "Well, we're on it now, so before I forget to mention it to you I've invited one of my business buddies to join us for a drink at the bar after dinner."

"Oh for Pete's sake, Skip. You need to stop." Marlowe wasn't sure whether to be embarrassed at having to meet someone or whether it might just be a good idea.

"Let's see, you're how old, Marlowe? Yes, I seem to remember you're about twenty-eight, a really busy woman with no time to seek out the important things in life, like a nice husband. Big brother is just helping his kid sister along, that's all."

"Okay, fine, Skip, fine!" She sank in her chair a bit, realizing there was no stopping this train.

"Would it help if I told you he's good looking?" Skip asked, with a huge grin.

"*Stop!*" Marlowe said, leaning forward to her dinner partner, her eyes flashing.

"Back for a moment to Duffield." Skip said, corralling himself back into normal dinner conversation mode. "My personal opinion, not supported by any specific intel, is this whole situation is larger than may be generally believed. I don't know where to go yet with such an idea. If I find out anything I'll call you. In the meantime, be businesslike in your efforts. The killers could be anybody. Watch out for anything odd, out of character with someone; these could be clues."

"Have you talked to Luca Pasquale?" Marlowe asked, remembering her brother had been on the Shelter Board of Directors a couple of years ago.

"I talked to him this afternoon. Apparently the FBI has an interest in the case. He wouldn't tell me why he wasn't happy about it. He said he has some leads. The chances are good whoever did the Lancaster fight did Duffield. Whoever they are, Luca said, they are pros at it, organized. Other than that I don't know anything. There's nothing definite yet. They'll get them, Miss Marlowe. You can count on it.

"You need to concentrate on your Wynne clients. Think of it this way. The shelter always needs money, a lot of it. If you keep building your book of business you'll have the money with power to create something for the shelter. Otherwise they wouldn't have the money to do by themselves. Something big. When the time comes, my sister will know what to do. I know you. You can do this, Marlowe."

Marlowe held back tears. For a few seconds she bowed her head, taking it all in. The one person who could have really helped her in all this was sitting right in front of her telling her she was good, she was smart enough to do something for animals that was really meaningful, through her own work she would have the power to make some sort of major change for all the animals she loved. In quick succession the bison and the dapple made a mental appearance then left, uplifting Marlowe like she hadn't been since before the Anglesey meeting. She had hope now.

Their entrees arrived.

Skip took a few bites of his stuffed flounder. "By the way, have you continued to practice your shooting? I always forget to ask you. Still have your thirty eight?"

"I have my boys, yes, I go to the range from time to time, just to keep my edge. How about you? Oh, never mind, how could I forget you imagine yourself one of the founders of the NRA."

"Your boys?"

"Yes, Smith and Wesson," Marlowe said with the slightest of smiles.

"Can you be any more like a girl? Calling your gun 'the boys?'" Skip asked, both tickled as well as proud of his kid sister at the same time. "Really, Marlowe! Though I have to admit, it's kind of cute. I'm still at the Whitehall Gun Club. You still go too, don't you?"

"I manage to get out three or four times a year."

"That's great, Marlowe, keep it up. I can remember even when you were a kid you were incredibly accurate. I remember when we had the three hay bales out in the field stacked with empty soup cans on top for targets. Remember what happened?"

"If memory serves I wanted to try tuna cans." Marlowe was tickled at the memory of shooting with her brother.

"Because they were smaller targets. My memory is you never missed."

"You've a bad memory, Skip. I missed some."

"Maybe one. Hey, let's talk about current events instead of that crazy childhood. What I want to talk about is Parker. What's going on? We haven't talked about him recently."

"Recently? We haven't talked about him for a while because there is no Parker in my life anymore."

"I heard about Parker. You seemed great together. I was sure he was the one for you."

"He hinted a couple of times maybe it was time to get married. After a while I realized I just didn't feel that way about him. I did have an email from him yesterday though. He wanted to get together for lunch. He said something about having a question for me about Nick." Marlowe frowned a little. "He may he just trying to pull us back together. I didn't respond."

"Anybody new on the horizon?" Skip asked, mischievously cocking his head as he enquired.

"Well, yes, in a miniscule way," Marlowe responded, a little grin appearing.

"What does 'in a way' mean? Translates how? He's married? That's not your style."

"No, he's never been married. He's different. He's unlike anyone else I've ever met. The 'in a way' means he doesn't know I'm interested in him."

A man like Adam, Marlowe conjectured, would prefer the real deal, the real Main Line woman, not some reformulated hick from a country town. He would want a woman whose family had been here before the Mayflower was even built, who had gone to any one of the highly acclaimed private schools, whose family had been members of their clubs, the opera, the orchestra, *et. al.* since the beginning of time. He would want the kind of woman whose only possible complaint in life could be her titanic clothes closet didn't have enough rods for her ball gowns. Marlowe managed a giggle. She would have to muse later about why Adam potentially could ever have any real interest in her except she wanted him to.

"Well who is Mr. McDreamy?" Skip was waving his hand at her like a traffic director would. "Let's go! *Name!*"

"Skip! He's not Mr. McDreamy. He's just a *guy* I know."

"Ooh! The little feisty part in you is coming out—this must be serious. You know, Marlowe, you might be able to get away with such stuff with your Main Line friends. Disregard that, this is Skip you're talking to here. Do you really expect me to believe he's 'just a guy I know?' Let's go, Marlowe, details. Your turn to spill it!" Skip demanded, hitting his right hand on the tabletop, possibly a bit louder than he had intended. His head was forward, leaning in like he was a drill sergeant, still with a smile.

Marlowe tucked her chin and leaned back into her chair. Without mentioning his name, Marlowe briefly explained who Adam was.

"Well, whoever this no-name is, I have someone better for you to meet. Period, end of statement."

"I doubt it."

"We're going to find out in about five minutes."

"Really? How is that going to happen?"

"Simple. He's probably at the bar right now waiting to meet this lovely vision of my little sister. Besides, he's well connected both in Center City besides on the Main Line. You should talk to him about who he might suspect is the Duffield guy. It wouldn't surprise me if he had a good idea."

"Oh for God's sake, Skip," Marlowe snapped, glaring at him. "I don't want to meet whoever it is. I do admit I'd like to talk to him about the fight, no matter what a creep he is."

"Well good, you can't avoid it anyhow. We have to pass the bar to leave. Gotcha!"

Sounding as innocent as he possibly could, Skip suggested, "Let's get a Baileys at the bar, shall we?"

Marlowe gave him a dirty look.

When they got up Skip reached for Marlowe, gave her a good brotherly hug and a kiss on her cheek. "Love you, Marlowe. You're going to be okay. Sometimes you forget this. You're a rock. You're indomitable. Always have been, you just don't always see it." Marlowe knew he was talking about Duffield, She silently thanked him for it.

They walked through the wide hallway toward the bar. Marlowe suddenly stopped and hissed, "Skip, he's here!"

Skip stopped, turning toward her. "What?" He asked in a normal voice.

"Sh! He's at the bar!"

"Who?" His voice was quieter.

"McDreamy!" Marlowe whispered as she observed Adam talking to of all people Jack Danett.

"McDreamy? Adam is McDreamy? Let's go buy him a Baileys!" Grinning from ear to ear Skip turned to Marlowe to put his hand on her shoulder.

"You're kidding, this is the guy? Love you, Marlowe. This is the guy for you, I'm telling you. I don't know why I didn't put it together before. It's perfect. Let's go."

Adam looked up and saw Marlowe, who was still at a distance from the bar. She blushed. "I'm dead," she mouthed, checking to see if her dress was straight, wondering if she'd checked her hair in a mirror when she first got there. This is horrendous, she thought. I could have worn my black sling-back stilettos instead of these clunky, one-inch high pieces of old lady shoes I should have thrown out the day after I bought them on sale, marked down after that.

She watched Skip stride toward Adam and Jack. Her stealth discovery process of Adam was shot to smithereens. Skip, Skip, Skip, please don't say anything. Struggling to remain poised, Marlowe followed her brother.

"Looking lovely this evening, Marlowe," said Adam, shaking her hand. For a second Marlowe imagined he held her hand just a bit longer than would be usual. "Skip invited me here to meet his sister—he never mentioned your name. I never imagined you were his sister."

Was he just looking at her cordially or was it almost a kind of gaze? Marlowe wanted it to be a gaze.

"I understand your big brother took you to dinner, how nice."

"Well yes, he—"

"Signed your number. He told me! You know Jack, of course. When Skip called I judged Jack might like to test someone else's booze instead of his own at Harlech Gate, so asked him to come too. With warm smiles Marlowe and Jack shook hands. Skip was ordering Baileys for everyone.

Adam turned to Marlowe, leaning down a little to whisper to her. "We need to meet tomorrow morning at 8:30. Can you make it?"

"Gosh, didn't we already finish?" Marlowe whispered back.

"Not quite. You'll be there? It's important." Adam said, taking a half step closer to her.

Marlowe mentally hesitated. She hadn't noticed Adam had moved toward her, though she was looking directly into Adam's eyes. Something about them made her forget where she was. The pile of work she needed to do took a spin through her head. Add to that two scheduled meetings in the morning she'd have to reschedule. Could she do it? Unlikely. Wait, this is a second invitation to a meeting with this group. She needed to do this. And look who's asking—McDreamy! For heaven's sake, Marlowe demanded, snap out of it, you nut job—it's *Adam*. Do it!

"I'll be there."

Chapter 20

Marlowe's Porsche chirped as she opened the door. She felt excited for her second meeting with Anglesey. As she slid into the driver's seat, her phone rang. The screen indicated it was Sol, except the voice on the other end was Kim, his housemaid.

"What's wrong," Marlowe asked.

"Sol had a call last night around eleven o'clock that upset him. When he hung up, he said something like 'those people are just like the movie character.' I think he used the name 'Fran.' I didn't press him for more information. It was just so odd. The call came through so late, which upset him. I wanted to let you know."

Marlowe promised Kim she'd follow up with Sol later. Right now, she had no time to spare to think about who Sol was speaking with or what he may have meant. Marlowe arrived at Harlech at 8:25. The restaurant had not yet opened for business. When she walked in she saw Franny, Malik, Jack and Adam waiting for her in the foyer. They had no books or folders. They were standing talking in a close group.

"Glad you could make it this morning on short notice, Marlowe," Franny said. "Let's head down to the meeting room."

Marlowe had decided on the drive to Harlech that the room would be more aptly called "the vault." She'd already lightheartedly mused about the fact she could be taken to their room by the austere Anglesey Philosophical Society members. Were she to have disagreed with their philosophies of life, left in the vault to age like the portraits until she came around to their point of view. Marlowe felt her life concepts fortunately seemed to meld nicely with theirs.

Once again following Adam through the dining room then through the door wasn't a regular door, Marlowe mulled over how odd it was they insisted on having to have the *Candide* meeting conclusion immediately. *Candide* certainly was not going anywhere. Exactly what was omitted the day before? She'd no doubt each of the Anglesey members were as exacting as she was. On the other hand wasn't this overstressing about the novel's implications? At the same time Marlowe deemed it eccentric, strange, she was nonetheless quietly thrilled to be included. If her presence was important enough to be invited to this second meeting, perhaps it meant she was going to be a member. That is, if she wanted to be.

When everyone was seated in the Anglesey room, Franny convened the meeting by clarifying the reason for the second meeting. She looked at each person as she spoke.

"While we abundantly analyzed the novel itself, the discussion of *Candide* was unfortunately interrupted at the point where we would have considered whether any meaning from the novel might pertain to anything going on in our lives now."

"Oh, a fascinating idea," Marlowe agreed.

"Let's take something we became aware of at the time we were assembled last time, the Duffield Manor incident," Malik proposed. "Since it happened less than twenty minutes from here and we all know the Federsons, let's see if there is anything to be learned from *Candide*."

Marlowe's face fell. Her excitement about what she supposed would be the discussion changed to dread. The last thing she wanted to do was talk about what she had been mentally reliving ever since leaving the paddock two days ago. She didn't want to resuscitate those images. Depending on the direction of the discussion, she would get up to leave without so much as a word. At any time, she could just leave, she told herself. Reassured she had an escape plan from what she might hear, Marlowe turned her attention to Malik.

As the discussion had proceeded at the last meeting, the members discussed and then agreed on an action that would be taken in a certain circumstance.

Franny summarized the conclusion.

"The conclusion we've reached together is in the Duffield case, our specific case for purposes of applying our conclusions of the real theme of *Candide* is as follows. If the person responsible for the torture and deaths of animals as is the case of the animals at Duffield, is identified, he should be penalized to the greatest extent of the law. If the law isn't sufficient in its measure of penalty then it is incumbent upon those who observe this situation to make things right."

Malik, Jack, Adam and Franny were in agreement, though Marlowe had questions.

"Fine," Looking at each member, Franny said. "Thank you to everyone for coming on such short notice."

"Agreed, Adam?"

Chapter 21

Marlowe called Ashanti. "You won't believe the Anglesey meeting I just left."

"What meeting? The meeting was on Tuesday. What was this one about?"

"Good question. We talked about some really heavy stuff. I was both fascinated yet on the other hand uncomfortable. I can tell you one thing though. These people are some of the most erudite, intellectual, and engaged I've ever met, including the professors at grad school. From what I can see their conclusions are based on multi-layered logic. Given their wide breadth of knowledge it's like each one of them is a Renaissance man."

"Of course I've no idea what you're really talking about. I must say I'm thrilled you've potentially found a group of people you can enjoy. Can you tell me anything more about the meeting?"

"Not really. I can't lay my finger on it. Staying true to their standard of not discussing anything with a non-member, I can say they used the book we'd discussed to talk about a current event. I found it really intriguing."

"Wow, peculiar. I guess it does follow to use the book as a springboard to a meaningful discussion."

"If I could tell you the subject, Ashanti, you'd think it might be scary."

"I remember you said they swore you to secrecy. Sure they aren't just back in college having a bull session?"

"Yes, I guess it does sound questionable. No, these people are real. It seems like this was not just a conversation about the topic."

Marlowe stopped talking for a moment. She recalled they were talking about the Duffield killer. Marlowe was aware she was making a leap here. Were they talking about whether the law itself was going to mete out a sufficient penalty? Using the same logic they themselves would employ so well, Marlowe deduced what they were saying was it was the obligation of those who recognized the injustice to make things right. The killer had to pay. This had to have been their specific, albeit unstated, conclusion. If so, was Franny's parting charge to Adam connected?

"Ashanti, you there?"

"Yes, I know you well enough to know you were thinking about the meeting. I didn't want to interrupt. What do you think?"

"No, I don't have any idea what Franny said. Adam responded with just one word, 'understood.' It could have been about anything at all, the next meeting, the next book, some kind of business. It could have been about anything."

At this juncture Marlowe wanted to tell Ashanti everything, except she couldn't be certain her deductions were accurate. And even if they were, what did they mean precisely? Although she didn't know Adam well, she liked what she'd seen to date. She couldn't imagine Adam would do anything against the law. He was a lawyer, for heaven's sake. Skip had mentioned Adam might have some idea about the dog fights. Marlowe started to wonder if they fit into anything said at the meeting.

Did Adam have an idea who was responsible? When was she going to have the opportunity to ask him?

"It isn't like you have to do anything, right? Don't worry about it, at least for tonight. Go home and relax. Get a good night's sleep. Girls' night out tomorrow night, Marlowe! Just like we always do, we're going to have a blast."

"You're right. Marlowe adored Ashanti not only for her professionalism as an MD, but also her continuous ability to see to the heart of almost any matter to arrive at a sensible conclusion providing wonderful guidance. She was a true friend to Marlowe. She loved her. See you tomorrow. I'll be ready too. I might just wear my neat tank top I got through the Blazes Tops catalogue."

"Through a catalogue, Marlowe? You're incorrigible! Repeat after me. 'Shopping is fun. Shopping is relaxing.' I'm going to set up an intervention with the few friends you really have to force you to understand shopping is therapy."

"Catalogues are easy."

"You're *hopeless*!"

"Will it make you happier to know I spent a mint at Emerald Style at the mall to get my jeans?"

"Okay, I feel better. We may still have to do an intervention. Goodness, Marlowe, the Blazes Tops catalogue."

"Love you too. See you tomorrow. By the way I have a little something for you. I'll give it to you then."

"Cool!"

When Marlowe finally got home from Wynne it was about 7:30. She poured herself a glass of chardonnay and turned on the bath water. It was the end of a long day on top of the confounding meeting. Thanks to the conspiracy of the warm water perhaps the wine, Marlowe was finally able to relax. Strider was already on the bed waiting for Marlowe to reappear. To Strider, bedtime was the ultimate part of his day. It was when he got lots of pets from Mom as both fell asleep all snuggled in.

Strider would have to wait. Still in the tub Marlowe realized she had gotten a call toward the end of the Anglesey meeting. She hastily got out, got dried and put her sweats on. No messages appeared on her phone. Sol's number showed as a missed call. Marlowe tried his number. No answer. It was already getting late. Sol or Kim should be home. Marlowe called Kim's cell.

"Marlowe! I tried to call you. I'm at the hospital with Sol. He had another pain in his chest."

Marlowe was back in her car five minutes later on her way to the hospital. With everything going on with Duffield and Anglesey she was upset at herself for nonetheless not going to see Sol before this. Sol had encouraged her at Wynne from the day she had met him. Over the last few years Marlowe had learned Sol was actually an extremely wealthy, accomplished man in the tech area. He never wanted to talk about any of his accomplishments; he preferred to talk with her about the securities markets. He consistently encouraged her to become even better, more insightful about the markets than she already was. At the hospital after asking at the desk what room Sol was in, Marlowe ran up the two flights of stairs then down the hall. When she got to the room Sol was not there, nor was Kim. She started to hurry out of the room to find him just as a nurse was wheeling him on his hospital bed down the hall back to the room. The look on the nurse's face was not encouraging. Marlowe saw Kim following the nurse. She waited to talk to Kim before she talked to Sol.

"Kim?"

"Marlowe, thank goodness you're here. Poor Sol, I'm worried." Kim said softly. An anguished look was on her already tired face.

Looking from Kim to Sol to the nurse who was turning into the room, Marlowe asked, "How bad is it?"

"According to his chart this one is about the same as the prior incident."

Marlowe saw the relief on Kim's face, she felt it herself. When the bed was in place, Marlowe went over to Sol's bedside. He reached for her hand. A slight smile emerged. He was trying to speak. She leaned over closer to him.

She barely heard him say, "I'll be fine. I always am." He tensed his grip on her hand slightly. "Marlowe…." His eyes closed.

He momentarily dosed off. Marlowe knew he wasn't fine. He was pale, it was obvious he was struggling to put up a good front for the young woman he'd come to respect so much, the woman he'd watch grow at Wynne from a new graduate of Yale to a stellar money manager. In a couple of minutes he was awake again.

"I know I've said this to you before, I won't say it again."

"You know I was at a second Anglesey meeting, don't you," Marlowe interrupted him, ignoring the Anglesey code.

"I'm not going to talk about it. You need to just trust me, Marlowe." Both the nurse and Kim had left the room. Sol did the best he could to turn toward Marlowe. "You must ask yourself why you were invited the first time. Why you. I have no answers for you. You need to think about it, to be aware if they contact you again. Maybe they won't. If they do, pay attention to why, to what they want."

After seeing Sol, Marlowe went out into the hall to a lounge area reflecting on Sol's comments. For him to persevere about Anglesey was bothersome to her. Yes, Sol was ailing, which could account for his singleness of purpose. Nevertheless it could also be because he knew he was dying so was becoming centered on a matter he felt genuinely important. Marlowe was glad she'd had a chance to see him. At the same time she didn't feel she had to change anything having to do with Anglesey. She decided though, to be wary were she to have any further interaction with the members.

She also mulled over Gwyn's situation. Being a judge, she must have connections. She must have some idea about who might be responsible. Then there's Nick. He has to have ideas too, Why didn't he ever tell her about his daughter. The omission is effectively a lie. A big one. Can you trust him? You have more detective work to do, Marlowe. You need to get on this.

On the drive home from the hospital Marlowe questioned whether she was up for going out the next night with her girlfriends. She felt tired. The last few days of mental anguish were translating into physical weariness. On the other hand when she was talking to Ashanti about what she was going to wear, she was having fun. She figured going would be like so many times when she was scheduled to play tennis except didn't really want to go. She was scheduled, she had to go play. Invariably, strangely, by the time she started putting her socks on then putting her sneaks on and starting to lace them up, she was mentally all ready to go. There was something else nagging at her. She felt guilty going out drinking and dining after all of the animals at Duffield had been so brutalized. It was dishonoring their suffering, their death by forgetting about them even if for only one night. As fatigued as she was right then driving home, she had to go to Reynard Run tomorrow night. If she were going to remain engaged in solving the Duffield crime, she needed to be strong, resolute. That would happen if she were well rested and in a constructive, clear frame of mind. She knew it was the right thing to do.

I'll be there, Fox!

Chapter 22

Marlowe looked forward to the hiatus of an uncomplicated, fun evening with her girlfriends. No split-second securities decisions to make, no clients to impress, no CNBC to watch, no Anglesey Philosophical Society to ponder, no Duffield Manor to ruminate on, as awful as it might sound. She even intended to leave her phone in the car, which shocked even her.

Marlowe's plan was to leave the office by five o'clock then go directly home to get ready for the evening. Instead of staying until five, Marlowe decided to leave Wynne early. The powerful horses under her Porsche hood were whinnying to her to get a move on anyhow. She answered their call by leaving a half hour early. Besides she had to stop by the jewelry store to pick up the gift she'd gotten engraved for herself and Ashanti.

When Marlowe finally arrived home, she had just enough time to have some wine and relax for a few minutes before getting ready to go out. Home for Marlowe was a four thousand square foot Wissahickon schist stone home built in the nineteen thirties, then fully renovated by the seller who sold to Marlowe a few years ago. It was a perfect size. Then a short time later her funny, sweet, rescued Hudson, a Rottweiler/pitty mix, died. The vet had said it was just old age. Now the family was just her along with Strider, though she wanted to get another dog for herself and as a companion for Strider.

She poured herself a half glass of Jacob's Creek chardonnay to take up to her bedroom to unwind for a few minutes in her favorite chair.

A text came in from her friend Olivia who'd sent it to Lindsey, Rachel, Ashanti and Marlowe: "Let's break tradition. Let's meet at the bar for twenty minutes re Duffield. See you there. Logan not coming."

Looking at Strider Marlowe said, "This is good. I need help on this, Strider. Maybe I can make them into my Duffield posse, like the sheriff did in the old cowboy movies. We'll only talk for twenty minutes, It'll be enough." She smiled at Strider, who gave her a tail wag equivalent to a marine oorah.

Though determined not to think about bad things, Sol's comment about making sure she asked questions if she were contacted by any of the Anglesey members trotted through her mind. Just maybe Sol's source of bits and pieces of information was Franny, not that it mattered. Fortunately for maintaining her happy mood, she dismissed the thought of whether she would be acceptable to Anglesey. She wouldn't be invited back. Why would she, she questioned, frowning. Many other people would be better than she would, more conversant, better educated, more successful, just better.

Having dismissed her frown, Marlowe's eyes found their way to the portraits she dearly loved. Sitting on the chair opposite the portraits, she could view the three prints hanging on the wall to the left of her bed also the three to the right. They were large portraits matted with three-inch off-white matting framed in four-inch wide antique gilt, wooden frames. Whenever she felt the need to decompress, Marlowe gazed at the intricacies of the paintings.

Enjoying her wine, though she realized she could have poured a little more in the glass, Marlowe looked first at Queen Whippley, a portrait of a white and tan whippet. Looking every inch a proud queen, Whippley was dressed in a traditional, stylish black gown with an eggshell-white ruffled, wide Elizabeth collar befitting her station.

Next was Betsy, a stunning tan patrician boxer donned in a Renaissance style gown with a gray and black thin-striped bodice, red cummerbund along with delightfully puffy maroon and black sleeves. Her white fur below her head and the black fur around her mouth and eyes bespoke her status.

Beside her was the magnificently impressive Baron von Bullenbeiszer, a bulldog suitably sporting a mottled black and orange full cape and a rather flat, soft velvet black hat with a single long white feather extending into the air. The white fur of the Baron's muzzle extended upward in a narrow blaze between his dark eyes imparting a good-humored, cheerful look. When Marlowe had first gotten the portraits she mused that a man trimmed out like the Baron would be a perfect husband, or or at least the perfect dashing boyfriend.

And then on the right was William Pettibone, a sleek pewter-gray Weimaraner wearing a dark blue jacket with gleaming brass buttons, a cinnamon-colored waistcoat and a soft, old-lace colored silk shirt with a floppy bow at the neck. Sir Pettibone's head, befitting his prominence, was covered with a formal wig of lateral silver gray curls extending almost down to the bottom of his long, dangly ears. Marlowe admitted to herself that if as a man Sir Pettibone would consider losing the gray curls, he could be a boyfriend contender as well.

Duke Andy, a Bernese mountain dog, was in the center position looking regal in his thick, black, white and silver mantle with his shimmering, lacy shirtsleeves peeking out from underneath. With his steady, unrelenting gaze made more direct by the two scallops of brown plus a thin line of white in his otherwise black forehead, the Duke was a figure to be admired highly respected.

The last of the portraits, Nathaniel Setterton, an Irish setter, with his numerous, glistening medals of excellence appropriately positioned hanging around his neck with his ruby-red sash over his shoulder, looked mighty, stalwart in his black military jacket replete with golden epaulets.

The joy in seeing these six portraits always forced whatever might be negative in her mind to the far back. The combination of them along with the incredible Strider always released Marlowe to a happier state.

Marlowe changed into her new jeans. She thoroughly enjoyed these evenings with her friends because they talked about the important things in life, like where do you get the coolest jeans, not that Marlowe herself would actually go shopping for them, who does the neatest haircuts, what are the new foods with fewer calories. Then after a drink or two, the most important topic inevitably reared its glorious self. Men. Marlowe could not wait to let her hair down, relax, have a couple or more pinot noirs, eat some good food, and enjoy the camaraderie of her friends. Instead of the tank top she decided on her American SPCA white T-shirt with a sweet cat with "We are Their Voice" in the center. She loved wearing it because you could see the cat along with the message under her linen, cream-colored, cropped blazer.

She slipped into her black three-inch sling-back heels. For once when she looked in the full-length mirror before she left, she admitted she looked good, not hot, although good. That was enough. She worked on her hair to encourage some curls and a slight flip at the ends, then sprayed lightly so it would behave itself all evening. Grabbing her black clutch, with one last look in the mirror, she was ready.

Back in her bedroom, seeking final approval from those who demonstrably understood fashion, she glanced at each of the six large personage portraits. She concluded they *in toto* pronounced her ready for the evening.

Strider was getting excited because, although he may have judged high heels were extravagant, it was after all, he was pretty sure, Friday night. That meant he was going out for another walk. Sadly, as Marlowe went downstairs to pick up her keys from the table in the foyer, poor Strider knew he was not going for the walk. Anytime he saw his mom pick up keys, he knew he was not going out. He knew he now had a serious mission until she returned. He was happy because now he got to guard the house for Mom. Of course Mom knew if someone got in the house Strider would most likely invite him into the kitchen to share a bowl of vanilla ice cream.

Chief of Security: Strider Evans—ice cream is in the freezer.

Chapter 23

At seven o'clock the Porsche cruised into the parking lot at Reynard Run Pub, a popular destination on Friday nights, in the heart of Wayne. Just short of gourmet, the food at the pub was excellent, the liquor was top shelf. By now, the bar would be filled with professionals celebrating the end of the workweek.

Marlowe was excited about having fun with Ashanti as well as seeing her other good friends of the Rolling Hill Gang to boot. They were all of different ages. It didn't matter to any of them. These friends were her closest. They believed in themselves, all type A's, as the alpha dogs. They were clear on the concept. It really doesn't matter whether you think you're an alpha dog or whether you are one. It was no matter to these women. They knew they were undeniably alpha dogs, pure and simple, no doubts, no discussion. Despite her accomplishments, every now and then Marlowe questioned, as she had all her life, whether she could really run with them.

Ashanti was her closest friend. The others were not distant seconds. Rachel Cohen from Gladwyne was the administrator of Whitefield Hospital. Olivia Holland from Haverford, a former marine, was the CFO of Penn Printers. Lindsay Dugan from Bryn Mawr was a partner at Greyford Haddington, LLC, a major Philadelphia law firm. Logan Bell from Wayne was the retired founder of Bell Ruddington Law.

Ashanti and Marlowe both had houses in Haverford, so they all lived relatively close together so could carve out time for dinner. One of the things Marlowe loved about these women was they had full personal lives yet were still standouts in their vocational fields.

About five years earlier Marlowe fortuitously met Rachel, Olivia, Lindsay, Logan along with their dogs at the off-leash dog park at Rolling Hill Park in Gladwyne on a brisk fall Saturday afternoon. As they chatted they realized they shared a love for animals, were committed to their families (whatever form it took) along with their vocations. They hit it off so well they agreed to meet every quarter at a restaurant to catch up and have a good time. It was when Ashanti joined the group they began calling themselves the Rolling Hill Gang.

Knowing they normally would never make it to the dining room if they went to the bar first, they had agreed at each dinner they would meet in the dining room instead of the bar. Tonight would be different.

Although Marlowe was five minutes early, the others were already seated in the bar area at a high-top. She hopped onto the chair next to Logan.

"Let's get right to it," Olivia said. "Marlowe, we know you and Ashanti were there. Knowing you love animals as much as we all do we suspect you aren't just going back to Wynne business. My question is, what do you know?"

"And my question is, how can we help you find this jackass?" Lindsey asked. They were all looking at Marlowe. No one had ordered a drink.

"This is where I am. I've talked to Officer Alten, who was at the scene, I've tried although not gotten any information from the Main Line Animal Shelter, I've had a conversation with members of a group who are strident in their belief the punishment for this jerk must be commensurate with the crime, I've spoken to Ginger Federson, I've spoken with a judge who is outraged at what happened not only at Duffield but also Lancaster, and I've talked to Skip since he was on the shelter board. Nothing all around. To be honest with you, and with you Ashanti, I've had a mental breakdown because of this."

Marlowe's friends were each commiserating with Marlowe as she was trying not to show it right there at the bar.

"Let's draw the line right there," Marlowe continued. "Understand and be assured I've recovered. I'm back to the same Alpha dog we all are."

"Okay," Olivia said. "We're done here for now. We have nothing yet. Let's get dinner. Anyone who gets any ideas or information, let us all know."

Marlowe was quietly disappointed none of her friends could provide any clues about Duffield. However she was encouraged these friends would be truly on the lookout for anything which just might be useful. So while not good responses, nonetheless potentially they may well provide something useful.

Getting seated in the Wily Fox room at a round table dressed in a white tablecloth with a ten inch, perky looking, smiling tan fox in the center, the friends ordered drinks and chatted at about a variety of topics for the first few minutes. Then they settled down to look at the menu. Throughout dinner they unwound from the week's responsibilities. They talked about the Phillies, the cute new pitcher who had come up from the farm team, about the new incoming crop of sexy tennis pros at the various clubs, about the new exhibit at the Philadelphia Museum of Art and about the Radnor Horse Races. Per their usual, they were having a great time.

When Marlowe got up to use the ladies room, Becky Stanfield, who'd been sitting two tables over followed her into the hallway. Somerset had about three thousand members. While Marlowe played tennis, squash, also paddle, Becky didn't play any sports, so Marlowe had just a social relationship with her so never had a lot of interaction with her. Marlowe half jumped when Becky said hi from behind.

"May I talk to you about something?" she asked.

"Of course."

"I don't mean to intrude in your business," Becky said hesitantly, "I've heard you recently met Malik Beresford."

"You intimated you didn't know anything about Anglesey," Marlowe said accusingly.

"But—but I do."

"Yes, I don't know how you would hear, I recently met Malik. He's a brilliant man."

"Yes he is. Since you know him I suppose you've met Franny Barrett."

"What's this about, Becky?" Marlowe always supposed Becky was a little strange, on the third ring of Saturn.

"Well, I don't know exactly how to say this. If I hadn't seen you I'd never have said anything to you. But… but I did see you."

Slightly irritated at Becky's characteristic mannerisms, additionally anxious to get to the ladies room to be back to her friends, Marlowe responded, her eyes widened, her eyebrows up in a questioning look, "And I *am* here seeing you too, so…"

Becky paused, looked down, then from side to side, seeming to search to see if anyone might be listening. No one was there. Frowning, shifting her weight from one leg to the other, as if she were cornered possibly thinking about quickly walking away.

"Well, let me put it this way. If I'm right, I did hear a rumor which may be incorrect, you've most likely been invited to a meeting of the, of the Society."

Looking around again to see who might be listening, she whispered, "You know the one I mean, Marlowe."

Annoyed at Becky's drama, Marlowe cocked her head.

"And?"

Taking a step away Becky turned taking a few steps backward toward her family at her table. She then swiftly turned back facing Marlowe.

"I was too. I went to two meetings…. Then I left."

Becky spun around looking intent on hurrying back to her table almost knocking over a tray of desserts a server was carrying. Marlowe sprang after her. "Becky, wait a minute." Smiling now, Marlowe took her arm gently pulling her back to the hallway.

Becky was flustered. Her face was red. She looked like she felt trapped.

"Calm down just a minute."

Becky started to regain some composure regardless she still looked at Marlowe as though she were expecting to be interrogated. Marlowe had a question for her as she was trying to undo her admittedly impolite action from before.

"Let's start over. Still CFO of the pharmaceutical company?"

"Yes." Becky looked nervous.

"Good, glad to hear it. They need your mega brains over there to keep the company on the straight and narrow. Now about Anglesey."

Becky froze.

"I'm not supposed to…"

"I know. You were right. I was there. We're not supposed to talk to anybody about anything. I understand. I have a question for you. Please answer it."

Becky was standing there facing Marlowe, feet together, hands clasped in front of her like she was in silent prayer.

"Okay." she said in a small, barely audible voice.

"Do you know if Sol Hirschfeld definitely *is* or *was* a member?"

"Yes, he was a member. His name was mentioned at a meeting." Almost unperceptively easing her posture.

"Past members can opt to be kept apprised on what Anglesey is currently doing. They won't be told all of the details though if something is being considered."

"Being considered?"

Breathing out, leaning back a little from the hips, Becky said, "I've already said too much. I will tell you past members take what amounts to their oath of silence, of not communicating about any business of the Society, seriously."

Becky turned, walking slowly back to her table.

Marlowe stood staring after Becky. All she could think about was, yes, Sol had been a member, so he did know things, though not everything according to what Becky had said. Marlowe realized she'd never asked Becky why she didn't want to be a member. Marlowe dismissed the question because she figured though Becky was on an intellectual level with everyone, she probably would want to spend more time on her computer looking over company tax returns than talking about timeworn books. She couldn't think about it anymore because Olivia was striding toward her.

"Hey, what did Becky want?"

"Nothing really, just to say hello."

"Weird as ever, isn't she? Well, are you going to stand there all night or are you coming back to the table?"

Smirking in reply, Marlowe said, "Going to the ladies room. Don't you worry yourself, Miss Olivia, be back in a jiffy, don't you touch my drink!"

Dinner was what it always was. Pure fun. Rachel Cohen hammered Ashanti about leaving Eastbury Hospital, going to what Rachel referred to as the finest hospital in all of Philadelphia, her hospital, Whitefield. For the zillionth time Ashanti said no even after being bribed with a date with the new gorgeous Eagles football team quarterback. Lindsay Dugan teased everyone about who the widely known person was who her firm was going to sue on fraud charges the following week. The women always had topic after topic to talk and kid about.

After dinner which included a couple rounds of wine, the Gang went to the bar sitting at a corner table. Marlowe was afraid their conversation would eventually turn to Parker, Marlowe's ex-boyfriend. It did.

"So, Marlowe," Lindsay started in, "have you seen pretty boy Stirling lately? Is he still working out at the gym maintaining his incredible physique, you lucky dog?"

"Lindsay, you have a one-track mind. Just because you are blissfully married to your cute husband doesn't mean we all have to be married."

"Whoa!" Rachel chimed in. "We're just talking here about a boyfriend not a husband."

"Ex-boyfriend, Rachel!"

"You've not seen him?"

"No, I really haven't."

Ashanti was mum on the subject. Olivia wanted in on the conversation. "Girls, maybe she's found a new suitor since we went out last time. Fess up, Marlowe. Who is he? We demand having a right to know every minute detail."

"Do you really want to hear?"

In unison everyone including Ashanti leaned forward, "Yes!"

"Well, okay, I'll tell you. Two Saturdays ago I went by train into Center City to go to the Reading Terminal Market to shop for some vegetables and some other stuff. I was in Penn Station waiting for the R5 train back out to the Main Line when I saw a sailor. He was in uniform. He was maybe six feet tall, brown hair, average looking with a pleasantness, almost a wholesomeness, about him. He was just milling around. I looked at him with a look that over a period of one minute turned from a casual glance, to a soft smile, to a look of 'yes.'"

"No way!" interrupted Olivia.

"I approached him. He turned to look at me. Then he smiled. I decided, why not? He seemed to understand what I wanted. He took a step toward me. Then another. He took me gently into his arms, kissed me, said he had been waiting for me his entire life. He asked if I would go with him to his room at the Loews Hotel. I gazed up at him.

"Of course, my darling, I'm yearning to go with you. And then—my 6:30 AM alarm went off!"

The women roared raising their glasses, "To sailors!"

Finally when the din quieted Marlowe said, "I sincerely wish I had something to report to you girls. The reality is I don't. I'm too busy to be out looking for a guy."

"Hey, Marlowe, you have to get over yourself, girl, just get moving," Lindsay advised. "No guy is better than Parker, no one. Think about it. You know he's pining over you. Get a move on, live! What about chapter two of your life, the part where you have a husband, maybe rug rats. You always talk about making a difference in a significant way, well start with Numero Uno. That would be you, Marlowe."

Rachel, Ashanti, Olivia and Lindsay raised their glasses in a second, this time noisy, toast with Marlowe laughing along with them. "To Numero Uno!"

They had drunk a few wines getting a little loud. Three guys at the bar quickly raised their glasses and in unison cheered, "To Numero Uno!" It was around ten. Everyone at the bar, by now, had been close to being over-served. The other twenty or so revelers joined in. Before long the entire bar, including the bartenders were toasting and chanting, "To Numero Uno!"

Marlowe leaned over to her friends. "This is going to get worse. I can see it coming. Let's leave while we can. See everyone at Nick's Rocking Horse Downs party!"

"Good idea." Lindsay was already standing up. "Let's go."

The friends were talking and giggling as they walked out the door.

Marlowe leaned over to Ashanti. "Come to over to my car. I have something for you."

At her car Marlowe reached in picking up the box from the jeweler. She handed it to Ashanti.

"Marlowe, what's this?"

"This is something I wanted for myself as well as for you too."

Ashanti opened the box. With a look of astonishment she picked up a four-inch silver-cased pocket knife with "Ashanti" engraved down the length. She looked surprised, confused and happy all at the same time. "I don't know what to say to you, I love it!"

All smiles Marlowe nevertheless felt the need to explain the gift. "Here's the thing, Ashanti. I've been thinking after Duffield. Living on the Main Line has made us more casual than we should be. We need to be using our home alarms. We need to be alert to the possibility of danger. Little happens here. You just never know. I got one for myself too."

Ashanti hugged Marlowe, "You're right, Marlowe, as you always are about things. Thank you so much for making me part of your life." Looking at the knife again, she said, "The size is perfect to keep in our purses, isn't it. That's what I'll do so I'll always have it with me. Love you, best friend Marlowe. This is really sweet of you."

"Glad you like it, Ashanti," Marlowe said, grinning from ear to ear.

Driving home more slowly than normal because of the wine, Marlowe smiled about what a great time she'd had. She pulled into the garage, went in the house and turned off the alarm. Strider greeted her with a single bark. After taking him out she made her way up the curved staircase and flopped onto her bed. Suddenly she remembered she hadn't hooked up her phone to recharge it.

She saw she had a voicemail. It was from Adam. Instantly she was wide awake. She retrieved the message.

"Marlowe, this is Adam. I'm a little concerned about the Anglesey meeting we had yesterday. I sensed you might have been uncomfortable at times. If you don't have other plans, let's have dinner at Penleigh tomorrow night to chat about the meeting. If that's okay, I'll meet you there at eight."

Marlowe squealed, which catapulted Strider off the bed in protection mode. Quickly reaching out to pet him, she explained, "Strider!

Dinner! With Adam Mansfield! At Penleigh Creek Country Club? Oh my gosh, what shall I wear? I don't have anything to wear! I have to go shopping tomorrow! I shouldn't have had dessert tonight. I definitely shouldn't have ordered the pasta! This is too good to be true, this is too awesome—it can't be happening! Can this be happening?" she asked the ceiling. Strider was now at the ready, sure some sort of fun was to begin even this late in the evening.

With that she pulled herself up short. "I'm meeting him at the club. That means he isn't picking me up. He wants to talk about the meeting. This isn't a date. This is a meeting over dinner. Suppose maybe not! Maybe he wants to ask me out on a date yet after all doesn't have the courage to ask me outright. I bet that's it, so it *is* a date! Hold on, this is *Adam Mansfield*. Why would you ever think he wouldn't have the courage to ask anyone out—movie stars even—let alone a little Somerbury hick named Marlowe?"

Emotionless, she texted Adam, "See you at eight."

She went to bed, her head still shaky from the booze, the food and the loss of something she never had. Hoping for even a modicum of encouragement about Adam she lay back and made a sleepy, quick sweep of her portrait dogs. Nothing.

Sensing something was wrong with mom, Strider snuggled in extra close.

Chapter 21

Marlowe was looking forward to her Saturday nine o'clock tennis match at Somerset. As unfortunate luck would have it, when she arrived at the courts, she saw Parker Stirling playing three courts away. She told the others she'd need to leave directly following their match because she had an appointment. In reality, she simply wanted to avoid running into Parker.

During her doubles match she had the opportunity to sneak some looks at Parker when he was playing his singles. On one point he served a kick serve that was returned wide to his forehand, that he drove back with tremendous top spin to his opponent who barely got it back to Parker who then hit a perfect drop for a winner. He was such a fabulous player, exciting to watch. One of the reasons she liked him in the first place was he was like a ballet dancer on the court. He had the grace of Roger Federer. He typically moved smoothly to each shot then, usually effortlessly, crushed the ball over the net. His serve was pure, nimble athleticism. The arch of his broad back, the sheer power of his legs pushing his wide, solid shoulders up, then the wrist snap all coordinated to drive the ball to his opponent's backhand. Even as a spectator she couldn't really see his serve, it was so hard. Flat, slice, kick serves, he had them all. He was a thing of beauty, an Adonis. Every time she saw him play, she couldn't take her eyes off him, he was that good. That morning was no exception.

After the last point of Marlowe's match the players shook hands. Marlowe headed straight to the women's locker room, to her anti-Parker safe haven. As she was showering and dressing, her analyzing naturally centered on Adonis. After seeing him play once again, how could she not. Okay, I'll give you he's extremely physically attractive. No argument. So what's the matter with him? He's well known for being one of the best lawyers in the city. You spent a year with him, he was supportive and loving. He doesn't need your money either. He lives on his hundred-acre farm in gorgeous Grasmere. How much do you imagine it's worth? Plus the fact he has two horses you love and Ragtag, an adorable golden retriever mix he rescued. What's not to like, Marlowe? What's the big deal with Adam? Parker is every bit as good looking as Adam, not that looks matter. He may even be more athletic than Adam. You always wanted an athletic husband, right? Okay, Parker qualifies. He's as sharp a dresser as Adam is. Plus he's got a Ph.D. in economics Even "Skip the Protector" approves of him. If that doesn't clinch it, what about your friends loving him. To boot in the last six months he's not gone out on one date with anyone else. At least that's what everyone tells you.

By then she was applying light rose gloss on her lips, then taking one last look in the mirror. Marlowe left the locker room. Next stop was Magnolia Place Mall to shop for a dress for dinner with Adam.

Shifting her tennis backpack into position as she opened the locker room door, she looked up to see Parker standing ten feet in front of her in the tennis lounge. He was beaming his charming smile straight at her. Her cheeks grew hot.

Parker acted as if he didn't know how awkward the meeting was.

"Hey, how about lunch on Tuesday at Élan, the new restaurant in Wayne? We should catch up on things. I've something I'd like to talk to you about. It's about the dogfight. I've heard some things. I'd like your opinion on them. I understand you were there."

This is shocking. Why would Parker have any interest, legal or otherwise, in Duffield. What could he possibly want to talk to me about. I don't know anything. Oh, wait a minute, Marlowe reconsidered, just wait a minute. He's still not given up. Everything she'd been thinking about, all the things that made him perfect, were right there in the front of her mind, as well as in front of her physically. He was perfect. Despite that she said to herself, I'm not going out to lunch with you, Parker. I'm not going to sleep with you. I'm not going marry you. Then drinking in his eyes she heard herself saying, "Yes, how lovely. I haven't been there yet."

"See you there at high noon. Have a good weekend, Marlowe, gotta run!"

He trotted off down the hall in his sweaty, clingy tennis whites, even from behind looking like an NFL MVP.

Chapter 25

Back to Adam, would it be business or pleasure, Marlowe ruminated on her way out to her car. She'd no sooner clicked in her seatbelt than she'd already made the decision.

"I'm going for it—I mean, I'm going for Adam," she announced to no one other than herself. She was going to try a stealth assault on at least getting Adam to notice her as a woman not just a reader of scholarly works. Maybe it was a business dinner. A lot of romances start out as business lunches or dinners. Nothing ventured this evening, nothing gained.

"I've got a shot. I'm going to take it!"

Although she was on "Mission Adam," her quest to find something to wear to Penleigh that evening, Marlowe would probably have gone to the mall anyhow. When she got to the mall in the early afternoon she spent some time looking around in the funky "It's All about You," a new clothing store with rather outrageous clothes, browsing in Lilly Pulitzer then Macys. Though Marlowe's weekday dress was typically suits, she really loved fashionable clothes. The problem was office attire was professional. Weekend attire was a tennis dress and shorts. There wasn't much room for fashionable clothes in her real life. She didn't pay a great deal of attention to women's magazines so she had little idea of what to wear for Mission Adam. After Macys she wanted to take a break to just to relax, maybe do some people watching.

Having chosen a soft chair outside Glenmoor Valley, a fabric shop, Marlowe allowed her eyes to gradually close. Gwyn popped into her mind quickly transporting her from the mall to Snowdon. She landed in the horror of what happened to Raspberry. Marlowe involuntarily drew in her breath hard holding it, trying to fight the Gwyn hopelessness. As hard as it would be to do, she had to call Gwyn to maybe find out what clues or suspicions she might have to solve the fights. She should have done it before. She just didn't have the courage to do it. She drew in a second breath, easier than the first, softly holding it a little longer. Her mind was beginning to clear. Gone were the constant darts dragging her along demanding attention with the constant immediacy Marlowe had grown used to. Something always said, look at me, I'm important. You must think about me because there are consequences if you don't.

"Hello, Marley!"

"Nick!" Marlowe cried, as she jumped up to see him.

"I'm really glad I ran into you. I still haven't seen your name on the RSVP list for the party. You're definitely coming, aren't you? Because if my doll can't make it the whole thing is off, done, cancelled."

"Of course I'm coming. How could I miss a Nick bash? No way."

"Excellent."

"The usual dress of black tie and tails and evening gowns?"

Nick laughed. "Yes, the usual dress. I have a reputation to uphold you know. Glad you can make it."

He nodded toward the big Home Depot across the way. "In a rush. Need to get in there and get out, so I need to go. You look good. I'm thinking you've a new guy in your life."

"Would that I did!"

"See you, Punkin!"

Nick had started calling her *Punkin* because, as a toddler, she had difficulty pronouncing the word "pumpkin." She loved the term of endearment, which he used every so often.

She knew he was in a hurry, even so here was her chance to ask him about the Duffield also Lancaster fighting.

"Hey Nick, I know you're in a hurry, a couple of questions for you."

"Sure, what do you have?" Nick was focused on her.

"We've never talked about the dogfighting incidents. With everyone you know, you must have had conversations with some of your professional friends about what happened, who is responsible."

Nick continued to focus on Marlowe with a little grin beginning to appear on his face. "Marley, don't you worry yourself about these things. What is done is done, you can't do anything about it. Just let other people take care of it. You have lots of other things deserving your attention. Pay attention to them."

Taking a step toward her, he reached out, gave her a kiss on her forehead, then started to turn toward the store.

"Okay, what about your daughter? You haven't wanted to talk about it with me."

Turning back, Nick said, "Marley, Marley, Marley. Same thing. What's done is done. Yes, I loved her, aside from that we were never close. I'm sorry she died, to be honest, it's painful to talk about it. I need to let it alone to move on in my own way. I love you, know I always have."

He turned toward the Home Depot.

Marlowe was relieved Nick was doing okay about his daughter, even so she was disappointed he had no interest in helping or even talking about the dogfighting. This didn't seem to fit her self-made profile of him. Nonetheless she watched Nick heading toward the store, marveling at how he was able to make money, how he seemed to be happy with his life. It seemed like whatever he touched turned to gold. Her dad had told her years ago about Nick's parents, so she knew Nick didn't always have money.

Her father had told her the two had become friends when they played football together in high school. He knew Nick's father had declared bankruptcy when Nick was about fifteen years old, his mother cleaned houses by day and offices at night to help them survive. Also Nick's dad began to drink. One day he drove into Philadelphia, parked on the Ben Franklin Bridge and jumped off. Just like that. His body was recovered later in the day. It was badly cut up. No funeral. He was just buried.

The day his dad jumped off, Nick quit school to go to work to try to help support his mother and himself. It was not until several years later, after Marlowe's parents married that Nick called his old friend. The way her father told the story it was as if nothing ever happened. Nick, still living with his mother, had a house in Farm Hollow, a town near Somerbury. It was like those years had evaporated. The friendship was renewed. The only reference Nick made to all he and his mother had been through was to swear he would never be poor again. Whatever it took, is was what he'd have to do.

As she strolled around the mall again her attention was caught by a white dress in the window of a small, stylish boutique. Once she was inside she decided against it—too low cut. Not exactly her style.

She went back into the mall to continue her dress quest. Though unequivocally not on her buy list type of store, Marlowe went to Sneaker Mania and looked in the show window. She spied dazzling pink sneakers looking right back at her. Cracking a smile, she wondered how they'd look as stiletto sling-backs. The women at Penleigh would think she was a slut. If she weren't at Wynne it would be a great thing to do just for the fun of it. With an idiotic grin on her face she checked her watch. She knew she'd better get shopping for real.

She knew exactly what that meant.

This evening, whether it was or wasn't a date, it was Saturday night and she was going to his club for dinner. She needed something sophisticated yet stylish. What it would be, or whether she would even recognize it when she saw it, remained to be seen. She was pretty sure she wouldn't see it in the kinds of places she'd been looking. Face it. She needed Needless Markup, where a single outfit could cost literally thousands of dollars. She would tell the probably snooty saleswoman what she was doing tonight, and let Ms. Snooty tell her what to wear. Foolproof. She was set. Of course she wouldn't spend thousands. If the dress she was supposed to have cost five hundred dollars, so be it. Five hundred dollars well spent. Marlowe was thrilled. She had a *guaranteed plan*! Because they were dining at Penleigh, Marlowe wanted to look smart, fashionable, still a touch conservative.

"I understand what you are looking for, dear. You're welcome to try on any dresses you think you might like. If you are asking me for my advice, I think you are, I highly recommend this one," the saleswoman said.

She reached for an above-the-knee, black silk dress, slightly low cut with a flared skirt. "To be sure of your effect, Ms. Evans," the saleswoman, who turned out to extremely nice, said, "You must also get the sterling silver necklace from the jewelry department right over there. I'll go with you to show you which one."

"Many, many thanks for your guidance."

Ms, actually "not-so-snooty," said with a self-satisfied grin,

"This guy won't stand a chance!"

Chapter 26

Marlowe arrived home late afternoon with her Needless Markup dress, jewelry and new pair of obligatory three-inch pumps with silver buckles on the toes. She already had similar shoes still, considering the stakes, she didn't want to take any chances, so she got new ones. Marlowe entered the house to great fanfare from Strider. She related the entire story to him of her amazing day exclusively focusing on herself until she realized his urgent need to visit the back yard. Off they went for a stroll outside. She could have let him out by himself because the whole property was fenced. Nonetheless Marlowe liked to go out with him. Strider was the constant in her life. She adored him.

She started to get ready to go to Penleigh Creek keeping an eye on the TV in her bedroom. She was hopeful she wouldn't see any new developments about the raid at Duffield. She told herself she'd been too busy to watch the news or read anything about the dog fighting. In reality she didn't want to watch anything to do with what she'd witnessed. Now that a couple of days had passed she supposed she might be okay to watch if something were to come on.

Within minutes of her turning on the TV there it was. An interview about Duffield. Luca Pasquale, Director of Law Enforcement at the Greater Philadelphia Animal Shelter. As the Director of Law Enforcement at the Shelter, Luca was the one who had been providing updates to the media. Although she didn't see him often on the Sundays she was there, Luca was a favorite of Marlowe's because he was hard, unforgiving with anyone he or his agents found mistreating animals. Out in the field Luca had heard all of the excuses in the world from these people. None was acceptable to him. Anybody who hurt an animal was going to have to deal with him besides his officers.

Dressed in his official uniform including his gun, was being interviewed by Kimnese Webber on Fox. Jamie Mahoney, the township Chief of Police was at Luca's side. They were standing outside in front of the shelter headquarters sign. Marlowe remembered Luca was at Duffield watching what the township policeman suspected might have been FBI agents standing in front of the barn. Marlowe liked Luca from her times at the shelter when she walked the dogs there. She was anxious to hear what he had to say. Luca was the head of the dozen plus law enforcement agents who investigated abuse situations for the shelter. They had full arrest powers, carried guns. As important, they were dedicated to their jobs.

"Director Pasquale, what progress has been made in this investigation? The public is horrified at what was found at Duffield Manor and outraged no one has yet been arrested."

"We've been working alongside the township police. Together we've determined a couple of things. The incident at Duffield Manor took place while the owners of the home were out of town. Neither they nor any staff were at the house. We've strong reason to believe they're in no way involved or connected to the dogfighting at their estate."

"Then what can you tell us about who's responsible?"

"At the moment we're questioning a person of interest about aspects of what we found at the fighting site."

Kimnese turned to Jamie. "Chief Mahoney, what would you add? Does the township have any leads on any suspects?"

"For this investigation Luca's team has the lead. The township however is working side by side with the shelter. We are careful to share all information or suspicions with each other. All questions need to go to Luca on this."

"So any other suspects, Director Pasquale?" Kimnese said, turning back to him.

"No."

"Do you think others were involved?"

"Yes, we do."

So there was the answer to Marlowe's earlier musings. Luca *did* think others were involved. Marlowe had been thinking about the questions of who was responsible for the fight moreover what his punishment would be. The possibility of the barbarian not being punished, not going to jail, maybe just being fined, those ideas continued to stir deep anger and resentment in her. That these people could get away with inflicting so much hurt on top of death on animals was more than she could bear. She understood what the Anglesey crowd would say. That was taking things into one's own hands, a step over the line Marlowe didn't think she could ever take.

On the television Luca was refusing to say anything more about other suspects. Webber tried a different tack.

"Three months ago a smaller fight took place in a barn in Lancaster County. No one has been arrested yet. Do you think the two fights are related?"

Marlowe sat down on the bed, riveted by what she was hearing. The fight in Lancaster was where Gwyn's dog Raspberry was found mauled, worse, dead.

Luca hesitated before responding. With a voice devoid of emotion, he said, "We can't speculate about that question at this time."

Webber wasn't going to let him off easy.

"It sounds as if you are considering the possibility. So what might indicate a connection?"

"Look, all I can say at this time is we're working hard to find out what happened at Duffield Manor. When we do, it's possible we'll have a better understanding about Lancaster."

"Director Pasquale, are you saying a dogfighting ring might exist here in eastern Pennsylvania? Is that what I'm hearing you say?"

Marlowe felt ill. She was sitting on the edge of her bed still in her shorts and tee shirt from shopping, listening to every word, merging her own suspicions into what Kimnese was asking plus what Luca was saying.

"I'm afraid I can't say more at this time," Luca insisted. He wasn't looking at Kimnese, he was looking down, steeled, his jaw set as though he were a boxer about to step in the ring. Anger was creeping into his face. Marlowe saw it. She knew it wasn't aimed at Kimnese, it was directed at whoever was responsible.

Webber didn't let up. "But it's possible."

"Anything is possible. I'm afraid that's all I can say," Luca said, looking back at Kimnese then turning away heading for the shelter front door. Jamie was right behind him.

Kimnese yelled after Luca, "You haven't mentioned anything about abuse, what kind of person does it. Who are you looking for based on what you are saying, Luca?"

Luca kept walking going right in the door.

Upset and worried Marlowe got up off the bed, muting the TV. "Others?" she questioned aloud. "*Others*? Who are these monsters?" she demanded of the TV. "Why are they still walking the face of the earth," she shouted, her arms extended pleading for an answer. "I want them found. They need to be convicted, further, sent to jail for life, or worse. No possible excuse exists for this."

Marlowe's cell rang. It was Ashanti.

Marlowe blurted into the phone, "Did you just see the news? This is so God-awful. It's so upsetting I can't think straight."

"I know, Marlowe, I've been watching it during the afternoon. I heard Luca Pasquale's interview earlier. Think about it, Marlowe. They are obviously working extremely hard on this moreover they are real professionals. Between these agents and the township police, they will get to the bottom of this. Someone will be identified and caught."

Marlowe had sat back down on the bed, listening to everything her dear friend was saying. With every word, Marlowe began feeling less frantic, the outrage was dissipating. She knew Ashanti was right. She started to feel much better. "I know you're right, Ashanti. I'm sorry for carrying on like I did. Thank you for making me see things are no worse off right now than they were before."

Calming down, Marlowe asked, "One other thing. What was Kimnese trying to get at with her last question. She's smart, she was looking for Luca to talk about abuse. What was she looking for?"

"What makes all of the worse is something I remember from psych class. I almost don't want to tell you this, Marlowe."

"Ashanti, you have to be kidding me! You took psych?"

"Yes, I needed a gut class. Got an 'A' in it too, I'll have you know."

"Gosh, Ashanti, you should never admit something like that to anyone. Okay, Miss A-in-Psych, what do you remember? Give me the Psych 101 class lecture—I'm listening, try not to bore me to tears, okay?"

"Oh Marlowe! You're a mess. Now listen, will you? Psychiatrists believe some people have a disconnect interrupting the feeling of empathy most humans have. Those people don't perceive, recognize, the real pain they're inflicting on others even if their victims are their own children."

"That does make sense."

"Regarding animals, those who abuse animals have no sense of the real suffering they're inflicting when they torture them in animal fights or torment them in other ways."

"I never conceived of it that way. God, this is more than horrific, Ashanti."

"This is the worst part. Just as abused kids will eventually abuse their own children, animal abusers will continue to abuse animals even though they're caught. Violent abusers will continue to be violent abusers."

"Translating the psycho-babble I want to make sure I get this straight, Ashanti. What I hear you saying is whoever instigated the animal fighting at Duffield has been responsible for past fights. He will, in one way or another, torture animals in the future."

"Precisely what I'm saying."

Marlowe realized this was helpful in the investigation. It would explain how whoever ran the fights could just do it with no conscience.

Like Pharaoh, hard hearted. She was concluding it was highly likely a woman couldn't have done it. Nor could she have been any part of it. So just men. Men who were cold-blooded killers. Now that, Marlowe assessed, was a real clue. Sure it was true, she instantly deduced her Rolling Hill Gang was not going to be a help to her as she had hoped. She highly doubted given their kinds of work and their families they would know anyone who would be close to being a suspect. She'd lost her posse. She was on her own. Jayla did enter her mind at this point, could she be any help whatsoever, in any way? Marlowe concluded that was unknown, even though she had offered help if Marlowe said she needed it.

"Marlowe, are you there? Are you just thinking?"

"Ashanti, guilty as charged. I'm sorry."

"Well, good, young lady, you better start thinking straight! You're supposed to be at Penleigh at eight. It's almost seven. Are you ready?"

"It's what?" Marlowe sprang off the bed heading for the bathroom. "No, I'm not ready for Pete's sake. I need to shower, do my hair, the whole nine yards. Go away! Hanging up. Love you—wish me luck!"

"Hey Marlowe, wait one moment! You don't need any luck. If this guy has any sense he'll grab you for himself before Parker worms his way back in. He's—"

"Ah, about Parker…" Marlowe had stopped dead.

"Oh no, you didn't! What did you do, Marlowe Evans?"

"It's just lunch" she said in a small voice.

"Marlowe, will you make up your mind, or do you have to have two hunks fawning all over you?"

"I know. I think Adam may be the one."

"Right, exactly what you said about Parker. Six months ago, just to remind you, you broke up with Parker. Any vestigial memory of that?"

"I know, I know..."

"Perfect, then stop watching television, get showered, dressed and go get Adam!"

"Okay, on it, boss!" Marlowe said as she trotted into the bathroom.

"Hey, what are you wearing?"

"I got a dress plus three inch sling-back heels from, you should be sitting down, Needless Markup."

"Excellent, this guy's dead in the water—he just doesn't know it yet!"

"How delectable!" Marlowe said as she opened the shower door.

"Bye! Full report to me in the morning, unless of course he's still at your house."

"Shut up, Ashanti!" Marlowe barked as she tossed her phone on a towel on the bathroom floor.

As she did that she realized she was finally getting an understanding of what was behind the fighting. She stood there in her shorts and shirt as she began to piece together what she was beginning to believe would identify the fighter. With dealing with clients at Wynne Marlowe hadn't stolen time to read online about the general subject of abuse. Whether animal or human abuse she was sure Ashanti's opinion was right. Those who have no respect let alone love for the lives of animals were extremely likely to continue to abuse and kill them. They think nothing of it. The bottom line was to allow them back on the street was to permit them to torture and kill repeatedly. Period. Such a notion ripped Marlowe's heart out. She believed it was likely the authorities would get whoever was running the actual fighting. Was it the whole story?

The sheer magnitude of the fight at Duffield, the fact it took place there said to Marlowe a single individual couldn't have funded and organized such horror. She felt sure Luca had already figured that out. Some other guilty party would have to have been behind this. Her further realization was the organization, the execution of the fight, was almost flawless, businesslike. There had to be quiet advertisements of the fight, someone finding a site, someone organizing, bringing the dogs and other animals, someone running the fight, finally someone to fund the costs. Tons of organization. Whoever ran it had possibly run one before. Or maybe more than one. Maybe Duffield was one of several. Maybe Duffield was part of what Kimnese just called a ring of fight sites.

Looking at the bathroom clock Marlowe realized she had even less time than she'd had before to get ready.

Showered and ready to put on her dress Marlowe mused about what she would say to Adam and how the conversation would go. She really didn't know anything about him except for what was generally known. Parker, on the other hand, was a known quantity. She loved being with him. They always had such fun with easy conversations. It was more like Parker was her dear friend besides her lover. In love? She had to find out what Adam was all about first. She picked up her phone and typed a text to Parker, "Parker, I've something else I must do on Tuesday. Sorry I can't make lunch." Her finger was raised to send her message. She deleted it. It's only lunch. She texted Parker, "See you Tuesday."

Of course Marlowe knew her problem was, like all women, she was attracted to the good-looking, athletic males, ergo Parker, now McDreamy. The chances were, however, Adam had any number of girl-friends. It was most likely all for naught. She still had to see for herself. She had to take it as far as it would go, which could mean the end of this evening. Whatever was going to happen was going to happen. Marlowe, true to her style, was going to try to make it happen the way she wanted it to happen. She just didn't know exactly what that way was yet.

Having finally gotten herself together Marlowe was pretty sure she looked set for her Mission. In addition to the Needless Markup ammunition, Marlowe added her Rolex. She was ready to go. She would make it to the club by eight.

Marlowe got into her 911 and put in her favorite CD of all time, even though it was old and she'd heard the Moody Blues song a thousand times. She opened the sunroof enough to let in the cool night air, of course not enough to blow her hair, then put Black Beauty in gear, and was euphorically off to Mission Adam.

With "I Know You're Out There Somewhere" blaring.

Chapter 27

At 7:50 Marlowe rolled into the club. A premier, private golf and tennis club, Penleigh Creek Country Club oozed wealth. Penleigh was different from the other Main Line clubs. It had been founded and built in the early 1950's by a fresh crop of newly wealthy entrepreneurs. To call them *nouveaux riche* would be a mistake. These people were intelligent, cultured and fiscally conservative. The group funded an endowment to maintain the club as well as for possible expansion. Beyond their contributions to the club, these philanthropic founders set up their own individual foundations to further the arts, hospitals, animal shelters, cinema, various museums, in addition to other charitable needs. It was the club where most of the major business deals in the Philadelphia region were executed. A good number of the chief financial players were members including numerous of Marlowe's Wynne clients.

Pulling in to the club at ten of eight Marlowe had just enough time to pull over to the curb. She checked her hair then took a minute to look at the club itself. Massive, architecturally imposing, the entire club had much less of the historic look than most of the other clubs. It was built, however, of Pennsylvania fieldstone, as many of the newer Main Line mansions were. The founders had spared no expense. Marlowe, as well as everyone else, was impressed with how well the overall property design looked simply like a country farm setting. The guiding design feature of the main building where the restaurants were was of a Pennsylvania country farmhouse, on a balanced yet grand scale. The indoor tennis and squash courts building was designed with the same stone to look like a country bank barn. All flawlessly conceived. There was no stucco or siding on any of the buildings comprising the club compound.

Not wanting to be one minute late, not even one second late, Marlowe valeted the Porsche. Adam was waiting at the bar chatting with several people. When he saw her enter he excused himself.

"Marlowe, so terrific to have you here," he said when he neared. "I'm so glad you could make it."

Marlowe extended her hand for a shake. "I'm happy to be here." With a wry smile she added, "You didn't bring *Candide* with you, did you? Let's leave him in the 1700's, shall we?"

Adam brushed Marlowe's hand to the side rather embraced her in greeting instead. "I couldn't agree with you more. Just between us he's a little boring, don't you think?"

He was incredibly attractive in his gray pinstripe suit and white shirt, which was her favorite suit/shirt combination. She recognized the Penleigh club tie. The pattern was crossed golf clubs and crossed tennis racquets in green and gold on a maroon background. He was such a lovely sight especially after the week she'd had. She didn't care if they talked about politics or the Eagles' Super Bowl chances, it would be fabulous to sit down with him, have a drink or two with dinner. Beginning to unwind, she was ready for whatever the evening was going to bring.

"Our table overlooks the golf course. Shall we go there or we can stay here for a while, whichever strikes your fancy."

Marlowe opted for the dining room. It was still light out. The sun was setting creating what Marlowe viewed as a romantic setting. The server arrived with a rather full glass of red wine for Marlowe and a Johnnie Walker Black for Adam.

Smiling up at the server quickly noting her name on the tag, Marlowe inquired, "Maggie, how refreshing. What kind of wine is this?"

With a look of concern Maggie glanced from Marlowe to Adam and back. "It's a pinot noir, Ms. Evans."

As Maggie turned to leave the table, Marlowe started to say, "How did you—"

Adam interrupted, turning to his guest, "Marlowe, I must say you look stunning this evening. Gorgeous!"

Marlowe took a good long drink of her wine more out of nervousness than thirst replying, "You're nice to say that. I decided my Wynne uniform of old-school suits and

with white blouses ought to remain in the closet for this evening."

"I applaud your decision."

"If *I* may say, you're looking exceptionally debonair this evening. How could you possibly know I love gray pinstripe suits?" How do you know I like pinot noir? You must have ordered it for me before I even arrived at the club.

"A lucky guess. How are you doing? How was your work week?"

"Jam packed. It's nice to be here in such handsome surroundings to be able to unwind." Okay, I'll buy "lucky guess" on the suit, for the pinot noir, he's either psychic or he's been talking to some friend of mine. Hmm.

"I know the market was a rollercoaster this week. I can imagine your clients were calling, which is probably no fun for you."

"Well some of my clients did call. They're financially sophisticated. They wanted to make sure I was buying for them. They leave it to me to know what companies to buy."

"What are you buying with the market at these levels? Any banks?"

With an engaging smile, a twinkle in her eyes, Marlowe parried, "My dear Adam, when you move your accounts to me at Wynne I'll be more than happy to share those shrewd ideas with you."

"*Touché*! I'll have to think about it."

"If it wasn't the market, what made your week so busy?"

She responded slowly. "It wasn't busier than most of my weeks as much as it was distressing. The raid at Duffield has been on my mind. I feel helpless." She took another sip of wine.

"Yes, it was bad. The police are working hard on it. They should find out who's responsible. A couple of my buddies and I have been tossing ideas around about who the ringleader might be. We think we might know. We aren't sure at all, mind you."

"Wow, who is it?"

"Not appropriate to say right now. Here's a hypothetical question for you we talked about too. Would you be willing to help catch the ringleader? Given everything happening at Duffield, this was a question the guys tossed around."

"It's a loaded question, though with no hesitation, yes. I guess it does depend on what is meant by 'help.'"

This was a strange question to ask right out of the blue, aside from that other things about Adam were strange. He was still single at maybe early to mid-thirties, he was a member of the peculiar Anglesey Philosophical Society, a member of the prestigious although boring Beaumaris Club then to top it off, he was out at his other club Penleigh on a

Saturday night with a woman who wasn't a date who just was a person who happened to be invited to the aforementioned dusty book club. Although his question fit right into the few strange things she knew about him. So let's move on, Marlowe, she concluded. Not sure what he is. Whatever he is he is. At that moment, considering the amount of wine she'd drunk, it seemed to make perfect sense.

If it does make perfect sense, then what, Marlowe?

Chapter 28

"Switching gears, what did you think of the Anglesey meeting? Did you enjoy the discussion of *Candide*?"

Here it is, even after we agreed at the bar, Marlowe recognized, her spirits dimming. He said he wanted to talk to me. Here we are about to have the "dull book" talk. I'm thinking coming here, despite how incredibly sexy this guy is, was a bad idea. I could be watching *Caddyshack* for the five hundredth time rather than being here. Marlowe had to control the smirk and wink to herself that were about to cross her face.

She took another longer drink of wine replying without much enthusiasm, "It was interesting."

Hearing the absurd answer she'd just given, it was all she could do to contain a laugh which was ever so close to disclosing itself. It was only then she realized Adam had barely drunk any of his scotch, worse, she'd made a real dent in her glass of wine. Oops. She'd better be careful. Slow down to let him catch up. She didn't want him to think she was drinking too much. Otherwise Mission Adam would be on the verge of being busted.

"Interesting?" Adam said, cocking his head, looking intrigued by her word. "Aren't you sweet. I was just kidding by the question. If I never heard the word Candide again I'd be happy. Let's leave him in the library stacks as agreed!"

"I'm curious about Anglesey though. No one knows what it is beyond knowing it exists. It seems like it's some kind of secret society. If you're just talking about books, though I don't mean to minimize it, why the secrecy? Or perhaps I shouldn't be asking."

"We're aware this is the impression many have of Anglesey. It isn't exactly accurate. To understand you'd have to know the historical background."

"I always like a good story. Yet doesn't this fall into whatever the secrets category of Anglesey is, things are not discussed, even mentioned, to non-members?"

"You have a delightful way of politely drilling down on things. It's remarkable," Adam said smiling at Marlowe. "Thank you for asking. No, this is just history, though no, we don't normally talk about it because it just doesn't come up in conversation. It's a long history. It would take a bit of time to explain it. It's fascinating though involved."

"Please tell," She was thinking maybe Adam's willingness to talk about the Anglesey was a hint she may be being considered for membership.

"Let me start at the beginning with the short version. Do you know what Anglesey means?"

"I know it's an island off Wales."

Adam became more relaxed starting to drink his Johnny Walker, which allowed Marlowe to loosen up too. She didn't know how, even so she seemed to have passed the first test, though she didn't know what the test was. She began to enjoy the conversation, especially because Adam was doing the talking. While she was listening, she had the opportunity to look at him. Adam/Parker, Adam/Parker went through her mind.

Maggie came over to take their orders. Having not even looked at the menu, Marlowe asked Maggie to recommend a fish or seafood. Maggie suggested grilled shrimp, to which Marlowe nodded in agreement. Adam chose angel hair pasta with shallots, tomatoes, mushrooms in a champagne sauce.

"Anglesey is a rather large island off the coast of Wales. The focal historical time for the Anglesey Society is the end of the thirteenth century."

Adam took some time to explain in detail that many castles were built during that time. European labor, carpenters and masons, was brought in to Wales to work on the decades-long construction process.

Marlowe was absorbed in the story. Their entrees had arrived. Maggie automatically brought additional drinks. Adam was engrossed in relating his narrative. Marlowe was equally engrossed, to her surprise, not in Adam now. Her interest was in his history.

"To use our word of the evening, 'interesting,' here's where the story will become interesting to you."

Both Adam and Marlowe became aware Maggie was standing facing them about ten feet from the table. Adam looked at Maggie, who then approached the table.

"Mr. Mansfield, is something wrong with your dinners? Please let me know so I can bring you both something else."

Marlowe and Adam looked at each other giggling. They were so absorbed by the events in Wales of over seven hundred years ago, their meals were sitting cooling regardless of the enticing aromas.

"Maggie, no, they're fine, delicious in fact. Thanks for reminding us to eat them."

With a confused expression, Maggie replied, "You are welcome, sir," as she backed away.

Marlowe suggested, "I guess we better eat then get back to the story."

Enjoying their meals at a quicker pace than they normally would have, neither said a word until they finished the last morsel.

"The shrimp was delicious, I think."

"I'm pretty sure my pasta was perfect!"

Bringing another glass of pinot plus a Johnnie Walker, Maggie came to clear the dishes.

"So we were talking about skilled carpenters and masons."

"Excellent memory, Marlowe. Yes, the carpenters and the masons. We're going to slightly switch gears here to move for a moment to Europe. Naturally you've heard of the Order of the Knights Templar?"

"Of course, with all the many movies about them probably most people know at least

something about them. They were among the most famous, recognized of the western Christian military groups in the Middle Ages. That's about all I know."

"It's a good start. After Jerusalem was captured in the First Crusade many Christians wanted to visit the Holy Places. While Jerusalem itself was safe, traveling to Jerusalem was not. To control the robbers on top of the killers of those travelers, in the early twelfth century a few men created a monastic order of warriors to protect them. It was the beginning of the Knights Templar."

"How do you know about all of this, Adam? It really is fascinating."

Marlowe was more and more enthralled by the story. She was full and the wine had made her slow down to the point where she was no longer nervous. She felt maybe she did belong here at Penleigh with Adam Mansfield after all.

Adam went on to say the Knights grew in numbers in Europe. As a group they eventually fell out of favor. Many of them who had occupational skills that could be used anywhere made the choice to move out of the broad geographic areas where the Order was dominant. Some of the masons went as far away as England then Wales. The important ones for us were those who ended up on Anglesey to help build the castle at Beaumaris.

"What happened next, Marlowe, was the beginning of the Anglesey Philosophical Society."

"Anglesey is definitely not a book club a few people started to discuss books or debate philosophies, or is it?"

Adam hesitated before answering. "The answer is 'no.'"

Marlowe's attention was piqued. Her mind was spinning. She knew it. The discussion on *Candide*. The meeting in the basement of Harlech behind closed doors, the portraits, the second meeting had to happen quickly, Franny's talk of "obligation," had given her the distinct feeling something else was the real topic of discussion. Was the discussion on *Candide* a ruse to talk about other things, to draw conclusions on potential future actions? She realized she might have been invited for a particular reason.

Adam leaned forward to take a sip of his scotch. His attention was fully on his dinner companion. There were no glances at the other diners or those arriving or leaving the dining room. His eyes were on Marlowe. For her part, Marlowe focused on Adam, captivated by everything she had learned about him at the first Anglesey meeting.

Now, his depth of knowledge of events of centuries ago. She was trying to make sense of who this man was and whether he could be the man she'd been looking for all these years.

"As time went by the Welsh made it clear the Knights were no longer welcome because they feared the Knights' military background might surface which could mean they might try to take over Wales as their own new country. Not wanting to go back to Europe, a few of the Knights on Anglesey made the extraordinary decision to try to flee to a land which was more myth than anything else—America. They took with them the most important thing to each of them, the Knights Templar principle of protecting those who couldn't protect themselves."

"How astonishing! How do you know their coming to America is true? Why isn't it in our history books?"

Her eyes were riveted on Adam. No class or book she had ever read had described anything like Knights from Wales sailing to America.

"An easy one. Because of the harshness of the trip, the freezing cold of the first winter only ten people survived."

"Okay. Does any evidence exist about these Knights landing in America?"

The question she was not asking, at least not yet, was what does this have to do centuries later with the Anglesey Philosophical Society other than the name? Where is this going. Why does he want me to know about this? This isn't normal dinner conversation, captivating though it is. I'm more confused about the Anglesey meeting and *Candide* than I was before, and I was pretty confused with just that.

"I know it from a descendant of the courageous little group. Records were kept from the year they landed."

"A descendent? Where does he live? I'm assuming on the U.S. east coast?"

With Marlowe staring at him, Adam sat back and looked down. When he raised his head he leaned forward. Not knowing why, Marlowe unconsciously leaned in, somehow thinking it was the right thing to do, maybe the situation called for it.

"I can't tell you at this point." The unwavering look on Adam's face was one she hadn't seen before. His jaw was set. He was motionless. Each of them was looking at the other as though a decision might have to be made about a life-and-death situation. Neither was moving. Neither had any expression on his face.

At that moment, Maggie arrived back at the table, wearing a smile and a bearing two pieces of devil's food cake along with two glasses of port. With relief, Marlowe welcomed the reappearance of Adam's slightly crooked grin, which she adored. The cake and the port went down easily for Marlowe. Despite the food, the pinots and the port had worked their magic. She lounged back in her chair taking in the enchanting view of Adam and the gorgeous Putter Grill Room. For a few moments she looked out on the golf course with its soft nighttime lighting. For now, it felt as if she didn't have a care in the world.

Looking back at Adam she said, "Thank you for recounting the remarkable story, Adam. I had no idea all of this was going on back then."

"It *is* intriguing, isn't it. Leaving the Knights on their own for a while, what else shall we talk about?"

Marlowe was thinking "us," in any case didn't dare.

Chapter 29

"It seems your conversation with your buddies was of interest. Are they some of your law firm colleagues?"

"Yes, they are. More interesting is while I was waiting for you this evening at the bar a couple of guys mentioned your friend Nick Gavin made bad investments about a year ago. Since then has been in trouble with shady lenders on some real estate deals. I heard before he tried to refinance them through ordinary lenders except was turned down. Apparently he owes the wrong people some money. Did you know that? Wouldn't it be something if he went under?"

"Who told you stuff about Nick?" Marlowe answered, a bit defensively, putting her port down, sitting straight up.

"A couple of the real estate financial types around here have talked about it. Maybe it's all rumor. Sometimes guys just like to talk about things even if they don't really know what they're talking about."

"I've known Nick my entire life."

Marlowe was remembering Adam had almost hung up on her when in the phone conversation on her way to Duffield she'd said Nick said the dog fighting was overblown by the media. Now this comment from Adam.

"I can tell you he doesn't do business with any shady lenders. He's a marvelous man who has an instinct for lucrative business deals, that's all. Whoever told you those things *is* spreading rumors."

"Oh, good, glad we got that one squared away," Adam responded with a broad grin.

"Sorry, I didn't mean to be brusque. Nick has been very good to me. Whatever people think, it isn't true. People are jealous of Nick's accomplishments, of his money."

"That's probably accurate." Putting his napkin on the table, Adam said, "We should go. Before we do, I can say something else to you about Anglesey. You aren't originally from the Main Line, correct? Somerbury I think it was?"

Marlowe nodded, wondering what was coming.

"Do the names Cynwyd, Llanalew, Glynwynne, or Bryn Mawr mean anything to you? I'm suggesting you use your marvelous deductive reasoning capabilities."

After all the booze, Marlowe's deductive reasoning was about shot. She made a mental note to think about it later. Just then it dawned on her. "Sure. They're towns or roads on the Main Line."

"Remember I explained the Knights loved their adoptive home of Wales? Those and many other names in the area are of Welsh origin."

"Are you saying the Knights who sailed to America landed in *this* area and eventually used Welsh names because they loved Wales?"

Adam sat back. "Precisely what I'm saying. A gold star to Marlowe."

"Holy cow." Marlowe was dumbstruck. She was staring back at Adam.

"Please keep my story also the comments about the Welsh names to yourself. It's just better for people not to be talking about these things. I know I can count on you. Thanks, Marlowe."

Marlowe's head wasn't spinning. It wasn't clear either. She'd never had a better time with anyone. Though she remembered Adam's entire story, she had little idea of why he'd told it. Her only hope was she would remember it tomorrow. She could sort it out then. As for the Welsh names, she could remember others, Gladwyne, Bala Cynwyd, Denbigh, Narberth. Welsh names abounded, she realized.

"Here's the last thing before I take you home."

"*I'm* taking me home. I have my own car."

"I *do* know that. Here's something for you to check out." Adam had an amused look. "I think you'll find it to be, to use our word of the evening, 'interesting.' What is the highest peak in Wales?"

"I didn't realize it had any peaks. Is this something else you've invented, Adam?" Marlowe asked, cocking her head.

"No it isn't. Let's go young lady. Let's get you home."

Marlowe's head was getting clearer. Adam wouldn't let her drive. The valet retrieved her car. Adam opened the door on the passenger side. Marlowe got in.

Getting his phone from his jacket, Adam speed-dialed a number. "Malik, Adam. Can you pick me up at Marlowe's place?"

"Ten minutes."

Marlowe sat quietly on the way home. It was clear Adam had driven a Porsche before. He knew exactly what he was doing with the gears. There'd been so much puzzling conversation over dinner, she didn't feel up to asking more questions. They were soon on Chatham Lane, Marlowe's street. She finally questioned, how did Adam know where I live? He didn't tell Malik where I live. So how does he know? Then she saw the black car again down the street.

"Adam, see that car down there? It seems out of place."

"I see it. I saw it when we turned onto Chatham. Don't worry about it."

"How do you know so quickly?"

"I just know. Don't worry."

First he wouldn't let me drive. That was probably a good call. I'm just getting to know him now, so how would he know where I live? How does Malik know where I live? Anglesey must have vetted me before they invited me to the meeting. For what? To talk about *Candide*? There's definitely something going on here I don't know about. Other than what he had insinuated about Nick, this evening was so lovely. Now these concerns are making me second guess his intentions.

Adam unclicked his seat belt and got out of the car quickly. He opened Marlowe's door. When she got out Adam took her gently by the shoulders viewing her with soft eyes. Malik was just pulling up at the curb. Adam's eyes stayed on Marlowe. Marlowe didn't know what might be occurring so she just looked back on him with no expression or movement, waiting for some indication of how to react.

"Marlowe," he said softly, pulling her close to him, "this was a beautiful evening."

He leaned toward her and slowly kissed her on the lips.

Caught thoroughly off guard, Marlowe barely responded, her arms were at her side. Then Adam pushed back gently, handed her the car keys and walked out to Malik's car. Marlowe stood there watching, having no real idea of what had just happened.

What just happened…

Chapter 30

Many Sundays, Marlowe drove the twenty minutes to the Greater Philadelphia Animal Shelter in Philadelphia to walk the dogs in the kennel waiting for adoption. Marlowe had just gotten a leash from the shelter equipment room when she saw Addison Duncan, the shelter CEO, heading to the critical care room.

"How's it going here?" Marlowe asked.

"Don't ask. It's bad," Addison said as he kept moving. "The entire medical staff has been working around the clock. Some of the dogs we tried to save died. Neither the little chicks nor the hawk with the broken wings made it. I have to say I've never seen anything like this massive destruction of living beings before."

Marlowe turned toward the kennel. She hadn't gotten fifteen feet distant from Addison when she heard Luca Pasquale approach him. They spoke in almost a whisper. Marlowe wanted to know what he was saying. It had to be about Duffield. She stopped pretending to look at a bulletin board showing the adoption procedure. She could barely hear their conversation. She heard enough to know Luca was talking about the FBI. His voice grew louder.

"If they're involved with this Duffield raid, it's highly unusual. I don't recall their investigating any cases like this. The only thing I can think of is Duffield is part of something else; maybe there is more to it than we see here locally. I don't care. They're not reaching out to us, they seem to be involved on their own. Maybe they have interest in some other kind of aspect. I don't like it. We need to nail the bastard who did this, we cannot let him get off scot-free somehow. I'm telling you, Addison, I can feel it. The police and our agents have some pretty good ideas as to who's responsible."

"Who is it?"

"I can't tell you, they're not sure. Cops want it hush-hush until they can prove it."

"You'll get this idiot."

"Yeah, well if we don't get him, and the feds get him, we're done. If this insufferable killer gets away with torturing and killing all of those defenseless animals, it's like their pain and

suffering means nothing. I'm not going to let that happen, Addison. God help me, I'll step over the line if I have to."

At that moment a veterinarian assistant came out of an operating room starting to walk down the hall toward the kennel. The two men stopped talking and went their separate ways. Marlowe stayed still looking at the bulletin board. She needed to think about the bits she'd just heard before she went into the kennel.

The FBI. That's what the police officer said at Duffield. Why would they be involved in an animal investigation, Marlowe questioned again. Based on what Luca said though, they *are* involved.

At that second she opened the kennel door to a welcoming chorus of happy barks. Entering the kennel Marlowe instantly focused on the dogs that loudly requested her to take them for a walk. She first saw the brindle pitty Molly, who reminded her of Strider.

An elderly woman's grandson had turned Strider in. Esther had lived in a rough part of the city. Strider had protected her home for her so had been her constant companion. When Esther died, the grandson had already lost his parents then his grandmother. He was unemployed so had no money to keep the dog. He had to take him to the shelter. The wintry Sunday Strider came in Marlowe was there. She saw him as soon as he was available for adoption that day. She'd already heard his story about Esther. She went over to pet him. She also took him for a walk. She knew a dog like Strider was exactly what she'd been thinking about adopting. She just wasn't ready to make the commitment yet. The following Sunday Marlowe found out a family had adopted him. She was happy for him. He was one of the lucky ones.

However, as it so happened, it was not more than a month later on a Sunday morning when the officers got a phone call from a neighbor of Strider's adoptive family. They complained their neighbor kept him outside in the freezing weather. Officers Taylor and Jose went out immediately to pick him up. When they got to the address, Taylor told Marlowe, they asked the wife why they kept the dog outside in the freezing weather. She replied after they had taken him home, they decided they didn't like him. They put him outside. They didn't want him in the house.

Marlowe was at the shelter when she saw Strider brought back to the hospital for treatment. She felt terrible for him first for having lost his loving owner Esther, then for having been tied up outside with no cover, almost no food. He was so thin he was on the verge of death. The vets and medical staff took care of him, they nursed him back to health. Marlowe had already let the staff know she wanted him. She adopted him the day he was discharged from the hospital.

After individually walking seven dogs, from a pug to a Bernese mountain dog mix, Marlowe came around to Molly's kennel. Marlowe was sure it was just a matter of time before a nice family adopted Molly. The family that had owned her was forced to turn her in because their uneducated neighbors, ignoramuses as Marlowe called them, were afraid of a pit bull. Marlowe knew pit bulls are wonderful, loving dogs unless someone treats them like fighting dogs or abuses them. Then they learn to defend themselves just as any other being would. Marlowe would have taken Molly because she wanted a companion for Strider. She was just too busy to take on any more responsibility. Marlowe put the leash on Molly. It was already one o'clock even so she wanted to make sure Molly got her exercise.

Just as they got outside to one of the walking trails Marlowe's phone rang. It was Kim.

"Kim, I'm glad you called. How's Sol doing?"

"You know he's getting weaker. He seems disoriented at times. This morning he got an early call from someone. I can't always understand him now. The only thing I understood clearly when he hung up was he wanted me to call a lawyer. He kept stammering, getting louder until I finally understood the name. He scared me, Marlowe. He was belligerent about it."

Marlowe knew it was odd because in their Wynne meetings early on they had reviewed Sol's estate plans. Marlowe had recently directed him to a competent estate lawyer for a review. What reason would he have to speak with a lawyer.

"Was it his regular lawyer, Aaron Spekel?"

"No, it was some new guy."

"What was his name?"

"His name was Adam. I'm so upset about Sol, I don't remember his last name. Should I have written the name down?"

Marlowe went still, almost rigid. "Was the name Adam Mansfield?"

"Yes, that's it. He came to the house right away. He's nice gentleman, handsome if I may say. They talked for about a half hour. I could tell Sol was trying to get him to agree to something. I was in the kitchen so I could see them. Not close enough to hear what they were saying."

"Were any papers signed?"

"None I saw. All I can tell you is Sol was not happy when Mr. Mansfield left. He seemed dejected, sad."

"Okay, Kim, don't worry. Whatever it was, Adam will take care of it. I know him, he's a good attorney. Thanks for letting me know, Kim."

Marlowe knew whatever it was it had something to do with Anglesey. Beyond that she had no idea nor any reason to pursue it. Sol wasn't going to tell her anything. Certainly neither was Adam. So that was that, she decided.

Molly was having a good time sniffing everything in sight. Her tail was wagging fifty knots an hour. In the meantime Marlowe was thinking about what Adam would have been doing at Sol's house. Why Sol was so insistent about speaking to him. She knew he had no needs on the legal front. It had to have been something else. She wasn't going to worry about it.

She took an ecstatic Molly back into the kennel then headed out of the shelter. She was looking forward to getting home because she'd remembered that Nick's invitation to the Rocking Horse Downs party was sitting exactly where she had left it unopened on the foyer table. She always took such delight in the wording of the annual spring party.

When Marlowe got in her front door Strider had great curiosity about the new smells on his mom's hands. Finally able to break away, her eyes lit up when she saw Nick's envelope. She carefully opened it.

The Duchess and Sebastian Gavin

Invite You to Their Home at

Rocking Horse Downs

1 Cherry Woods Lane

New Hope, Pennsylvania.

Attire for the Evening is

Shorts and T-shirts

Sneaks and Sandals

May 22

Cocktails at 6:00 PM at the Pool House

Dinner at the Pool

"I love it, Strider! The Duchess and Sebastian, isn't it cool?" One of her favorite things about the pair was the thin cross on their backs. Formed in dark brown fur on their otherwise light tan fur, the long part of the cross started at the top of the mane on the head then went back to the tail. The horizontal part of the cross was at their shoulders. It extended from the end of the mane down each shoulder. Marlowe made a mental note to be sure to take both carrots together with sugar to her favorite two donkeys.

The funny thing, Marlowe remembered, was May 22 was Nick's birthday. He would be fifty-five. Of course Nick wouldn't want anyone else to know, which is why he didn't put it on the invitation. If he had said, "No Gifts," the Main Line translation was, don't spend too much. A couple hundred dollars would be fine. Nick had everything he ever wanted or needed. She knew his present to himself was to spend his birthday evening with those whom he counted among his friends.

Marlowe made a quick chicken dinner for herself, took care of Strider and stretched out on the couch in her Great Room to watch TV. It was getting late, she was falling half-asleep. Suddenly she sat up. Was the black SUV outside? She never put the alarm on. She got up, turned the lights off in the front of the house then peered out a dining room window. No car. She went outside to be able to see farther down the street. No car.

"Marlowe," she chided, "you're such a fraidy cat!"

Chapter 31

Early on Tuesday of the following week Maria walked into Marlowe's office. She placed a cup of coffee on Marlowe's desk. When Marlowe looked up to thank her, Maria said, "Earl's here, down in the lobby. He's not sure he should, regardless he needs to talk to you."

"Why does your boyfriend want to talk to me? Is everything okay?" Marlowe asked, concerned.

Maria hesitated, then said, "it's about Duffield."

"*Duffield*? What about Duffield?"

"I told him right after it happened you were upset. Now you really want to help the police identify the guy."

"Okay. Let's go down to talk to him."

Earl was sitting on a settee when Marlowe and Maria got down to the foyer. He got up moving forward to shake Marlowe's hand.

"Hey Marlowe. I hope you don't mind me coming, even so there's something, a little thing, that might help you."

Maybe she'd been wrong in her quick judgment of him. He was taking his time to try to help her, really to help the dogs.

"You may not know I'm a commercial real estate broker in downtown Philly. I meet tons of business people in my job. I work with all of the banks down there to finance a variety of different buildings, from slums to high rises."

"Okay, didn't know that."

"Well about a year ago I became aware from more than one source about Mexican, shall we call them businessmen, had started to do business in the broad Philadelphia area."

Earl stopped speaking. He was looking at Marlowe.

"And?"

"Oh, sorry, Marlowe, I suspected you might make the connection. These guys are not the most honest people. They've been known to deal in businesses that could be termed illegal."

Marlowe stared back at Earl, finally making the connection. "The Duffield fight. Illegal. All cash. In and out."

"I need to be clear here. I've met some of these men. They conduct themselves just like ordinary real estate investors, they even wear suits and ties. If they are who I think they are you'd never know it. I've been in this business a long time. I've not been sniffing around. I'm not saying they were involved. I'm just here to say it may be a situation you want to keep at least in the back of your mind. Maybe in your detective work someone will say something and you'll remember what I'm telling you."

Marlowe reached to shake his hand. "Earl, this is information I didn't know. I admit at this moment I don't know what to do with it. I'm definitely going to keep it more toward the front of my mind. Thank you for taking the time to think about this the time to come talk to me."

Wow. When she got back to her office she wondered if she knew anyone who might fit Earl's description of being Mexican real estate entrepreneurs. She couldn't think of anyone. At any rate this was one more possible clue. The organizer was probably local, now possibly maybe Mexican. It wasn't much. It was a start. Though she was busy in the office Marlowe did take the time to meet her old boyfriend Parker for lunch on Tuesday at Elan in Wayne. She decided to get there early to look around since she hadn't been there before. She'd heard the outdoor dining was sensational so she was happy the weather was perfect, sunny, not humid, with just a few clouds drifting by in the sky. It occurred to her that lunch there might have been much more fun if she were meeting Adam instead of Parker. She readily admitted though the jury was still out on Adam, more importantly the kiss on Saturday evening was likely just a good-night kiss, not a kiss kiss. Besides, good-looking Parker was lovely to sit across from. Best, she reminded herself, to keep the drinks to iced tea, not wine. Otherwise lunch could turn into an afternoon delight, which would turn the Adam/Parker state of affairs into something more muddled than it presently was.

Having gotten there first Marlowe took the liberty of choosing a table. The name of the restaurant, name, Elan, was perfect as the restaurant theme, both inside out. Marlowe didn't know a great deal about gardening or shrubs. She did know the center piece for what was designed to be a country garden was an Eastern redbud, a small, handsome, multi stemmed tree about 30 feet high. The spring rosy-pink flowers massed to create a wide crown providing some relief from bright sun. The tree had been trimmed to permit fine-looking, well-constructed bamboo dining tables to be clustered around the base of the tree. The perimeter of the dining area was replete with a circle of numerous spring flowering shrubs additionally wrought iron urns filled with fans of forsythia. Marlowe judged the Elan design to be a perfect ten.

Speaking of which, as she had just enjoyed the scene, the other perfect ten walked in. Dressed casually for the Main Line, Parker wore khakis with a light blue Philadelphia Racquet Club polo shirt with what Marlowe guessed were Ferragamo brown loafers. GQ all the way. She was painfully aware *she* didn't look Main Line Vogue in her grey suit and white shell underneath. At the least, had she been thinking at all morning, she could have put on her attractive, strappy heels. As a result, Marlowe felt she looked matronly. Where was Miss Snooty from Needless Markup when she needed her. Marlowe made a mental note to get Snooty's cell number, have her come to Chatham Lane then probably throw out eighty percent of Marlowe's clothes. The only thing left would be her white tennis dresses, her white tennis sockies, plus white tennis sneaks. Marlowe was confident she'd made good choices on the Snooty front. Snooty would probably throw out a tennis racquet or two if she didn't think they were the right color. The rest would be heading to Goodwill. All her clothes were in perfect shape, they were just incredibly boring. Ergo, Miss Snooty needed to be put on permanent retainer.

Parker came over to their table and gave Marlowe a kiss on her cheek. Not sure why, Marlowe was mildly disappointed. Not that she expected an all court press from the outset. A chicken peck wasn't cutting it either. On the other hand, just maybe Parker was no longer interested in her. That hadn't occurred to her. She'd been telling herself that good old Parker was no longer in the picture. Let's leave it so, you goof.

"Parker, such a fabulous idea to come to Elan—it's gorgeous!"

"It truly is. The food, especially the salads and seafood, is getting rave reviews. I already know I'm having the Cobb salad with chicken. I know you love shrimp, so I'd recommend the shrimp salad. It's fabulous."

Parker was beaming at his lunch companion. It looked like he couldn't take his eyes offer even for a second.

When the waiter come over Parker gave him the order along with iced teas. Iced teas—saved! Marlowe breathed, privately questioning whether she was or was not relieved.

"Nice Racquet Club shirt. Looks great on you."

Parker smiled softly at Marlowe. "Marlowe, I know you always think you look way too conservative in your Wynne Capital suits. You need to know, really, you look striking. You look exactly like you should look Monday through Friday. You manage an incredible amount of money. Your investors want a money manager who is professional whose look is understated. Your choices are flawless."

As he always had, Parker tended to support her in everything she did.

Wait just one moment here, Marlowe reflected. Seems like he really thinks so. It does make sense. Need to amend note to have Snooty in to just review my closet. She's the expert, no need to tell her to throw everything out. At NM prices I would be saving thousands of dollars anyhow. Good plan.

"You're so kind to say that, Parker."

It felt good to hear the compliment because she really didn't like clothes shopping even if it was at NM. If she didn't have to do it she'd be thrilled. For a few seconds she wondered how Adam judged her style. Of course he'd only seen her a couple of times, probably not enough for him to have any opinion at all.

"How are things at Wynne?" He was leaning back, legs outstretched to the side of the table. "The market's been behaving itself, just gentle movements."

"Yes, it's not been bad as long as you're in a balanced portfolio. What's new in your legal world?"

Parker straightened up then leaned in toward Marlowe. He dropped his voice to just shy of a whisper. "Let's talk briefly about Nick then move onto other fun subjects, like the French Open Tennis Tournament. Would love to hear your evaluation of the seeds. You may remember for certain things I'm Nick's attorney. Though my main practice area is real estate law, I don't help him in those areas. I don't even know if he uses a lawyer for the buildings he owns. I've been made indirectly aware of something which may be related to him. That's what I wanted to talk to you about." Parker paused. "Okay to talk about him, Marlowe?

"Sure, Of course. You would always do the best by him. I'm sure nothing has changed in that department."

Parker reached across the table to take Marlowe's hand. "You know, I don't think you've ever looked more beautiful than you do right now. I mean that."

Any onlooker would have seen Parker was one hundred percent sincere.

Marlowe smiled back without moving her hand.

Removing his hand, he said, "Sorry, dear, force of habit."

Marlowe looked back at him with no expression on her face.

"Yikes, sorry about the 'dear' too. Force of habit again. Hard to break some things."

He was trying to smile. Marlowe met his try with a real smile.

"Ah, it isn't anything Nick mentioned to me," Parker said, "It has the potential of being serious. I'm not comfortable asking him about it because it's none of my business. At the same time I can't just sit by doing nothing."

"Heavens, what are you talking about?"

"I'd much prefer not to discuss any specifics because this could be rumor and speculation. Here's my question to you. You've known Nick a long time. I know you don't see him except every month or so. If you've seen him in the last several weeks, have you noticed any change in the way he acts, or has he been the same as he always is? Does he seem anxious in any way? Has he been brusque at all?"

Marlowe considered it. "I guess I've seen him twice recently. Once he popped into my office at Wynne. He had a question about a stock and he wanted to deliver an invitation to his party at Rocking Horse Downs this Saturday. The second time was when we happened to see each other at the mall last Saturday. There wasn't anything unusual about him then either."

"Okay. I'm hoping what I've been hearing about him is just gossip." Parker paused to drink his iced tea.

"I'm glad to hear. You had me worried," Marlowe said as their lunch arrived.

She quickly mentally reviewed that Gwyn had inquired about Nick when she was at Snowdon, then on Saturday evening, Adam said his friends talked about him. Certainly Nick was fairly widely known in the greater Philadelphia area, so his coming up in conversation really shouldn't be a surprise. From time to time stories about him or one of his real estate holdings were in the media too.

"By the way a funny thing happened at the Philadelphia Racquet Club late last week. I saw Adam Mansfield when we both had squash league singles matches there. We didn't play each other, though it would really have been fun. He's really a nice guy. I'd never really talked to him before. When we were chatting about legal stuff after the matches were over he offhandedly asked me about you. He knew we were seeing each other for a long time. He seemed to think we were still together. When I told him we called it quits months ago he got the beginning of a smile on his face. I knew what it meant. I told him to go for it. So don't be surprised if he asks you out."

Whoa. A double game-changer for Marlowe. First, Parker either had given up, or was waiting to have the next guy come along for her to realize what she had in Parker. Either way, in her mind, she didn't have to think about him, at least for now. And second, now she was beginning to make some sense out of the unexpected kiss when Adam had dropped her off at home on Saturday night. Marlowe remembered the kiss because she'd just stood there like a mannequin. It was so bad she'd been almost surprised he hadn't picked her up sideways, leaned her against the front door of her house, and rung the doorbell for someone to come out and carry her in.

On the way back to her office Marlowe decided to call Gwyn at home. Parker asked about Nick. Gwyn had asked about Nick. Was there a possible connection of some sort with Duffield? It didn't make any sense to her. She needed to touch base with Gwyn anyhow after what had happened. Missy picked up.

"Is Gwyn in, Missy?"

"No, she's out for the day at a meeting in Center City. May I help?"

"Is she okay?"

"She's trying to stay busy so as not think about Raspberry."

"Any idea if Gwyn has discovered any clues about who did the Lancaster or Duffield fights?"

"Well, since you are involved, I guess it's okay to tell you yes, she along with some of her friends believe they have some information pointing to someone, as they say, of interest."

"*What*? Really? Who?" Marlowe jerked her car over to the side of the road and stopped so she could concentrate on what Missy was saying.

"It wouldn't be for me to say. I'm sorry. Understand, they aren't sure. It's more of a theory at this point."

Marlowe stared out her windshield at a groundhog that was in a pasture about twenty five feet from the road. She needed to think about who Gwyn's friends might be that Missy spoke of.

Who was their suspect? She realized she was not going to get any more insight by just sitting there with the groundhog. Just then the groundhog sat up and looked right at Marlowe. She took that as a sign she'd better get moving. It was possible Gwyn did have a good idea on the perpetrator. Marlowe needed to get on it.

The groundhog theory.

Chapter 32

By Saturday morning, Marlowe had gotten no farther with solving the Duffield murders. Gwyn had an idea, apparently nothing more than. On Friday she'd had some time to also call Skip then Luca to see what they might know. She posited even if she could get a little something she might be able to put it together with other things then come up with something useful. Time was rapidly passing. Nothing she knew about was happening with the investigation. Her next opportunity to talk to people to get some clues was Nick's party that night.

She played tennis and got her Saturday chores completed. She had plenty of time to get ready to leave at five for Rocking Horse Downs. She decided to wear her mid-thigh white shorts, yellow and white striped tank top and her white and silver sandals. She put her hair in a ponytail, which made getting ready a breeze.

At about six o'clock in the evening, as Marlowe turned onto Cherry Woods Lane, she was taken aback by the dozen or so cars in front of her waiting for the valet. Normally the valets made quicker work of the queue. Most of the cars were empty. The passengers in three cars directly in front of her were getting out. Marlowe finally grasped what was going on when her eyes lit on a four-in-hand team of light gray Percherons pulling a beautifully restored, antique hay wagon up the driveway. Even from a distance, she could see the guests onboard were holding flutes, which were likely filled with some libation. Leave it to Nick to outdo himself, she marveled with pride.

On her way to Nick's she'd speculated about who else might be arriving. Ashanti always received an invitation to Nick's parties as did her other friends, the Rolling Hill Gang, Lindsay, Olivia, Logan and Rachel. Marlowe had talked to Olivia briefly during the week. She, Lindsay, Logan along with Rachel were going. Of course, Ashanti would be there. Nick was careful to invite Marlowe's friends so she would be certain to have a great time. With the Gang there she would be able to talk to them to see if they had any ideas for moving forward.

About ten years earlier, around the time she'd come to the Main Line, Nick had built his magnificent compound in the country near New Hope, Bucks County, Pennsylvania, about an hour's drive north of the Main Line. The first time she saw the property she regarded it as spectacular. It rivaled Main Line mansions.

Nick said he mostly went to the house because it was located in a sparsely settled area so private. He said he could get a great deal of uninterrupted work done there. The Ritz condominium in Center City was where he said he stayed most of the time when he wasn't traveling.

As for his entertaining, it was nothing if not lavish. He was a master at throwing dynamic, entertaining parties. An invitation to Rocking Horse Downs was sought-after. Rarely did anyone turn down the chance to attend. Even the invitations were creative. For a party last fall the hosts were listed as Moxie, Bubbles, and Gucci Gavin. They invited you to their home at Rocking Horse Downs in New Hope. Jeans and T-shirts were specified, no high heels permitted. Moxie was a fawn-colored Mastiff, Bubbles was a Vizsla, Gucci was a Jack Russell mix. Sometimes it was the cows doing the inviting, or sometimes the horses. One invitation Marlowe remembered to an orchestra sponsors event was from "Mr. and Mrs. Gaston Longchamp, Resident Swans."

Nick wanted his guests to come to the country to enjoy their visits by being comfortable. The swans could be found in the pond at the entrance gates. Guests could visit the cows in the barn or ride any of the many horses or ponies—the tack room stable hand would provide a saddle and bridle. Cocktails would be available while all this was happening. Eventually dinner was served on the lawn provided by the master chef Nick employed year-round. Unless it was a big charity occasion there would be no more than a hundred guests. His real estate investments had obviously been good to Nick. His was a lifestyle to which few could aspire, much less achieve.

Marlowe pulled over behind the last car, left the key in the ignition, got out to walk toward the driveway to join the others in front of her. Newly arriving guests were queuing up behind her. One of the valets handed her together with the other empty-handed guests a glass of rum punch. After one sip Marlowe quickly discerned the rum punch was more rum than punch. Oh, well, she decided, let the fun begin.

Waiting to climb aboard the wagon, Marlowe saw her friend Aaron Spekel, one of the up and coming trust and estates lawyers in the city. He was the attorney whom Marlowe had recommended to Sol. The wagon was on its way back down the driveway to carry the next group to the house. Marlowe had time go over to Aaron.

"This is fabulous, isn't it?" Aaron said. "Leave it to Nick to come up with something like this. You have to love it."

"Nick is something, isn't he? How's the law these days, Aaron?" she said, leaning forward to shake his hand.

As the wagon driver turned the wagon around in a wide circle in the middle of Cherry Woods, Aaron teased with an amused grin, "Join me for this ride, maybe I might tell you."

"You drive a hard bargain, Counselor. I'm in."

"Great, then let's board if we can manage it without killing ourselves."

Just then the valets adjusted a portable set of wooden steps for each person to carefully make his way onto the wagon. Aaron got in first extending his hand to Marlowe helping her negotiate the tricky boarding process.

The two-hundred-yard paved driveway went up a gradual hill to a courtyard in front of the house. Designed by a renowned local architect from nearby Doylestown, Rocking Horse Downs had the look of the typical upper Bucks County farmhouse. Constructed of fieldstone plus a few sections of light brown fiber cement clapboard, it did look like a farmhouse. It was the largest farmhouse by far in the entire area. The fieldstone springhouse was at the sizeable swans' pond near the road. A stable for the horses and donkeys along with an outsized, stone bank barn for the Ayrshire cows were part of the property. To Marlowe, this was paradise.

Marlowe and Aaron settled in on a layer of straw piled so thick it was like a pillow mattress.

"Things have been really great," Aaron said. "You may have heard I just made partner."

"I did *not* hear. Fantastic, Aaron, I must say you deserve it. You have to be the youngest partner at your firm. Just great," lauded Marlowe as she tried to give him a congratulatory hug. The Percherons were trotting up the driveway and, as Marlowe found out, sitting on massive piles of straw trying to lean in any direction was not conducive to maintaining an upright position for long. She ended up falling over on him.

Obviously delighted at the turn of events, Aaron declared, "Well, I'm beginning to like this country life. I could get used to this!"

Marlowe started to separate herself from Aaron as the rest of the other twenty or so guests on board started to giggle.

A man at the other end of the wagon said in a voice loud enough for everyone to hear, "Why do we all get the feeling you two will be staying on the wagon for the trip back down perhaps then back up?"

"Hey, I'm not going to fight it! I don't even know this woman, aside from that I sure would like to get another rum punch or two for her!"

Marlowe swatted at Aaron. Everybody especially Marlowe enjoyed a good laugh.

Righting herself, she asked, "So how did you do it? Become partner, I mean."

"Same as your business. It's in the numbers you generate, I guess word has gotten around I may know what I'm doing, at least when it comes to law. Thanks for the referral of our mutual client, Sol. He's referred several clients to me."

"His legal papers are taken care of, aren't they, Aaron?"

"Yes they are."

So Sol had no legal issues to discuss with Adam. Her analysis had been correct. Then why was he at the house? What subject was so important Sol insisted on seeing him.

The horses slowed, then halted at the top of the driveway. Marlowe made her way around the house to the pool to the pool house, which was itself the size of a substantial house. The two Har-Tru tennis courts were in the back to the right of the house. The barn, other farm outbuildings, including the pastures were to the left.

Constructed of the same fieldstone used for the main house, the pool house was two stories high with a hip roof. As Marlowe looked around, though she had been to Rocking Horse Downs numerous times, she never tired of gazing at all of the features of the property. She'd decided a long time ago she could easily move out there to live a happy life in the country with all of the animals with such a stupendous house. She'd even have more animals at the house, maybe even bring some in from the Greater Philadelphia Animal Shelter.

She marveled at how the side facing the pool was practically all glass with a southern exposure. It was always flooded with light. The first floor glass was retractable Nana walls, which allowed the first floor to be open on warm days. A magnificent bar made out of walnut topped by scintillating black, off-white and gold-colored granite was directly inside in the center of the pool house. Behind the bar was a huge television screen along with bottles of every kind of liquor imaginable. Built to accommodate twenty bar stools, the bar took up about a third of the first floor. A gorgeous billiards table sat to the left of the bar. To the right rested one of the fanciest ping pong tables Marlowe had ever seen. Behind these to the left was a kitchen which would be the envy of any chef. To the right were rattan dining tables and chairs for at least a hundred people. The second floor was a movie theater with separate plush chairs for each viewer. A smaller secondary bar with a kitchen used to prepare snacks and hors d'oeurves for moviegoers was tucked along the back of the theater. A marquee read "Double Indemnity" was playing at 6:30.

Chef Gabe Martinez, Nick's Certified Master Chef, was in the lower kitchen whipping up a myriad of seafood appetizer dishes. Servers were carrying trays of mouthwatering morsels to offer to the guests.

It was six fifteen. Most of the guests who had arrived had made their way to the pool house bar. Dinner was at eight so Marlowe had plenty of time to chat with other guests as well as wander about the farm. She decided to first go to see The Duchess and Sebastian, the formal party hosts to deliver the carrots in addition to the sugar cubes she had in her pockets.

She found the donkeys in a small paddock near the barn. One of the stable hands was there to let guests in to pet or brush the animals. Marlowe went in to offer them the treats which they gladly accepted. She was rubbing Duchess behind her ears when Logan came up to the fence.

"You look fabulous! I hate you!"

"Right back at you, Logan!"

A lawyer herself, Logan's husband, whom she'd married after college, had also been a lawyer then a judge in Philadelphia. He'd died three years earlier from pancreatic cancer. Logan decided the day she received her husband's diagnosis to retire from her law firm. Since then she filled her life with those things she loved including her favorites, gardening and landscape painting. Recently, Marlowe knew, Logan had speculated about finding a partner with whom she could spend some time.

"Nothing like losing ten pounds, working out at the fitness center, then going to an Arizona spa to make a woman feel young!"

"Whatever you're doing is working, Logan, that's for sure. Isn't this a delightful farm? Come meet your hosts. If I may, I present The Duchess and Sebastian."

The donkeys gave a quick look to see who had come over to their paddock. Not seeing any carrots, sugar or anything else of interest, they refocused on Marlowe, specifically the hand holding more carrots.

"Come on in, they won't bite!" Marlowe opened the gate, waving to her friend to join her in the paddock.

"I'm afraid they will, either that or kick" Logan said, backing away. "I grew up in the city. I'm not a country girl like you. When you're finished with the creatures, come take a walk with me."

"You're so disappointing, Logan," Marlowe said, shaking her head. "You're supposed to be this tough, take-no-prisoners lawyer, yet after all here you're afraid these fine donkey specimens will not be polite to you. Shame on you." Marlowe was looking sternly at Logan.

Logan stood outside the paddock, arms akimbo, looking at Marlowe with her head cocked giving her a playful stare.

"You're a little country snob. Now get out here. Let's do some proper hiking up this hill here."

"You're pushy to boot for heaven's sake. Alright, we'll do this your way." Putting the remainder of the treats back in her pocket, Marlowe said, "They've had enough for now anyhow. Just so you know, this the *only* reason I'm coming along."

The stable hand opened the paddock gate for her as Logan said, "You're a mess, Marlowe, don't you ever change."

Marlowe and Logan embraced as long-time good friends do.

Turning back to the sweet, furry kids Marlowe said, "See you two later. Behave yourselves!"

They were watching her, their ears back, slightly down. Marlowe was certain they were telegraphing their discontentment of the end of the carrot and sugar treats.

Marlowe looked around the compound. "Which direction shall we go?"

"Let's go up this way," Logan said, pointing up the slight hill away from the buildings.

"Sounds good. What a lovely way to catch up with my old friend."

"Watch what you say, Miss Marlowe. At fifty eight, I'm not old!"

Logan barely looked fifty. She was always beautifully dressed. Her dark brown hair was in the new fashionable, shorter, layered cut. At about five feet four inches appearing to weigh no more than one hundred ten pounds, Logan played tennis or squash daily also went to the fitness center three times a week at Somerset. She took care of herself.

"How are your gardens? I bet your hostas are up and your peonies are about to bloom. This is such a gorgeous time of year."

They were leisurely making their way slowly up the pasture hill by themselves. The other guests were around the house, pool or around the various stables. When the Gang met for their quarterly dinners it was all about having fun, all about not having serious discussions about anything. It was an informal law all agreed on. The stroll up the grazing field toward the back of the inner compound was picture-perfect for private chatting between close friends.

"I'm afraid the gardens have expanded to the point I have a full-time gardener working on them. I often have my morning coffee out on one of the patios to see what's grown or bloomed since the prior morning. You must come over. It's lovely in the morning."

"I'd like to. Don't expect me to bring my garden tools. Been there, done that as a kid back in Somerbury. Not doing it, Ms. Bell."

"You really are funny, Marlowe. I'm glad to see you happy. I know breaking up with Parker was hard on you even though you were the one to call it quits."

"How about you? Has any man caught your interest?"

Taking in a deep breath, coming to a halt after a couple of steps, Logan said, "Well, that's what I wanted to talk to you about."

Marlowe stopped walking. She turned around facing her friend. "Really? Tell me!"

Chuckling, Logan answered, "No man is in my life. Don't get excited! A businessman has…" Logan started to walk again.

"Has…" Marlowe said waiting, lightly touching Logan's arm.

"Become of interest," Logan restarted diffidently. "He has no idea I'm attracted. This man is charming beyond words, soft spoken, extremely successful, maybe available. He's younger than I am, though I don't think it would matter to him. You know me, once a lawyer always a lawyer. I've been doing some checking first. I have a concern or two."

"Looks good so far. What are the concerns?" Marlowe asked as they slowly wended their way up the field toward the woods, arm in arm.

"One misgiving is one of his houses is owned by an offshore entity, which I believe is based in the Caymans though I'm not sure. It's down there some place."

"Lots of people have Cayman entities. The government is fairly easy to work with, even accommodating."

"Doesn't it seem odd though? Why not put it into a trust of some sort? Another thing is he owns a great deal of other real estate."

"That's a good thing, right?"

"Ordinarily, yes. Would you think it strange if some of the real estate had no recorded liens against it?"

"By 'liens' you mean what precisely?"

"I mean regular old liens. No liens. No mortgages, no notes, nothing."

"Maybe he has enough money to invest cash in those properties he wants to own."

"It's possible. I'm not saying it isn't."

Marlowe unhooked arms, faced her friend gently asking, "Logan, you know I love you. Are you sure you aren't just apprehensive about putting yourself out there, about exposing your feelings to potential hurt?"

"I won't deny that," she said with a little frown. "I admit I'm apprehensive. It's been a long time since I even looked at another man. Gary was the love of my life."

By this time they were at the back fence of the pasture. "I know. You're fearful, nervous, maybe feeling a little guilty about thinking about developing a relationship with a man other than Gary. Remember, Gary loved you. He'd want you to be happy, wouldn't he. He'd want you to meet someone and fall in love."

Logan's expression changed on a dime to one of impending joy and excitement.

"What is it? What's going on, Logan? You okay?"

"I feel encouraged by what you've said. It's Nick, Marlowe! Nick!" Her face was full of expectation, hopeful anticipation of Marlowe's reaction.

Marlowe stopped in her tracks, spinning around to look at Logan with a broad grin. "Is Nick the man you're interested in? You have to be kidding me! Is he?"

"The one and the same!"

Marlowe threw her arms around Logan almost crushing her in exuberance. She grabbed her arm. They twirled around like they were in the midst of a square dance, both laughing like little kids.

"Fantastic, Logan!" Marlowe said when they calmed down. "Oh my gosh! I don't know what to say! Of course, I should've figured him out for you myself. You two would be *perfect* together. Let's go find him!" This time Marlowe was looking expectantly at Logan.

"You're making me feel much better. I was reticent to ask you. I knew you'd be here. I didn't know if I would have the courage to talk to you about it. Something else though really draws me to Nick."

"Wonderful, what is it?"

Logan's voice became softer. "The rumor is when he was young he fell in love with a woman who was married. She wouldn't divorce her husband because they had a son. What I've heard is Nick's heart was hers forever after that. In a way it's so touching, so endearing. Any idea about this?"

"Don't know about any early love life, I was little then. Now you're thinking straight about Nick—forget all the other concerns, they don't mean a hill of beans. Let's go find him!" She was already starting to trot down the hill toward the house.

Right behind her, Logan added, "I agree, I think as guests at his home it's entirely fitting at a minimum for us to say hello."

Picking up the pace, Marlowe shouted over her shoulder, "And ask him out on a date!"

"Marlowe Evans, don't you dare!" Logan managed to get out as she ran to catch up.

Because they had walked so far it was a couple hundred yards run to get back to the pool. Marlowe arrived at the pool terrace with Logan just a few seconds behind.

"Hey, we're in better shape than we imagined, Logan!"

"Squash and tennis players are always in great shape!"

"I have an idea." Marlowe moved closer to Logan, leaned over whispering so no one else would hear, "I think it would be better if you talked to Nick by yourself. If I'm with you it might end up being a conversation more between him and me. I'd love to have him talk just to you to see you for the fabulous woman you are. You go. I want to check out the goats anyhow. You go, young lady, shoo!"

"On my way, goats! What do you want for treats!"

Chapter 33

Marlowe helped herself to different salads, a lobster roll from the buffet and found a table in the pool house where her friends Lindsay, Olivia and Rachel were already sitting. By the time dinner was over Marlowe had chatted with her friends along with many of the other guests. She went to the pool and sat on one of the surrounding, white marble benches and stretched her legs out. One of the new people whom she'd just met was a friend, as it turned out, of Gwyn's. Marlowe saw him sauntering around the pool. She invited him to join her on the bench. Willy Phillips had mentioned in general conversation he'd known Gwyn when she was a judge, he was an assistant DA and had helped her with several cases.

When he sat down he picked up from what he'd said before. "She was an excellent judge, very fair. I assumed she'd stay on the bench forever because she was dedicated to putting criminals behind bars. I think she would've stayed if her dog hadn't died."

Marlowe unconsciously quickly drew in her legs.

"Raspberry?" Marlowe asked, incredulous, twisting around to look at him intensely, like she was searching for any possible clue she could glean. Willy knew about the dog?

"Yes, do you know about Raspberry?"

"Only a little," answered Marlowe not wishing to betray her friend's confidence.

"You know what happened then. Raspberry was about to give birth to her first litter of puppies when she was stolen."

This was news to Marlowe. Gwyn hadn't told her that.

"She was one of the ones they put out for bait, you know, to get the other dogs, the fighting dogs, ready to fight. Sometime afterward the police raided the site. It was too late. The animals still there were dead. The police caught a man running away. When they got him to stop, he turned around and held a newborn puppy in his hands. He said he'd been told by a man he didn't know to get rid of the bodies. That was all. He said he couldn't kill anything and wouldn't kill the one live puppy he'd found with a dead dog. The police made him show them the dead dog. It was Raspberry. She had a microchip in her neck. They were able to trace her to Gwyn. They took the pup to Snowdon and delivered him to her. The last thing I heard was she named him 'Raspy' in honor of his mother."

Raspy! Marlowe's face momentarily contorted in shock and horror. Her jaw tightened, her teeth clenched. God damn it, Marlowe, you should have put it together. The little red spots on Raspy's white coat look like raspberries. Her mother Raspberry must have had the same coloring. Gwyn is living with her treasured puppy who is a constant reminder of what those felons did to her dog in addition to the other animals. Then Duffield happens essentially in her back yard? I realize *I'm* so distressed by all of this. Poor Gwyn. No wonder she's in such a bad way. No wonder she has nightmares for God's sake.

Willy couldn't help noticing Marlowe's reaction. "Are you okay? I'm sorry, I never should have told you about that, please forgive me, Marlowe."

Still breathing heavily, she said, "I'm okay, it must have been so awful for Gwyn."

As calmly as she could, she asked, "Willy, why do people do such a heinous things like dogfighting? I don't understand it."

"Easy one to answer. It's money."

"What do you mean exactly, 'money?'" she asked startled by his quick response. She looked around the pool hoping no one was there. She didn't want this conversation to be interrupted. Guests had begun to leave, so fortunately no one was around, not even any staff.

"I mean big money. Certain wealthy people come to bet on these kinds of fights. There can be big money, I mean a million dollar night, with no expenses for the organizer. The big time fighter dogs are worth hundreds of thousands of dollars. The animal fight in Lancaster where Raspberry and the others were killed would have had betters waging many thousands on just one fight round. These private fights exist in various locations."

"You can't be serious." Marlowe was dumfounded.

"Dead serious."

Marlowe looked at him with a piercing stare. She'd had no idea. Gwyn did. That's what she can't get out of her mind. Her imagination keeps repeatedly unfolding these images of these fights. Trying to get more information, Marlowe asked, "Have you followed what's going on out at Lancaster? Do they have any idea of who's to blame?"

"Not officially. The word around the office is the police believe they've identified what they refer to as 'a person of interest.' Information gets a little complicated because the Lancaster police are involved. At least one person in our office thinks the FBI might be involved."

The FBI. "Because the Lancaster dogfighter is the same as the Duffield guy?"

Marlowe seemed to have more information than Willy, albeit she wanted to keep pressing to see if he knew more than he was saying.

"No. The only reason would be this guy is involved with fights in more than one state. The person in our office thinks, whoever this guy is, he's involved in other crimes. He's using the fights only as a part of his other illegal activities."

"Fights like in like Pennsylvania and New Jersey?"

"In like maybe the whole east coast, Marlowe, from Massachusetts to Florida. Maybe beyond. They don't know. They have suspicions."

"You're talking about a whole organized dogfighting ring."

"That's what she says."

"How does she know this?"

"All I know is her uncle works in some capacity at the FBI."

Oh my God, the FBI again, Marlowe repeated, doing her best not to react.

Willy smiled at Marlowe. "Gotta go, good to meet you, Marlowe."

"You too, Willy."

Her mind was reeling. Still sitting, she felt dizzy. I've been looking for information and now I think I've just gotten it. Money is driving this. What did Earl say? Illegal activities. Could the people he was talking about be involved in this? These guys would be methodical, they would be slick. *They* could have done these fights. How do we get the proof.

At this point Marlowe decided to leave too. Logan's questions and concerns added to Willy's comments about Raspy. The fights apparently in addition to Duffield were overwhelming Marlowe's already overloaded brain. She needed time to try to sort this out. The valet brought her car up to the parking area at the compound. She remembered she never did say anything to Nick. She decided he'd be busy with his other guests so she'd call him in the morning.

She drove down the driveway about to make the right turn onto Cherry Woods Lane, when out of the corner of her eye she caught sight of a car down the road at a distance to the left. She tramped on the brake. It was a black car. Her first impression was it was just a security car. Why security out in the country? Her second guess was it might be an FBI car like maybe was at Duffield. Animal issues out here? Made no sense. It seemed like everyone was talking about the FBI like it was all part of a police TV action series.

"I have to know." Marlowe was getting overwhelmed, too many major issues going on. She had to do it, she had to. She turned her car around driving back up the driveway. Asking the valet to leave her car where she was parking it, Marlowe found Nick. Giving him a hug and taking his hands, she took him aside from his guests.

"Nick, there's a black car out on Cherry Woods," she said, still holding his hands. "It's sitting pretty far down the road. It's just sitting down there."

"Hold on, Marley!" Nick took her face in his hands and kissed her on her forehead. "How'd you like the party? Did you have a good time? I saw you were over with the donkeys."

"Fabulous party, Nick, I loved it." Marlowe was so concerned she had to force a grin. "Nick, what's the black car doing out there?"

"It probably belongs to some guest who didn't want the valets to take his car."

"No, Nick, it's too far away. It looks like what I saw—" She slowed her speech. She changed her mind. "It looks like a cop car."

Nick's omnipresent grin vanished for a moment. It quickly returned. "Oh that, that's a security car, not that I need it with this crowd. If I call them they're here in ten seconds."Marlowe looked at him. His smile had disappeared. He shot a quick look back to the house. He looked around at the remaining guests around the pool. Only five guests in conversation lingered.

"Don't worry your pretty head about these things." He was smiling again. "You should enjoy yourself."

"Okay, Nick, sorry to have rushed over to you. It was a sensational party. Another incredible Nick-bash! Thanks! Love you!"

She felt somewhat better after talking to Nick about the car. Sliding into her own car, Marlowe turned back to wave at Nick. He wasn't looking at her. A valet approached him, nodded, then spun back around toward the five-car garage. Nick made a call. His normally neat red hair was disheveled in the strengthening breeze. He threw his free arm up in agitation. Marlowe watched him curiously in her rear-view mirror. After a minute, he tucked his phone in his pocket then hastily walked back to the house. Parker's question about Nick came to the forefront of Marlowe's mind. Did he seem nervous? She sat for a moment. He said the black car was security. That was smart of him. Invited guests probably wouldn't create any security problems. to the contrary a gatecrasher might. She guessed the valet had headed quickly off to get one of Nick's cars for him to take to the city that night. Maybe Nick had business in town the next morning. Maybe the phone call had been with a caterer or a vendor who didn't deliver to Nick's satisfaction. Marlowe admitted to herself she had no idea what was going through Nick's mind. Was he nervous, agitated? Maybe it was caused by something going wrong at the party, or maybe not. Did the black care make him nervous?

She finally started home. Within not more than five minutes of getting on Route 611 south toward the Main Line area. She noticed, in her rearview mirror, a black Bentley coming up fast behind her on the four-lane highway. She'd no sooner seen it than it passed her as if she were standing still, like it was going at least a hundred twenty miles an hour. As it went by, she managed to see the license plate: "RHD." A vanity plate, Marlowe concluded. With such a fancy car, it could have been a guest from the party. Who could it be? Probably no one she knew. Who would have those initials? Richard Dreyer. No, not that much money. Rita Drury, no, she has a Mercedes.

RHD, RHD….

"I know what that is. Rocking Horse Downs. That was Nick!"

Chapter 34

Instead of going into Wynne right away on Monday, Marlowe decided she needed to work on the Duffield case. She'd already considered what happened when she left Rocking Horse on Saturday night. She felt this was her Nick, her lifelong mentor, who people were talking about. She knew Nick. He was amazing, nothing like what some were half insinuating. She moved on in her investigative process.

According to Luca they had been making some progress, though it didn't sound like they were really on to who did the fight at the Federson's or Lancaster.

The first thing she needed to do was talk to Sol. One thing she wasn't going to do was mention Franny. It didn't matter anyway. Maybe Kim, though with the best intensions, shouldn't have told her about the call to Sol. Sol had been clear about his opinion of Anglesey with regard to Marlowe's involvement in it. What might he know about the fights. He and Marlowe hadn't talked about it. Maybe he might know something that would be helpful. Her plan was to talk once and for all about Anglesey. Duffield was infinitely more important.

She'd called Kim who said to come right over and go directly to the back yard. When Marlowe got to Sol's he was in the back lawn near Kim's vegetable garden. He was drinking water sitting propped up in a lounge chair with his legs stretched out. Kim was picking some of her lettuce from the garden and then went into the house.

"Sol!"

"Marlowe, so nice to see you, I'm so glad you had time to come by."

"Just checking up on you to keep you out of mischief."

"Do I look like I'm going to get into any trouble, young lady?"

"You can stop right there, Sol. I know you. You have a reputation a mile long, you can't fool me!" Marlowe said, pointing her finger at Sol. She sat down on a lounge chair near her friend.

"You're a funny girl, missy."

"Sol, you have me concerned about things you have only suggested to me about Anglesey," Marlowe said, reaching for his hand. "I understand you don't want to talk specifics with me or anyone else. I've known you a long time. As you well know, I have great respect for you. I wanted to stop by to see you. I also wanted to tell you if invited I'm going to decline attending any more of their meetings. I really like each of the people I met, yet there's a little something that isn't hanging together for me. I can't put my finger on it. That combined with your comments are enough for me to forego Anglesey."

Laying his head back onto the lounge chair, Sol smiled a heartfelt, contented smile. "I can't tell you how pleased I am about your decision."

Marlowe knew she'd made the right decision about Anglesey. She didn't know why, nonetheless she knew it was right.

"If you're up to it I'd like to ask you about something else. How are you feeling?"

"Right now I feel pretty good. Doc's got me on some good meds, so go ahead, ask away."

"I know you mostly watch CNBC for news. You must know about what happened at Duffield."

"I've seen reports on the local news. Luca looks like he's going to get them."

"He's definitely a good guy. I've known him from the shelter for a while now. He's dedicated, first class all the way. I know Luca with his crew are working with the police, still it disturbs me they still don't have the guy. I know their forensic work takes time. Maybe by this time it's too late to find him. I've been doing some digging. I think whoever ran the fight also likely the one in Lancaster is a local guy."

"Gee, Marlowe, a guy from around here? That would be surprising."

"By around here I mean center city Philly also the suburbs. Someone told me there are some criminal types who are new to business in center city. Do you have any speculations on that? I remember you had friends, connections at city hall."

"Well sure I did. I still have a couple down there. Let me make a call or two. Can't promise anything. You never know if they've heard some bits that might help you."

Marlowe left Sol's at about ten o'clock heading for the Wawa in Bryn Mawr. The convenience store had the best kind of fast food. She decided to get a twenty-four ounce hazelnut coffee also one of what she called a "hockey puck," which was a rather large, undeniably pure bliss, glazed apple fritter. Sure it was over five hundred calories, Marlowe rarely allowed herself to indulge. With her late breakfast in hand, she was about to get in her car to head for a church parking lot about a half mile away when she saw Officer Alten from the Duffield fight scene walking toward her.

"Marlowe, hello! How are you doing?"

"Doing well, regardless Duffield is always on my mind. Anything new on your end about who did it?"

"Without going into it, we have more clues. One of them from the work I did at the site. Can't say more, I think we may get him, not sure though. I gotta get some coffee and run. Take care Marlowe. Thanks again for all the work you and your friend did."

There were no cars in the church lot allowing Marlowe to have the property grounds all to herself. She parked near one of the few wrought iron benches overlooking the adjacent grounds, took the coffee and treat and went out to sit and mull over something about Duffield.

She called Ashanti first just to say hello to check in. She left a voice-mail. Marlowe wanted to know at this point if Ashanti or any of the Gang had any ideas at all.

After about fifteen minutes of absorbing the quiet countryside along with the sounds of squirrels rustling in the underbrush on a pleasantly warm day, Marlowe was about to begin her think tank about Duffield on the exact question of who was responsible for the fight. As important was her corollary question. If she couldn't figure out who did it, then the next question was, what *type* of person would be likely to have done it.

She hadn't had a chance to follow up with Ashanti with her psych class background, which was one of the reasons she wanted to talk to her. Marlowe reasoned if she could define the person type, then maybe she could identify who would be a prime suspect. She was sure all the authorities were working slavishly hard to identify the person.

Maybe, because she wasn't a shelter agent or a police officer, rather someone who worked in a totally different field, she might have an advantage. She might see things just differently enough to be able to add to the identification process. Worst case if she had even only one idea about who to investigate, she could share it with Luca. Sol could potentially be some help too.

Aaron had given her what was an obvious clue, though on her own she'd been oblivious of it. Fights weren't about dogs. They were about money. Big money, he'd said. Marlowe managed money, millions and millions of dollars' worth of money. What Marlowe had begun to realize was it wasn't her money management ability that was valuable. Maybe something else she knew could be valuable.

She understood individuals who had substantial money to invest. She was thinking that was the key. Investors weren't always the same in their investment outlook. Some wanted their money to be safe for their families, for their charities. Others were much more emotional about their money. Some wanted merely to make even more money than they already had. Others bordered on being intense, almost frenetic, about being certain not only to lose no money but also insisting on making a lot more money.

These last clients were difficult for her or any financial advisor to work with because their outlook was constantly changing depending on what might be changing in the world or a company on any given day. Their money mentality seemed to Marlowe to almost be an oxymoron kind of mindset. They wanted to make sure they kept the money they had. They wanted much more. The result was they couldn't tolerate the big "r" word. Risk. It made them consistently agitated, anxious about their money. For some it was to the point where they couldn't help themselves, they were consumed by the possibility they wouldn't have enough money. As soon as she had sorted this out, it was clear to Marlowe that the investor type to run a dog fight would be, to one extent or another, the intense, frenetic type. She also reasoned it could be that while they had these tendencies they might not be obvious to a casual observer.

Believing she was on to something, Marlowe wanted to mull over her own clients as a test of her theory. Could she tell whom of her clients, or even her friends, fell into that category? Lounging on her bench with a full stomach and her remaining coffee, she started off handedly, in no order, to mentally run through her clients, acquaintances and friends. The quick survey produced a relatively short list of names.

The bench she was sitting on was a long one, so Marlowe decided to lie down on it, close her eyes to think better. Even though her approach was a worthy one, the only people who really popped into her mind where the people she knew well or knew what business they were in, people like Malik, Jack Danett, Nick, some of her Wynne colleagues who'd done financially extremely well. Then there was, as improbable as it might sound, a sleeper, Becky. Who knew what she might be capable of. Marlowe remembered, as many Main Line residents did, Becky had a trust fund set up for her when she was a baby. She had oodles of money. So far it wasn't a promising list.

She had no belief any of them would be anywhere near being a perpetrator. Reflecting further, there was Maria's boyfriend, Earl. Marlowe had met him only recently when she came to pick Maria up at Wynne. Something about him still put her off. Maria was sure she wanted to marry him, yet they'd been dating for two years. Earl still hadn't popped the question. Because of the way he dressed, the expensive Mercedes he drove, Marlowe suspected he had money. She never wanted to ask Maria anything about him. It would be inappropriate since Maria worked for her. Marlowe admitted Earl did have the characteristics of what she was now calling an oxymoron investor. Earl went out of his way to speak with her about the Mexicans he said he'd heard about. He knew she was persistent. Suppose he was the guy so was trying to throw her off the scent. It was possible, Marlowe concluded.

How would she investigate him? Other than through Maria, she had no access to him or anything about him.

She was sure none of the others on her short list would ever have done anything like Duffield, let alone Lancaster or any other place. Marlowe ended up sitting back up, frustrated that her incisive idea wasn't fruitful in the least. She decided she'd better get back to Wynne to get something productive done there for her clients.

In the ten minutes it took Marlowe to drive to her office she decided she'd look for an opportunity to carefully ask Maria about Earl, just to rule him out. No sooner had she gotten into her office Maria came over.

"Sorry to burst in on you. I just found out Compliance is doing an internal audit of margin accounts."

Marlowe knew this was not the opportunity.

"You know how they are, when they say jump we jump! Here are the questions they have," she said, handing Marlowe the form. "I'll start making calls to your other clients. I assumed you'd like to call a couple of them yourself. Let me know which ones. Don't forget Nick even though he doesn't use his margin."

"I'll call him first Maria, thanks."

Marlowe was about to dial Nick's number. She stopped. Despite knowing people were talking about Nick because he was relatively well known, she was still bothered by the vaguely insinuating comments regarding him. Gwyn and Logan had asked her about Nick, about how he made his money. Gwyn had revealed to her Nick's holdings were specifically real estate. Marlowe tamped down her gestating suspicion that she didn't know Nick as well as she should have. She and Skip had known Nick forever. He was kind, sweet, generous, definitely support-ive. He'd started his life with a bad hand, worked incredibly hard to make his money. She felt resentment toward the people who were seemingly intimating her cherished, lifelong friend was not what he seemed. On the other hand, maybe they weren't implying anything at all. Marlowe didn't want to focus on any negativity surrounding Nick any longer. Who would have imagined dismissing the tiniest lingering concern she had about Nick would be provided by such an unlikely source, the Wynne Compliance Department? Marlowe finally placed the call. She laid out the form on her desk.

After a few pleasantries about the party, Marlowe explained Wynne was doing an internal audit for quality control of their clients' accounts."

"Ouch, sounds like a lot of work," Nick joked, adding quickly, "What do you need from me?"

Nick sounded as if he'd just had a good round of golf. He was typically in a cheerful mood whenever he chatted with Marlowe.

"Okay, it's just a few questions really affecting margin borrowing," Marlowe explained. "I don't use margin."

"You could, that's what these questions pertain to." His account had been set up for margin so he could borrow quickly if he needed to, without having to sell anything. A single call to Maria and money would be wired to wherever he said it should go.

"Got it," he said, "Shoot."

"Major source of income?" An easy, straightforward question to start with.

"The companies I own."

"The type of companies these are? Manufacturing, transportation, what?"

"Nothing like that. They're commercial real estate companies."

"The income is from rents primarily?"

"Yes."

Marlowe hesitated, shifting her weight, feeling uncomfortable. Then she stood up, nervous, brows softly knitted. Her chair rolled back. It softly touched the wall behind her. The questions she'd asked were the only ones on the form. She thought she had a chance to get answers to her own nagging questions about why Nick had been the subject of conversations. She felt bad, like she was sneaking around Nick, behind his back. She had to do it in order to put these issues to rest. She decided to push further despite the fact none of these subsequent questions would be questions an investment firm would want to know about a client just for a margin account.

"These companies are triple-A rated companies?" she asked, going off script.

"Far from it. You see, the way I've become successful is I buy commercial buildings, warehouses and old manufacturing buildings needing huge renovations. Typically the area surrounding these investments has gone downhill. I sufficiently renovate the buildings then lease them to whatever stores, offices or little start-up companies will pay the rent."

"Sounds risky, Nick." Marlowe started shifting her weight back and forth, her cheeks were getting warm as she pressed Nick for answers Compliance didn't need. Nick didn't seem to care. It was quickly occurring to her it was almost like they'd never talked about it before because it just never came up in conversation. They always talked about fun things.

"Thanks Nick. I have the answers I need for the margin watchdogs."

Marlowe sat back down in her chair. She felt bad she'd lied to Nick to get him to talk about his financial affairs. She did get some answers though. She was glad to know more about his business. Now, as she had always been, she was sure he was a legitimate businessman. She'd stood up for him when questions had come up. She'd done precisely the right thing.

No word from Ashanti from the message she'd left earlier. It was high time to harass her. She called her cell again. Voicemail again. "Ashanti Ba, where are you? Why haven't you called me? When I speak to you, I'm going to tell you off then never speak to you again. I want my present back. You don't deserve it. I give you a little gift of a cool silver knife, now you're on to your other friends. You're such a little gold-digger. If you don't call me back, I'm going to tell Andy about the new, handsome intern at Eastbury. If you don't know who he is, you better find out 'cause you'll get questions from Andy."

With an enormous grin on her face about the fake new intern, she said into the phone, holding it at arm's length,

"*Good bye!*"

Chapter 35

The next morning Marlowe was hoping to catch Maria to have a cloaked conversation about Earl. Maria was sitting at her desk looking through a file.

"Morning, Maria!"

"At seven o'clock in the morning the market still looks like it's going to open normally, seems no one is panicking about anything, at least not yet."

"There's still time before the market to go crazy before it opens at 9:30. Hey I wanted to ask you a little bit about Earl. He seems like a total gentleman. Is he from around here, what does he do?"

"He really is a gentleman, Marlowe. I met him at a 5K race in center city. He slowed down for me. We finished the race together. That was the beginning. He's thirty-two. His parents' family sold a railroad equipment parts company a long time ago. He has a degree in economics from Villanova University. He spends his time being on a number of charitable boards. You'd be interested that one of them is the Philadelphia Zoo. Neither he nor his family need to work. Earl does anyhow—he loves putting real estate deals together. His family are lovely people. I have the feeling sometime this summer, maybe on my birthday on June 29, we'll be engaged."

"Fantastic! I want to be among the first to know!" That was that, Marlowe concluded. Earl was ruled out as a suspect.

Just as she walked into her office her cell was ringing. It was Adam. Marlowe sat down on the edge of one of the client chairs.

"Marlowe, I need you to do something for me. I need you to call Nick right away. Tell him to meet you at the cul de sac on Grays Mill Lane at ten o'clock. I'm going to pick you up at 9:30, don't say I'll be there."

Shocked Adam was calling her so early, add to that confused by what he wanted, she didn't know how to respond. She moved back in the chair then hunched forward, not understanding the call.

"Marlowe, are you there?"

"I'm here. What's this all about?"

"I know you don't know me well, even so I'm asking you to trust me. Please call him."

Having listened to all of his credentials at the Anglesey meeting it was clear Adam was a class act, that he was trustworthy. If he was this insistent on having Nick meet her and Adam, though it was peculiar, Adam must have a good reason. To meet at Grays Hill was also peculiar, even though it was only about ten minutes from her office. Maybe there was something at or about that particular road which made it better to meet there. So, as enigmatic as it sounded, it seemed like it was okay to call Nick to meet him there.

"Okay, I'll call."

Marlowe called right away. It went to voicemail. She left a short message asking him to meet her at Grays Mill at ten o'clock. Ten minutes later she had a text from Nick saying okay, he could be there briefly.

Marlowe decided to call Ashanti to see what she would deduce about this request from Adam. Ashanti was usually in Eastbury Hospital earlier for rounds. Marlowe didn't want to interrupt her so waited until eight to call her. She didn't pick up.

"Damn it, Ashanti, where are you?" She left a voicemail to call right away.

Not wanting to wait, she called the hospital. The assistant, whom Marlowe knew at the neonatology nurses' desk, answered.

"This is Marlowe Evans. Is Dr. Ba available please?"

"Dr. Ba? Checking, one moment please."

Thinking she was with a patient, Marlowe was going to leave a message for her to call as soon as possible.

"Ms. Evan, I'm sorry, Dr. Ba isn't here. I'm told by one of the nurses she came in early then left abruptly around seven thirty."

Marlowe hung up. If she was to leave the office at nine thirty she'd better to get some work done in her clients' portfolios.

At nine twenty Adam's number came up on her cell.

"I'm outside in my Range Rover. Come down please."

"Okay, I'll be down."

"Hurry."

Odd. What could be so important that I have to hurry?

Marlowe was out the Wynne door quickly. She saw Adam right away. She got in his car.

"Look, Marlowe, I know this was short notice, and you've lots of things to do in the office. This can't wait."

He was smiling like he was glad to see her. She was thinking there was no place she'd rather be than sitting beside him in his Range Rover.

"Got it. What's up?"

Adam was now not exactly looking at her, he was looking out the front window to her side.

"Sit with me a minute. I have some important things to explain to you. We need your help right now. This has unfolded much faster than we anticipated it would."

"You know I have no idea what you're talking about. Who is 'we'? Why are we going to Grays Mill?" Why aren't you looking at me?

"I know what's there. It's a dirt road a quarter of a mile long through a woods ending in a cul-de-sac. The only thing at the end is an old, dilapidated little stone springhouse not too far away in the woods. Everybody knows what's there," she said with a growing edge to her voice.

"No one goes down there."

"What's this meeting about? I obviously don't know. If it concerns Nick, I want to be there. Recently a couple of people have been asking questions about him. If I can help straighten these things out, I'd like to."

"Let me lay out a little background for you. First, we know for a fact Nick is a big time gambler."

Marlowe's voice rose. "No he isn't. Don't say that, Adam. I've talked to a bunch of people like Logan, Maria's boyfriend Earl, even Gwyn, Ashanti, Skip of course, even Parker. No one thinks bad things about Nick."

"Parker? Are you seeing him again?"

Marlowe stared back at Adam.

"Forget that, Adam. I'm trying to say Nick is not a bad person like you are suggesting he is. He's not.

"Marlowe, please listen to me. We know Nick has been a longtime associate of a highly profitable Mexican cartel headquartered in Cabo. It has a gambling arm based at the Silver Club in Las Vegas. He met the management as well as some of the cartel members when he was at his home in Cabo. The cartel wined and dined him. He became a regular at the Silver Club."

Marlowe turned her shoulders to fully face Adam. She didn't like what she was hearing.

"You may not be aware the cartel takes tremendous drug profits then lends them at high interest rates to borrowers like Nick who need lots of cash for their investments. Those investors have no sufficient, acceptable collateral on which to secure the loans with a bank. Nick approached the cartel. They set him up with the loans he needed to buy even more distressed properties to expand his real estate empire. He deals in cheap real estate in bad neighborhoods so can't get bank or pension-fund financing for his projects. Borrowing from the cartel has allowed him to make a fortune over the years. This cartel wants to remain invisible, under the IRS radar so they put no liens on any property. It's however clearly understood by borrowers like Nick the cartel must be paid their interest."

"Are you saying, because Nick took money from the cartel, he's considered dirty by the police?"

"He's been complicit with the cartel by knowingly accepting laundered money. He's guilty, yes. It's illegal. And it isn't the police who are involved, it's the Federal Bureau of Investigation."

"The FBI?" said Marlowe instantly remembering the black car at Rocking Horse Downs. The black SUV at Duffield. "What about the car you saw on Chatham when you took me home after dinner? It didn't seem to concern you."

"I saw it. We're going astray here. Yes, that was the FBI. They'd been watching you as a known associate of Nick's because you manage his Wynne money."

"'A known *associate*'? I'm a nobody!" Marlowe snapped. She sat forward on her seat, further twisting around to look directly at Adam who was now facing her, full of seriousness of purpose.

"They know that now. There's another reason they were on your street. I didn't want to tell you this part. You keep asking questions so I'll tell you. Remember I took a call at the Anglesey meeting. It was about Julie Hudson?"

"Yes," she said slowly, remembering Julie was murdered.

"She was Nick's daughter." Adam showed no emotion as she stared at him, not comprehending.

Marlowe's color drained.

"The cartel found out about Nick's having a daughter. They executed her."

Adam explained with the straightforward expression of a TV news reporter covering a mob hit. "It was a brutal warning to Nick because he's late on his interest payments. You would not have detected this. When we found out about that at the meeting we were incredulous. We were afraid for *you*, You could be the next cartel hit if Nick didn't pay."

Marlowe blankly stared at Adam, it was too much for her to take in.

"The FBI realized the same thing. They were there to protect you. The hit wouldn't have happened right away, the cartel would give Nick time to pay. The FBI was at Chatham to monitor the normal kind of activity on the street so if something out of the ordinary happened they would recognize it might be a cartel action.

"This is all crazy. Nick's a gambler, he does business with a Mexican Cartel, his daughter is killed, the FBI is involved, I might be a cartel hit target. All of this in the ten minutes we've been sitting here about a man I've known all my life?"

Marlowe was gesticulating with her arms, waving them all about. A deep frown etched itself on her face.

"Can you see where I might think you're making this up, that this is going to be one of Franny's movies?"

Adam sat back, looking down, trying to release his frown. "I hear you, I do. We need to get back to Nick. This gets worse."

"I don't know you well. I do know you're smart. I tend to believe you are honest, that you wouldn't have me out here to tell me things that weren't true, no matter the subject matter. It's just it's so upsetting. My whole world is being tossed upside down."

Adam put his hand on her shoulder looking back into her eyes. She was at full attention, not knowing what to expect next.

"Even though the Anglesey meeting was only a few days ago, we had reason to believe then Nick might have been involved in some way in the Lancaster dog fight. If that were the case, then we needed you, as his money manager and trusted advisor, to be available to us if we determined we had to meet with him to see if he was involved. We would have to use you."

"You have to be making this up now. It isn't funny." This latest accusation made her angry. She glared at him.

"You've no idea how I wish I were—I know you're becoming a reluctant participant in this," Adam softened. "This is all real."

"How do you know this? You keep talking about 'we,' and 'us.' Who are they?"

"The 'they' is the Anglesey Philosophical Society."

"What are you talking about?"

"We'll talk about Anglesey later."

"Anglesey?" she asked, calming down. "How does Anglesey figure in this?"

"All I have time to tell you is the meeting at Anglesey was a test for you. We used the discussion of the themes in *Candide* to gauge your reaction to the principle we discussed. It was clear at the end of the meeting your belief is the same as our key belief. As human beings we are obligated help someone if no one else will or can. Remember?"

Marlowe was speechless. She sat motionless, scrutinizing Adam's face, her green eyes searching for something that looked familiar to her, that looked like the Adam she'd met. The one she was already starting to fall for. This person sitting next to her was a steeled man she was seeing for the first time. This person was saying things to her that disrupted, intruded into her life. Her reality was no longer authentic. Maybe it was non-existent. Either her life was collapsing, or Adam was spinning tales. To what end—she knew it wasn't possible.

"We have connections in the Manhattan office of the FBI. We have deep connections where we need them, Marlowe. You have no idea who we work with across the country as well as internationally. Let's concentrate on what is about to happen. It's almost nine thirty. The meeting with Nick is at ten. Here is the reason we must meet with Nick and why we need to meet with him now. Okay?"

Taking a deep breath in, Marlowe managed an "Okay" in a small, reticent voice. She was slumping, nearly collapsing in her seat, looking straight out the front window.

"We believe the FBI doesn't really want Nick. He's guilty. They really want the cartel members. Nick is their way to get to them." Adam sat straight up as though he was in a court room lecturing a jury. "What they want from Nick is to question him to get more information on the cartel so they can make arrests. After that, they don't need him. Assuming he cooperates, the government will take all his assets even though he'll do no jail time. He'll go into witness protection. Make sense?"

"It seems straightforward, yes." she said, talking to the window, hands clasped on her lap. Motionless waiting for the other shoe to drop. Wasn't witness protection a good thing?

Maintaining his lawyerly demeanor about to lecture, Adam took his phone out of his shirt pocket and handed it to her.

"I need to show you a photograph I received from a friend. Marlowe took the phone. She couldn't believe what she saw. It was a photo of Nick, standing beside a bloody dead dog. She stared at it, paralyzed.

"We've identified the background. It's the barn where the animal fights were in Lancaster. All we know is Nick was there, we don't know anything else. No one is jumping to the conclusion he was involved with carnage."

Marlow broke down and started to sob. She slid back in her seat. Her whole body was shaking.

"It's possible Nick is a cheat on top of an animal killer?" She felt just like she'd felt in the gazebo at Gwyn's, only this time betrayal had been added to the rest of the horror. Who was Nick, the man she adored?

Adam started to take her into his arms. She pulled away screaming. "Why are you doing this to me? This could've been photo shopped. Nick could have been inserted into a photograph. Why would Nick have been at such a place? It can't be Nick in this photo, it can't be." She shrieked at Adam, "What are you saying Nick did?" Looking at the photograph, Marlowe doubled over weeping uncontrollably. "Oh my God, Adam, no! *No!*"

Adam reached for her. She jerked away.

"Marlowe, you need to understand we don't know why he was there. Hang on now. This is *precisely* why we're meeting with him right now. At this moment all we know is he was at the barn. It could've been *after* the fight for all we know. All we want to do is talk to him. We knew he wouldn't agree to meet with me—he doesn't even know me. We knew he'd meet with you if you asked him. Then I get the chance to ask him just a couple of questions, that's all. If in fact he was involved in any way with what occurred at the barn in Lancaster, what we want to know is who is *organizing* the dog-fighting ring. Maybe it's Nick's cartel buddies, maybe not. Maybe it's someone else altogether. Any problems Nick may have with the FBI are his problems. We don't care about them. All we want to know is who massacred those animals. He was at the barn. He knows something. Whatever it is, we want to know it. If the authorities can't get him, Anglesey is going to get the bastard who did these fights."

Marlowe's eyes were closed tight, trying to take it all in. Maybe it wasn't as bad as she had first expected. The photo was unsettling. Adam was right, it didn't prove anything.

She moved over close to Adam, putting her head on his shoulder for comfort.

"I'm sorry I've reacted in such a dreadful way. My life is a simple one. Duffield, Lancaster, everything is upside down. Add knowing my Nick has some serious financial issues—it's all so saddening, incredibly distressing. I don't know why Nick was at Lancaster. At any rate you're right. It could have been for some other reason. If he'd heard about the fight he might have gone there to stop it. Maybe he got there too late. The photo could be for evidence to the police. I'm sure it was something like that. Let's talk to Nick. We'll get this straightened out."

She was looking up to Adam's face, looking for assurances she was right.

"You may well be right, Marlowe," he said, stroking her hair.

Marlowe was still leaning against Adam, a thousand thorns coursing through her mind.

"Marlowe, what I am going to tell you right now is extremely important," he said, gently helping her sit up straight, his car still sitting in the Wynne parking lot. "I had to give you the background first so you would understand everything. What I am going to tell you is why I called you this morning, why you are here with me right now, and why we are going together to Grays Mill."

She was being dragged in to accuse her beloved Nick of monstrous things.

Chapter 36

"The reason we had to set up this meeting right away is because we think the FBI is going to move in sooner than we believed to take Nick in for questioning about the cartel. You need to understand through our sources we know the FBI has been working on two separate, independent investigations led by two different FBI teams. One team is investigating Nick the other the cartel. The other team is investigating the dog fights we know have rapidly spread from Lancaster to New York, New Jersey, Delaware in addition to other states, making them an interstate crime."

"*Two* teams? That explains all my confusion. I assumed your referring to the FBI was about their animal investigation. I had no idea there was another team working on the cartel investigation. This is now all starting to make sense."

"The whole FBI situation is irregular. This is what we believe has been happening."

"You're telling me there are Duffields and Lancasters in other places?" Marlowe half probed flatly, overwhelmed at this point.

Adam bypassed her question. "What I'm going to tell you next is critical, Marlowe, it's the heart of the matter. What's at stake is enormous. We wanted to make certain we had the opportunity to talk to

Nick about the fights *before* he finds out the FBI is on to him for his business with the cartel. We have no idea how much he knows, if anything at all, about the cartel investigation. It's paramount we talk to Nick right away, *right now* to determine what he knows."

Marlowe nodded her head, then sat up. "Wait a minute." She was again staring out the windshield saying nothing.

Adam sat looking at her, waiting.

"Rocking Horse Downs."

"The party?"

Marlowe was still looking out the window, perfectly erect, not moving a finger. "The *car*." She was still staring out the window. "The car on Cherry Woods Lane, Nick's street. It was just sitting there."

"What are you talking about?"

"It was a black car. Parked down the road, away from the driveway. He said it was security."

"He?"

"Nick. But… but he didn't wave goodbye to me. My Nick always waves goodbye to me. He didn't." Tears were appearing in her eyes. Still staring, "then his Bentley…. It flew by me so fast I almost couldn't see the license plate."

Turning to look at Adam, she said in a whisper, "He knew right away it was the FBI, didn't he. He didn't realize then which FBI team it was or there were even two teams who were on to him."

It was Adam's turn to be silent. Each was looking at the other, searching for answers. Adam spoke first. "Here's our critical issue. Assuming he realizes they want him for the cartel, he'll panic. He knows he's guilty. He knows they'll seize all his assets, all of it. He's rich today, tomorrow he'll have no money. *That's* our problem, Marlowe. We're not sure. He may try to run."

"Run? Run where?"

"If he runs he'll try to go into hiding."

"Like to one of his homes, like Nantucket?"

"No, he'd know the FBI knows about his homes. No, he wouldn't go to one of those. He's been working with the cartel for so long without being caught he may not even have a plan set up. We think he thinks he's been flying under the cartel FBI radar. If he does have a plan, he's smart enough to have set it up so he would have the wherewithal to execute it at a moment's notice."

Adam's phone rang. Marlowe saw a name come up on the phone. She couldn't read it fast enough.

"Yes? When? Malik, how do you know? Where are they now? How soon will they be there?"

Hearing Malik's answer, Adam said, "About eleven? Shit! How did they find out? Never mind—it doesn't matter."

Adam hung up. "Put your seatbelt on. Our information is the FBI will be at Grays Mill around eleven. I don't know how they found out about the meeting. We still have a chance—they have the meeting time wrong. We have to go!"

Adam put the car in gear and screamed out of the Wynne parking lot. His face was tight, his lips pressed together.

His phone rang again. "Franny, what? I'm on my way to Grays Mill."

Adam listened for half a minute. "Wings Airport? The question is, has a flight plan been filed, if so to where?"

As Adam listened, his frown became deeper.

"Exactly what we were afraid of. That's it then, Franny. Tell Malik and Jack. It's the game changer. Tell Jack I'll be at his place in five minutes." Adam disconnected.

"I have to stop quickly at Harlech."

He was doing sixty out Lancaster Avenue.

"What's happening, Adam? Was that Franny Barrett? Why Harlech? You're driving too fast!"

"You just blew through two red lights! Adam!"

Chapter 37

Adam sped west on Lancaster Avenue toward Jack Danett's Harlech Gate Inn where the Anglesey Philosophical Society had met.

"Sorry about the red lights—can't be helped. I'll explain when I get back in the car at Harlech."

Marlowe's phone indicated an incoming call from Maria. When she answered, she told her assistant to just take care of whatever it was.

"You're on speaker, Marlowe. The manager needs to talk to you. It's about Nick."

"What about him, Tammy?" Marlowe nearly shouted.

"Your client, Nick Gavin, just wired *all* of his money to an account in Scoto Island. What's going on?" the manager demanded.

"I know nothing about it, Tammy," Marlowe cried, squeezing her phone tighter, wanting to crush it.

"Well find out what the hell is going on," Tammy demanded, ending the call.

"Adam," Marlowe said calmly, blinking back the tears, steeling herself, "Nick just wired all his Wynne funds to an account in Scoto Island."

She looked at him beseechingly, wanting him to tell her everything would be alright.

Adam pressed his foot harder on the gas pedal as he made the right turn onto Lancaster Avenue. Marlowe was thrown to her side window, a look of astonishment on her face.

"We figured that would happen. He's running. Scoto has no extradition. He'll be at the meeting place. He'll come because he loves you. This will be his only chance to say good-bye to you. Remember, he thinks he's meeting just you."

He looked across at her now, his own eyes tearing at Marlowe's obvious pain. He reached toward her with his free hand. She took it in both of hers asking softly, "Good bye?"

They reached Harlech. Adam parked right in front of the door leaving the engine running. He sat for a few seconds staring straight ahead. Then in a controlled voice, almost a whisper, said, "Wait for me here." He flung the car door open and sprinted into the inn, his suit jacket flying open.

With the chaos all around her, Marlowe decided to call Sol. Like Nick he had always been there to support her. She needed support right now. She also wanted answers about Anglesey.

Kim answered. "Sorry, Sol is finally asleep after a rough night. I don't want to wake him."

"Kim, this is important. Did Sol ever say anything about a society?"

"Yes, I don't know what he meant by 'society,'" Kim said. "I think about five years ago he was a member for about a year of some philosophy group society. The only thing he ever told me was they were not really a discussion group even though anyone who had heard about them assumed they were. He said they talked about important matters. He said he left because he didn't agree with how they did things, whatever that means. The only things he said he missed were the friendships he'd made with members in other cities."

"You said a philosophy group. Was the name 'Anglesey?'"

"Yes, that's it. It's a funny name. I just couldn't remember it."

"Kim, when you say members in other cities, what do you mean?"

"I don't know for sure. I know he used to get calls from people in New York, Boston, Chicago, L.A., cities around the country."

Marlowe's mind was racing about Anglesey as she hung up. Whatever Anglesey really was, there must be more of them. Just then Adam came running out of Harlech with a small shopping bag. Stepping hard on the accelerator, he sped out of the parking lot in the direction of Grays Mill Road.

"Nick knows. He may even guess the FBI team looking at him for the cartel arrests could be at Grays Mill because he now knows he's under surveillance. He must have figured it out because of the Cherry Woods car. Franny says he has a private jet waiting for him at Wings Airport in Bucks County, forty-five minutes from here. Now Maria says he just transferred his money out to an account in Scoto. He's going to meet with you, us, then rabbit to escape the FBI. That's clear now."

"What do you mean 'rabbit'?"

"*Run*, Marlowe, *run!*"

Adam called Malik. "Nick transferred his money to Scoto Island. Call Maria at Marlowe's office to find out which bank it's going to. Tell her Marlowe said it's okay to give you the information. Then take care of it."

Marlowe heard Adam giving orders to her firm. She knew whatever he was doing, she had to trust him.

Turning to Marlowe, Adam said, "We've got to get our answers from him and get them fast. Now we know he's made these escape plans, it may escalate, especially were he to see the FBI."

He handed Marlowe the bag.

"What do you mean, escalate?"

"Take these."

"What's this?"

"Push may come to shove." Adam's voice was hardened. "It's possible Nick may bring others along for protection in case he thinks he might need it."

"Protection from what? *Us*? He doesn't need any protection from us."

Adam's decibel level increased, "All I'm saying is we've seen this type of situation before. If he feels cornered in any way, things may turn worse. We need to protect ourselves. Get them out of the bag right now."

Marlowe peered in the bag. She saw two Colt forty-five semi-automatics. "What are we doing with these for God's sake?"

Adam, the gentleman attorney, was suddenly morphing into Adam a marine, barking orders, pulling rank. She imagined his seat belt suddenly looked like a bandolier. Marlowe was alarmed and frightened, not only for Nick. She was frightened for herself.

She was finally beginning to see what Sol had been strongly hinting at. Obviously felt he couldn't tell her. Anglesey wasn't the law, nor were they acting alongside the law. They were *making* themselves, moreover their beliefs, the law, vigilante style. She finally understood why Sol tried to tell her all along not to become involved with them. He must have been pleading with Adam to keep her out of it. Adam must have told him if they had to they were going to use me to get to Nick.

Adam was on the phone. "Did you go down the narrow farm road through the woods paralleling Grays Hill? You parked so the van can't be seen?"

Marlowe couldn't hear the person on the other end.

"Good. Things have escalated. Stay out of sight. Stay close enough to hear the conversation at the meeting. We're hoping it will be okay. Just in case, have your pistols prepared. Are you three ready?"

"Be careful."

"Adam, you're turning into a fighter out of a guerrilla movie. You're terrifying me."

Adam said nothing at first.

"Marlowe, this meeting this morning has gone from a meeting to get information to something potentially volatile and deadly. I told you I've seen situations like this before. It is deadly serious, I tell you. If it weren't important, I'd drop you off here then go on by myself. Given what we now know you must go. Otherwise he won't talk to us."

"This is so—it's all so upsetting. I'm not thinking straight," Marlowe said keeping her eyes on the road, seeing other drivers trying to stay out of their way as they came up fast behind them.

She tightened her seat belt and pushed her legs forward to keep straight in her seat.

Adam looked at his watch quickly. He abruptly pulled off to the side of the road approaching Grays Mill.

"Remember at dinner when I said some buddies and I had an idea who the fights ringleader was? Remember when I asked if you would help capture him if you could?"

"Yes, I said I wouldn't hesitate." Marlowe turned toward Adam.

"We have ten minutes before we have to be there. Here's how this will go down. We'll drive in Grays Mill. Nick will already be waiting. He will have arrived early to make sure no one else is around. That's why the others parked at a distance. We'll get out of the car and go over to Nick. It will be just the three of us unless he brought someone else with him. I'll start the conversation by asking him why he was at the Lancaster barn. You say nothing."

"Okay." She was resolved whatever was going to happen was going to happen.

"Can you do this?"

"I don't like it. I don't like any of it. Yes, I can do it."

"Marlowe, look at me." He reached over to her slowly, a gentleness in his eyes, a try at a small grin, drawing her shoulders toward him. "Another thing may happen here. I didn't want to load this on you. I know it's been a horror show for you from the moment I called you this morning."

Marlowe focused on Adam. Here he was, just as he was before all of this god-awful stuff had gotten started. The soft eyes, the sweetness she had first seen in him, the ever so slightly crooked grin. This was the Adam she wanted, the Adam she could fall in love with, the Adam she was already starting to fall in love with. Suddenly everything else melted away. Her only vision was Adam looking back at her, his eyes locked on hers.

Adam's face turned grave. "You need to steady yourself into the woman I know you to be. The photograph you looked at with Nick at the barn. Think about it. Why would he have been there? He didn't just happen along, did he, Marlowe. He was there because he wanted to be there."

"Was he betting?" she asked in a steady voice, her feelings quickly dissolved, her eyes narrowed, concentrating. "You're saying if he wasn't gambling he might have been running the fight."

"I'm saying it's a possibility. We don't know though. We think Nick learned about dogfighting from the sordid wealthy types of men attracted to high roller gambling in Vegas. We think he found out how easy it was to make major money for organizing on top of running fights. Because the properties he bought in the last year are so distressed, we suspect he began having trouble renting them. His empire began unraveling. At that point, he knew he had to pay the cartel or else. He had to get his hands on more money fast. That's when we believe he started the fights, including the one at the barn."

Adam hesitated like he was waiting for Marlowe's reaction. He got none. He continued, "Gwyn's dog, Raspberry, was one of the dogs there, wasn't she."

Marlowe looked away. She responded quietly, "Yes."

"Think about it. If Nick organized that dogfight, it means—" Adam faltered. "I'm so sorry, Marlowe. It means Nick must have had guys out picking up bait dogs in Rolling Hill Park when Gwyn was there with Raspberry. One moment Raspberry was romping around full of fun. The next moment she was on a truck headed for unbearable torture and death. We're almost positive Nick was the one who set up the Lancaster dogfight. This would mean Nick was responsible for those animals killed in that barn. He tortured and killed those animals. I didn't want to tell you this. Adam breathed in heavily. If it's true, I want you to hear it from Nick's own lips."

Marlowe looked intently at Adam, her eyes the size of saucers. She was strangely quiet, thinking about Raspberry. Raspy's mother was torn away from him before he was even born, He was ripped out of her by some dog that had been forced to lunge and crucify Raspy and his brothers and sisters. Raspberry herself, about to give birth, was torn asunder, unable to protect her puppies let alone herself. She was extinguished by some dog that had itself been kidnapped and commanded to kill or be killed. No dog had a chance in that ring. All were doomed to a hideous, ghastly death full of agony, attacked on all sides by dogs that had been turned by men to being vicious not because they wanted to be. Because men made them that way. None of these dogs was culpable in any of it. Some man was. That man needs to suffer, to die the way he drove the dogs to kill other dogs.

Marlowe's last image was of Raspberry, images of how she would have looked in the park, then sprawled out in Lancaster, her guts spilling out of what had been her round tummy, running all over the ground covering her soon to be smashed puppies. Raspberry.

"Duffield?" she asked haltingly, not wanting to hear the inevitable answer. Tears now streaming down her face.

"We'll find out in a few minutes when we talk to him. If he was the killer at the barn, then he was the killer at Duffield. Additionally many more sites. Nick owes a fortune to the cartel. He needs loads of money. The FBI dog fight team doesn't yet know who's responsible for either of those two dogfights. We know they've determined they were part of the same operation. The ring has spread in the last months across several cities on the east coast. That's why the FBI has been investigating the two local dogfights because all together they are taking place across state lines. It's a federal offense. However, they've never had enough information to identify who set up the ring. We suspect they're close."

Marlowe's tears began to go away. She listened intently to Adam.

"Here's the key part for us, for you, Marlowe. Again, this is crucial. It's crucial you understand this when we talk to Nick. This FBI cartel team of investigators has not yet pieced together that Nick, the cartel associate, is potentially Nick the dog fighter. Remember there are two separate FBI teams working on each one. They will, and fast. It's only a matter of days. Then the FBI teams will come together as one."

"They'd arrest him for the fighting, wouldn't they? Not the cartel business."

"Normally, if the dogfighting mastermind were someone else, yes, of course."

"If it's Nick?"

"No."

"Why?"

"This is where it gets a little complicated. This is the critical part, Marlowe. They would definitely *not* arrest him on animal cruelty charges. The combined FBI teams will want Nick for just one thing and one thing only. The cartel offenses have the priority. Those offenses are much much larger in importance than the death of some animals. They want the names and information on the cartel drug and money-laundering guys. The animals won't enter into the picture even for a second. If the FBI gets him, Nick will be forced to testify against the cartel members. He'll then go into witness protection as a free man though stripped of all his real estate assets and all of his money. If they think Nick will run, leave the country, they'll close in fast. They must have figured out Nick intends on fleeing the country. The FBI is smart with plenty of information resources."

Oh my gosh. Back in the hall at the shelter on Sunday. This is what Luca Pasquale was afraid of when he was talking to Addison Duncan, the shelter CEO. He said if it happened, the animals would never be avenged. Luca didn't have the details, though he'd known enough to already have figured out what could happen. Marlowe was starting to drill down on what all of this ultimately meant, what it ultimately meant for animals. Her oxymoron theory swiftly swooped into her mind. Did Nick fit into her theory? He kept telling her the Wynne money was his safe money that the real estate money was risky. He needed to do it. She asked herself if Nick fit the theory. She was afraid of what it might be.

"Adam, wait a minute. Nick will have no money because his assets will have been seized, so no assets to use to build his wealth again if he's in witness protection against the cartel members. He'll have only one way to make money again. That's dogfighting, isn't it, Adam?"

"Yes," Adam replied blandly. Sitting stone cold still Adam and Marlowe were solemnly looking right at each other's eyes.

"To set up dogfights you need just a place plus the animals," Marlowe offered. "You don't need any start-up money. It's exactly what he'll do. It's his *childhood* that's making him do this. You don't *understand*. He was—"

Seeing Marlowe starting to break down, Adam cut her off. "We've researched Nick, we know about his childhood. We started finding these things out after Lancaster. We had suspicions even then because of all the real estate he owns it doesn't have mortgages or liens."

Marlowe looked to Adam for answers. She pleaded, "I love Nick—I don't even know who he is anymore."

Adam took Marlowe in his arms, stroking the red highlights in her hair. "I know, poor Marlowe," he whispered to her. "I know how deeply this is affecting you. I'm so, so sorry. I'd do anything to save you from this misery if only I could. You have to believe me."

Marlowe slumped against him, her strength and resolve gone.

Adam looked at his watch. "We need to go," he said quietly. "Take those guns out of the bag. Keep one for yourself. Give me the other. Use the gun only if you need to protect yourself."

After five minutes of riding silently, they were about to turn down Grays Mill.

"How do you know I even know how to shoot a gun?"

"Skip."

"Skip told you at Penleigh last Thursday night?" Marlowe asked in disbelief.

"Skip? I've known Skip a good long time. I didn't know he's your brother. I met him at the shooting range where we both go. Keep your eyes open. There's Nick's Bentley at the end of the cul-de-sac parked pointing back out Grays Mill. He's set up for a quick getaway if he needs it. Two guys are getting out of it. Do you know them?"

"I think I've seen them before, maybe they were the valets at Nick's party."

"And there—who's getting out of the Bentley?

It's Nick!"

Chapter 38

Adam drove slowly down the narrow dirt road. Marlowe guessed he was assessing how things might play out. He slowed and parked on the side of the road about forty feet in front of Nick.

"Marlowe, tuck the gun in your belt under your suit jacket before you get out of the car."

Marlowe did as she was told. She saw Adam put his in the right pocket of his jacket.

"Get out of the car slowly. Walk a couple of steps behind me as we approach Nick." They got out. They walked up to within about twenty-five feet of Nick. Marlowe was a couple of steps behind and to Adam's right. Nick glanced at Adam with a scowl. As she saw them closer Nick's two friends did look familiar to Marlowe. She recognized them as two of the valets at Nick's party. She saw their recognition of her too in their faces. One of them was the valet who had helped her into the hay wagon.

"Nick?" Marlowe said with a pleading voice.

"Marley," Nick returned flatly, sorrow in his eyes.

"Nick, were you at the dogfight barn in Lancaster three months ago?" asked Adam.

Looking surprised, Nick answered, "Is that what this is about?"

"That's what this is about. Were you at the barn?"

Nick smiled that warm smile that had always made Marlowe feel loved. His jeans and camel jacket fit as if they'd been tailored for him. *This is my Nick. He looks like a model right out of GQ.* She started to breathe a little easier. *This nightmare is almost over. He'll explain whatever it is.*

"I presumed you wanted to meet to confront me about my investments, perhaps about my colleagues. By now you know the FBI has an interest in talking to me. Why are we at this meeting? I figured somebody, obviously you, whoever you are, wanted Marlowe to know the truth about what her Nick was doing. Whoever you are, stay out of my private business. Keep Marlowe out of whatever you're trying to do. This is a joke, let's go fellas." He started to walk to the back of the cul-de-sac toward the Bentley.

"I'm asking you nicely not to leave yet," Adam retorted with rising intensity.

After only a few steps Nick turned around, visibly nervous, "What about the barn, wise guy? Were you at the barn? I know what barn you're talking about. It was in the news. The answer is no, I wasn't at the barn. Satisfied?"

"No." Adam reached into his pocket. Each of Nick's men pulled pistols out aiming them at Adam.

Marlowe caught her breath. She backed up toward the Range Rover.

"I'm getting my phone. Take it easy." The men didn't take it easy. Their guns were trained on Adam.

Marlowe was astounded. In an instant Nick had become unrecognizable. Who was this man with henchmen on either side? "Fellas," "wise guy," these were not terms she had ever heard from Nick. Nick was sophisticated, refined. He never sounded like a hoodlum. What was this all of a sudden? This man standing before her was the Nick she loved, not some wretched crook.

"Well get the phone out. Are you calling somebody to help you here?"

"I've something to show you." Adam walked over to Nick. He showed the photograph of him at the barn.

"Where'd you get that?"

"I got it." Adam backed away toward the other side of the road from where Marlowe was standing. Sounding like the lawyer he was, he persevered, "You were there, Nick. What was your involvement?"

"None of your business."

"You weren't there to gamble, were you, Nick."

"I don't gamble," Nick said, glancing at Marlowe.

"No, you don't gamble when the bets are this small. You make bets with sometimes hundreds of thousands, don't you? You don't make these small wagers. You weren't at the barn to bet because you were there running the dogfight, weren't you? This was your fight scene, wasn't it? Duffield too. How about Boston, add Washington to that. They were yours, weren't they, Nick?"

Marlowe was staring at Adam, her mouth open, her brows tight. What was Adam talking about with these other cities. Rage began to surface. She was angry with Adam for thinking Nick would ever have done these things. She was angry with Nick for somehow being involved in this. Marlowe's whole life base was suddenly twisting into a hideous combination of lies and deceit. Who really was this Adam—who was this man she was realizing she might fall in love with? He was ruthless in his accusations. How did he know any of this for sure? Through some stupid nerd group called the ignorant name, "Anglesey?" Who were they? Nobody knew. How dare they accost Nick with these crimes. She could barely stay composed. She had to. She had to hear what Nick would say. She had to hear him show Adam and Anglesey they were utterly, undeniably wrong.

Nick looked from Adam to Marlowe. Her eyes were pleading for him to explain what was going on, to show Adam he would never be such a brute. She managed to get out a soft, beseeching, "Nick?"

Nick started to back slowly away toward his car.

Adam took several measured steps toward Nick. "Where are you going, Nick? If that barn fight wasn't yours, tell Marlowe you didn't do it. Tell her to her face."

Nick wheeled around toward his car yelling to his men, "Shoot the guy. Don't hurt Marlowe. Let her go. Then let's get the hell out of here!"

Marlowe screamed running toward the edge of the woods, away from Nick and away from Adam. Adam and the two valets were looking at each other. Adam hadn't moved to take his pistol out. The men were holding their guns leveled at Adam.

Marlowe had run a short way into the woods toward the end of the cul de sac. She didn't feel in danger. Albeit she took the forty-five out of her waistband. It hung dangling at her side. She looked at Nick. He was moving quickly. He was almost at his car.

"Nick!" Marlowe shouted.

He stopped and turned to look at her. "You know me, Marley. You know I didn't do this."

The pistol still dangling at her side, Marlowe's hands were shaking as she took the few steps out of the woods. She was about twenty five-feet from him now. She looked at her friend, her father figure, the man she adored, the man who were it not for his age could have been her husband. Then something came over her, something greater than herself. She quieted herself without consciously trying. Her body calmed. She wanted to believe Nick. Yet she had to be sure.

"Nick, I know that isn't true, otherwise you wouldn't have tried to leave. You brought your men with guns with you."

Marlowe slowly turned her body. Her feet were pointed directly at Nick. She squared her shoulders, just as Skip had taught her to do when she was a little girl when they practiced shooting at targets, first at soup cans, then later at tuna cans. She slowly raised her right arm. She extended her left hand to support the gun. Marlowe pointed her forty-five straight at Nick.

"Tell me, Nick. Tell me why you tortured and killed those animals. Tell me."

"Okay, okay," he blurted out. "I did it! I had to do it, Marley! I've been a gambler since I was a kid. It's how I saved my mother and me from being destitute after my no-good father jumped off the Ben Franklin Bridge. He should've done it years before. You've no idea what happened back then. I had no money for food even. I had no friends because they abandoned me when we were so poor. 'White trash' they called me. I told you about mom, how she worked those awful jobs just to support us."

Nick talked louder, more belligerently moving closer to Marlowe. "I couldn't take it. I didn't have a high school degree. No one would even give me a job. No one would give me a chance. What was I going to do?" Nick's arms were spread out to the side as he asked Marlowe.

"I damn well was not going to turn into a drunk like my worthless old man. I wasn't going to scrub floors for anybody either. Don't you see, Marley, I had no choice," Nick offered with tears starting in his eyes. "Poker and blackjack came easy to me so I gambled. I usually won because I'm smart. I got better and better at it. I started to make some real money. I knew it was not the right thing. Mom needed money. So did I. It became a way of life, see Marley? I built my money to the point where I'd never have to worry about money. Then I made huge investments in the real estate I told you about."

"Then about six months ago the cartel brothers, Eduardo and Raul Este, demanded I give them more. They wanted more than the interest on the loans. They wanted half of my profits on those buildings. They were forcing me under, ruining me."

Nick's hands were on either side of his head in obvious pain about what he was telling his dear Marlowe.

"I had no way to stop them. I was *trapped*. I needed more and more money. I didn't have it. They threatened to kill my lovely Julie if I didn't pay. The bastards ended up murdering her anyhow. They don't know about the money at Wynne. That's my safe money. Nobody's getting it. They said they would lay off if I did two things. First I had to pay them the interest I owed them. Second if I started the dogfighting ring and paid them seventy-five percent of the take. It was blackmail, I tell you. They told me how to do it. Men with a lot of wealth pay huge dollars to bet at these things. Don't you see, Marley, I had to do it. I had to survive. They were bleeding me to death. I had no choice, don't you see?"

Nick was crying, tears streaming down his contorted face, begging Marlowe to understand he had no other way out.

Marlowe was standing there motionless.

"You understand now. It was either the animals or my money at Wynne. My whole life's work. You have to let me go. I'm leaving the country. I'll never do this again. I'm leaving—my plane is waiting."

Still pointing the gun at Nick, Marlowe barked, "Stand exactly where you are, Nick!"

Settling down, Nick much more calmly said, "You have to let me go. I knew something was going on when you called to meet me here."

Pointing to Adam, he said, "Now I see this clown is somehow involved. I'm sorry, Marley. Now listen. I took Ashanti this morning—I had to. I was afraid you might not understand. I needed insurance if something happened here, if push came to shove, I could get away, you'd have to let me go."

"What do you mean, you took Ashanti? Where is she?" Marlowe was livid at her closest friend having been drawn into all of this. She rapidly pointed her gun into the air. She pulled the trigger to shock Nick into telling where Ashanti was.

"She's in a place where you'll never find her. I had to do something in case this meeting went south, see? Too much at stake. When I'm on the plane I'll call you to tell you where she is. She's okay. She's fine."

Adam yelled to Marlowe, "You okay?"

Marlowe glimpsed Nick's men crouched behind trees. Adam had shifted to behind his car.

"Yes."

Suddenly a woman's voice was screaming behind Marlowe. Marlowe twisted her head around to see Ashanti running toward them at the same time she lowered the gun to her side. It looked to Marlowe like she might be coming from the abandoned springhouse Marlowe knew to be back in the woods.

Ashanti saw it was Marlowe standing there. "Marlowe, Nick kidnapped me. He tied me up in the little shack back there. Stop him!"

Marlowe whipped back to Nick. He was striding toward his car. "Hold it, Nick! I mean it. Stay precisely where you are."

Nick came to a standstill. She kept looking directly at him. Ashanti rushed up to her.

Without looking at her, Marlowe asked, "Are you alright?"

"Yes, what's going on?" She noticed Nick's men on the other side of the road. "Who are these other guys?"

"What happened, Ashanti?"

"At maybe a quarter after seven this morning Nick called. He said he needed to talk to me about a surprise he was working on for you. We agreed to meet right away at the Bryn Mawr Starbucks. When I got there he said we needed to come here for some reason. Sounded weird. It was *Nick*. He told me he needed me to stay in the shack back there—that you both would come to get me. He said for part of the surprise he was going to tie up my hands to some old wood post in there. He didn't have to make the twine so tight!" She glared at Nick. "Then I got scared when I heard what sounded like a shot. I wanted to get out of there. I couldn't get the twine loose. Then I remembered the knife you gave me."

"The knife."

"Yes, Marlowe! I was able to reach it in my purse to pull it out. I was able to use it!" Marlowe remained focused on Nick as Ashanti hugged her.

"Nick, are the keys in your car?" Marlowe was gently pulling away from Ashanti. Marlowe shot a glance to make sure where Adam was.

"Yeah."

Without looking at Ashanti, Marlowe instructed her, "Look, Ashanti. As wacky as all of this looks, it's no more than a misunderstanding between Adam and Nick. It's all fine. Since you don't have your car Nick will let you borrow his. We'll give him a ride to pick it up when we leave here. So take Nick's car. Go tend to the babies in the hospital. Park the car in the parking lot at the hospital. Leave the keys under the mat. I'll call you later."

"I don't know what's going on. I'll take you up on that." Looking at Nick she said, "I'm mad at you Nick. It's going to cost you a dinner at White Dog Café."

She ran over to the Bentley. Nick turned to see Ashanti getting in his car. When he turned back toward Marlowe, his face full of love as well as fear, his mouth in a forced grin while his eyebrows pushed in a deep frown, Nick stared back at her. She slightly lowered her gun. Ashanti got in the car and started out of Grays Mill.

As Ashanti was leaving, an insistent, implacable tableau presented itself in Marlowe's mind. The critically injured black Great Dane she'd helped save, the other Dane she'd carried hoping for his salvation which was already dead; the bloodied bodies, pieces of bodies of slaughtered dogs, chickens and other birds outside the paddock; the vehicles transporting mutilated bodies toward potential recovery or the dead to their final resting place; the silent, eternal scream of the calves and their magnificent mothers and fathers in that old photograph of the thousands of needlessly, wantonly slain bison; in the field at Jackson Hole the passionate, compelling plea from the mother of the bison calf for not only her innocent calf but also for all blameless living animals; in Jackson Hole where those two souls, Marlowe's and the bison's, were prophetically merged in time over a hundred years after the merciless murder and torture of such rugged and majestic beasts; the barn in Lancaster, the image of defenseless, pregnant Raspberry, and the other animals being ruthlessly torn asunder alive and imploring for someone, anyone, to save them, being met with cigar smoke, callous sneers and catcalls of derision; Raspberry's babies, her progeny, gouged from her belly, just one surviving, the others without even a breath of life.

Marlowe saw the parade of horror in her head which would live on in her forever. She understood now there were many Lancasters and Duffields. It was all real. She was confronting it all head on now. No repression. Her innocence was gone forever. As for Nick, no question her once darling Nick would do it all over again.

He'd sacrificed what were surely thousands of animals. He'd sought them out to order them to their deaths, just as he had Raspberry. If the FBI got him for his involvement with the cartel, they would seize his assets and place him in witness protection a free man, which meant he would need to make money. The Wynne money, even though it was three million dollars, would never be nearly enough for Nick to reestablish his life style. Marlowe knew that now. Killing animals was easy, lucrative for him. In his mind dogfighting would be his only salvation. He would restart his fighting ring because he would still have his gambling contacts. If he escaped to Scoto, knowing Nick, Marlowe was one hundred percent certain he would be back in the U. S. shortly with a different identity. Either way Marlowe looked at it, Nick was about to get away with the mass torture and killing of those animals. Just as important, he would do it again. With one big difference. He would be smarter the second time around. No one would ever be able to prove anything he did. The torture, maiming and killing of more Raspberrys would go on and on, unstopped, unpreventable.

Marlowe had never been surer of anything in her life.

She faced Nick. She squared her shoulders. Her breathing was shallow and quiet. She was in a zone, like an elite athlete in the finals of a world championship. She heard nothing. She saw only one thing. She'd crossed over into a specific slice of time disconnected from every other slice of time by unimaginable distance. She was focused intently on Nick. If Nick walked away, she herself was condemning more animals to hideous deaths. Whether she liked it or not, her obligation was to come to the aid of her fellow beings to any length required by the circumstances. Those circumstances had presented themselves, a paradox of competing values. Right here. Right now.

She slowly raised her gun, left hand supporting her right.

Nick looked back at her. He started to raise his right hand.

"Don't do it, Nick!"

"Marley, you need to know—"

"I know all I need to know, Nick."

Nick hesitated, then quickly raised his hand and reached inside his jacket, a budding smile appearing on his face.

In a controlled, level, decisive voice, Marlowe pronounced, "I kill you in Raspberry's name."

She squeezed the trigger.

Chapter 39

The bullet landed squarely between Nick's eyes. Marlowe stood in a trance. She stared with no feeling, like a stone-cold gladiator. Nick had been the quintessence of Marlowe's standard of what a man should be. He had been the person who cared for her for as long as she could remember. This man was now before her. Dead by her hand.

It seemed like hours. It was only a few seconds. Marlowe stood still. Her arms were still outstretched. The gun was pointed down at the dead body that had been Nick Gavin. The difference was her arms were shaking. Tears were streaming down her face. Pay attention to what they want, Sol said. She saw Nick lying on his back with his arms outstretched, his right hand still clutching a piece of paper. He had fallen straight back. He looked like he was staring up at the cloudy sky expecting to see maybe a robin fly from one tree to another. Except for the blood oozing out of his forehead, spreading down over his red hair and down into his left eye and then off the side of his face, Nick looked like Nick. Marlowe unconsciously half-expected Nick to physically turn into the vile monster he was. He did not. He just lay there.

Suddenly shots came from behind Nick's men. Two other men appeared from behind two big trees, shooting at Nick's men. Marlowe, turning to see what was happening couldn't believe her eyes. Dominic and James. Gwyn's gardeners from Snowdon. What were they doing here? Nick's men ran for cover behind trees without firing. Adam drew his gun and ran for protection behind another tree. No one was firing now. No one moved. For the moment it was a standoff.

Suddenly she heard a woman's voice shouting, "Adam, Dominic, James, shoot!"

Several shots rang out. Nick's cornered men went down. Their guns shot high into the air as they fell backward in the woods. Marlowe's whole body swung around to see what had happened. The men's bodies were still. They appeared to be dead. Next she looked to see where Adam was. He, Dominic and James were racing toward Nick's men. Out of the corner of her eye Marlowe saw a woman emerge from the direction where Dominic and James had parked their van. It was Gwyn.

"Go, go!" Gwyn bellowed. "Dominic and James, get the van over here. Put these two in it. Clean up any blood. Adam, go get Nick. It's ten thirty. If our intelligence is accurate, the FBI will be here in one half hour or less. We must be gone. Let's move!"

Her mouth open staring at Gwyn in disbelief, Marlowe lowered her gun. She remained standing exactly where she was. She was dumbfounded to see Gwyn at Grays Mill shouting orders at Adam and her gardeners.

"Gwyn, what are you doing here?" she shouted in confusion.

"Where did you send Ashanti?" Gwyn asked ignoring Marlowe's question.

"To her hospital."

"The keys." said Gwyn alarmed.

"She's leaving them under the mat."

"Good. We'll take care of the car and everything else. You need to get out of here. Go with Adam when the bodies are loaded. Tell Adam to take you directly home. Don't go anywhere else. Go to the office tomorrow and manage money. Talk to no one about this. I'll call you tomorrow."

Marlowe continued to stand there, the gun at her side. Adam knelt at Nick's body. He picked up the piece of paper, looked at it then turned it over. His eyes were riveted on it. In an instant he was on his feet running toward Gwyn.

"Look at this. He must have been reaching for it when Marlowe shot him. It says on the back—"

"Adam, we don't have time. Whatever it is, take it. Go help Marlowe get to the car. We'll get Nick. We have to get her out of here."

"Wait—"

"Adam! Go!" she said, snapping her command.

Marlowe was in shock at what she'd just done, at the murder of the other two men, at Ashanti's kidnapping, at Gwyn, Franny, Jack and Malik being part of this. She was frozen in her tracks. It looked as surreal to her as her vision had in the Anglesey meeting room of the knights preparing for war against the rest of Europe. Her mind reeled with the memory of the rat-tat of the guns. Nick, Adam, Gwyn were involved in a shootout at the end of a dirt road. Who were these people? Who was *she*? Expressionless, Marlowe looked from Gwyn to Nick, to Adam, then back to Gwyn.

Gwyn reached out to Marlowe. "Give me the gun. Go. Get in the car, Marlowe. Do as I say."

Marlowe handed her the gun, her head shaken clear by the command. She ran over to the Range Rover, got in and put her seat belt on. James had pulled the van into the cul de sac and was loading a body. In minutes Adam jumped in the car, turned it around and sped back out Grays Mill. Marlowe looked back and saw James pushing another body into the back of the van. Dominic was still looking around on the road Marlowe guessed for blood, Nick's blood. Gwyn was in the van driver's seat with the engine running.

Marlowe sat in silence. Neither she nor Adam said a word as he drove her to her car at Wynne. Each looked ahead, detached.

When they got to the office Marlowe started to get out. Adam reached for her arm. "Don't discuss this with anyone. Don't go back into the office. Stay at home today. Go into the office tomorrow. Gwyn will call you. Marlowe, don't worry about this. This will be okay."

"Okay," Marlowe replied flatly. It was beginning to sink in that she'd just committed murder.

Marlowe did what Gwyn ordered her to do. She went home and sat on the sofa in her Great Room with Strider curled up on the rug beside her. Although it was just eleven in the morning, in her hand was not coffee, soda or juice. She'd rejected them in favor of the John-nie Walker Black she'd bought in the off chance Adam might come over at some point. Marlowe was much too dazed to eat any lunch or do anything else. She sat there. No television. No music. She started replaying what had happened. For her own sanity for the last time she had to review the series of events. She had to be positive she'd done what she had to do.

Mentally exhausted, Marlowe finally arrived at her conclusion. It was a conclusion she was not going to have rehash time after time. She could live with it. She had done, in the end, the only possible thing by preventing Nick from continuing his madness. Though her action had been harsh, she had had no other choice. It was the necessary outcome, given the circumstances.

What about Franny, Malik, Jack, Adam also now, obviously, Gwyn? She was the one giving orders after the three men were dead. Clearly they saw the horrific treatment of the animals was going to go unpunished. It was going to be resumed.

For its own reason, Marlowe was convinced, the FBI was going to let the animal butcher get away in this case. Adam had said he'd seen situations that were about to unfold like Grays Mill before. Marlowe wondered if they would call it exigent circumstances. They've all seen these situations before, Marlowe surmised. Malik, Franny, Jack, Adam, Gwyn and who knows whom else were part of Anglesey. Were these people the modern day Knights Templar who had fled to Wales, then fled to America?

By this time Marlowe's head was spinning. She had an enormous headache. She called Strider and went up to bed to lie down. She wanted to call Ashanti to see how she was. She was mentally too depleted to make the call. She would call later. She went into the bathroom, took two Excedrin PM and lay back down, one arm over her dearly loved dog.

At about eight that night, Marlowe awoke with a start. Where were the police, or the FBI, or somebody? She'd just committed murder for heaven's sake. She got up and looked outside. It was quiet. Whether justified or not, the fact remained she had murdered a man.

"What am I going to do, Strider? I killed Nick—I'm going to jail or worse. Gwyn is saying don't worry about it? I must turn myself in. It would be better for me if I did. Nick was not convicted or even a person of interest in the dogfights. I'm a cold-blooded murderer."

Marlowe collapsed on the bed. She got up in one second, took another two Excedrin, and flopped on the bed. She lay there, her mind moving in ten different directions. In a few minutes she propped herself up on one elbow. She looked at Strider.

"What about the future. Will there ever be these circumstances again? Could I ever do this again? Could I ever murder again? Is this the way it should be or must be? Have I become like the Anglesey people? Have I always been like them?"

Falling back on the sheets, she felt not. On the other hand, what if the same kind of situation arose? Suppose another predator who massacred animals was going to get away with it, free to repeat it. What would I do? *That's* the question. Maybe I could do it again. There has to be another way. There has to be.

What is it? I need my Advisory Board.

Chapter 40

Marlowe awoke at six in the morning. It hit her instantly—she killed Nick yesterday. She got up to look out the front window. "Nothing there, Strider—at least not yet. No cops. No FBI. No one."

Marlowe's only hope was Gwyn had said she would take care of the aftermath, whatever that meant. The Feds were supposed to have been at Grays Mill around eleven yesterday. The entire action happened so quickly Gwyn, Dominic and James would have been long gone by then. The FBI, seeing nothing out of the ordinary, probably turned around and left. They'd have no reason to believe Nick or anybody else had been at the cul de sac. From the FBI's point of view, when they couldn't find him, they would assume his plans had changed or he'd escaped.

If Gwyn were right they would have no idea Marlowe had been there either. She'd have to trust Gwyn. She was still extremely edgy. She tried to focus on getting herself together so she could get to the office. Gwyn had told her to go to the office as usual as though nothing had happened. That was what she was going to do.

The first question was, as it was every morning, what should she wear. Surveying her suits, Marlowe saw herself standing in her pajamas in the closet mirror. Her hands started to tremble. I'm worried about what to wear? *Whatever I wear they'll still arrest me. Forget about the*

Financial Industry Regulatory Authority, screw the SEC. I'm headed for death row. It won't matter what I wear!

Marlowe managed to put on her most understated suit, which was navy blue with a flared skirt and her navy pumps. That suit always made her feel better then she actually felt. What the hell. I might as well wear it, because I'm not going to need it in Rikers. Still nursing a headache, Marlowe headed for the office via WaWa.

She pulled into the Wawa parking lot after first glancing around to look for any police before she parked. "Wouldn't you just know it!"

An officer exited the store with a large coffee. Her heart skipped a beat. She was sure her whole world was about to come to a crashing halt. The officer only smiled at her. A wave of relief washed over her, just as quickly, panic reestablished itself. She imagined the officer with his colleagues were waiting for her to go inside so they could surround the building to impede her escape. No sense running, she decided. If they're here, *they're here.*

Marlowe went in half expecting to see more police. She saw none. Though fearful, she nonetheless succumbed to temptation. She got her hockey puck. She held it up and looked at it. This is the last one of these apple fritter babies I'll ever see.

Having survived the WaWa trip, Marlowe was at her desk by seven thirty. Tammy called Marlowe into her office. She closed the door. Tammy must have heard. The FBI must have called the Securities and Exchange Commission, which must have called Wynne Capital. Tammy Lopez had been her mentor from the beginning. She would be ready to tell Marlowe exactly what to do. She sat there in her best suit in her straightest posture waiting for Tammy's instructions.

"You okay? You look a little tired."

Was it possible Tammy didn't know?

"Just a long day yesterday."

"Okay, well I have good news and bad news for you." *Here it comes*, wondering how Tammy could seem so blasé about her forthcoming advice on how to beat a murder rap.

"Regarding the prospect you've been working with named Odie Thomas?"

"Ah, yes, of course," Marlowe managed to get out, thinking this was obviously the good news compared to the murder rap advice.

"The bad news is you aren't getting his accounts transferred in from Janney." Marlowe knew those were his retirement accounts, which were small. Fine, Tammy. Naturally I'm not getting the retirement accounts because I'm a felon! I'm pretty sure the SEC doesn't allow felons to manage people's money. I don't think we need to check that one. The good news has to be I'm getting life, not execution, because of exigent circumstances, my new word.

"The good news is you're going to get the considerable fee accounts including the trust accounts. Nice job, Marlowe. Maria is already processing the transfers. Congratulations!" Tammy said, getting up to give Marlowe a congratulatory hug. "You deserve it! At the one percent management fee on the value of these accounts, it's a pretty nice payday."

"Excellent!" Marlowe said, smiling in spite of herself.

Albeit still petrified, she did the math. At the same time, she knew she was about to get the electric chair or that heartless needle. Which did Pennsylvania have? Whatever it was, it was going to be the death penalty. Shocking herself she said almost too casually,

"Running the numbers, it's about five million in incoming assets. Not too bad, Tammy."

"Don't forget about the meeting with Martha and Edward Baldridge and Marty this afternoon at three thirty here in my office. Edward called yesterday afternoon to confirm to make sure you'd be here. He said it would take only fifteen minutes."

Gee, I did forget. What does the worthless, loveable colleague Marty Highland want? I wonder why I forgot—it isn't as if I've been preoccupied or anything. "On my calendar. I'll be here." Marlowe walked out of Tammy's office with a stride that belied her headache. Five million, electric chair, five million, electric chair, she weighed.

"Congrats, Marlowe! You worked hard to get these accounts," Maria said. "I saw Tammy pulled you into her office before you got coffee. Can I get you anything?"

Yes, of course, Maria. Three of those Dunkin Donuts chocolate munchkins I saw out on the table plus one bottle of strychnine, please. "No, thanks," because my head is still aching from the Johnnie Walker, and, oh yes, I'm about to be arrested for *shooting* our *client* Nick. Please get me a direct flight right now to some country with a sunny beach which doesn't have extradition to the United States. The Caymans are nice this time of year. Double oh yes, yours truly, the killer, *moi*, just, as you know, got a five million dollar account. Really who cares when you are going to the *electric* chair?

"When you walk in your office you're going to be pleasantly surprised. I bet they're from Parker. By the way, with the new accounts coming in this morning, I forgot to let you know a Mr. Hill from *The Philadelphia Magazine* called yesterday late afternoon. He said to return his call. He said you'd know what it was about."

The Philadelphia Magazine? Mr. Hill? I don't know this guy, never heard of him. He must be a reporter. They must have found out somehow. Gwyn said to go home. She didn't say go home and get drunk.

What was I *thinking* about? I should've done something, like stay to bury the bodies, kill everybody else, including myself. I don't want to be a drama queen, the headline most assuredly would have been, "Wynne Capital Financial Advisor killed herself leaving no suicide note. She also killed a retired judge, two gardeners, a prominent attorney, two Brazilian valets, and Nick Gavin, bon vivant owner of the spectacular compound Rocking Horse Downs in Bucks County."

"Thanks I'll call him later." After I commit suicide.

"Ashanti called yesterday afternoon too. She sounded worried about something. She wanted to talk to you right away."

"Got it, assistant extraordinaire! You're the best." I'm the worst.

Waiting for Marlowe on her desk were a dozen creamy white, long-stemmed roses surrounded by baby's breath in what Marlowe recognized as a Lenox vase.

"Oh Parker, what are you doing? The last thing I need is complications from you, gorgeous though you are."

She opened the little envelope and read the card.

"I owe a lot to you for your helping me manage my client accounts, Marlowe. My best, Marty. I look forward to our meeting with my parents in law, the Baldridges, this afternoon with Tammy. See you then."

"Marty?" she said, surprised. They're truly lovely. He should know I'll help in this afternoon's meeting with his clients the Baldridges with any tough questions Edward might ask. He didn't need to do this. I do have to admit they're brightening my day in a way the five million dollar accounts can't. I don't have Nick to call anymore for support. The roses will have to do.

"Marlowe, Doris Craven for you, line one."

I'm sorry, Doris. I'll have to call you back. It will probably not be today or tomorrow. It will be more like in forty or fifty years because I just *murdered* somebody. It could be longer because I'll most likely get the *chair* in the near future, which will somewhat compromise my ability to manage your investments.

"Doris, good morning, how are you doing? How is that little grandson of yours?"

A little after eleven she left the office. She had to get out to clear her head. She was getting in the car when her cell rang. It was Gwyn. "Can you meet at Buck Park?"

Marlowe's anxiety increased from nine to ten on a scale of one to ten. She fretted, out in the open where everyone can see? Squirrels will be bugged. Roving carrier pigeons with GPS on them will track my every move. Ground hogs will be taking photos. I'm done, I'm being lured out into the open for the kill—no, oh my God, don't use that word.

"The park?"

"Would you rather come to Snowdon?"

"Yes, I would," Marlowe said, sidestepping that one.

"Okay then, see you when you get here. And you'll stay for lunch?"

"Great, thank you, Gwyn." Marlowe was delighted to stay out of the office for another hour or two to have lunch with Gwyn. For one thing it meant there would be sufficient time for her to get the answers to her questions. She needed resolution. She needed to know Gwyn had in fact taken care of Grays Mill. Otherwise she'd have to face the fact she was going to be on the lam.

"I'll invite Adam for lunch too."

Startled by the possibility of having to see Adam so soon after yesterday, she questioned whether she should call Gwyn back. Maybe she and Gwyn should talk later in the afternoon after Adam would have left. Adam after all was the one who demanded she get in the Range Rover to go to Grays Mill where she shot a man. She was hesitant about the coming encounter. She didn't want to decline the invitation either.

She decided with both Gwyn and Adam at lunch, she should be able to pull together everything that transpired from the first meeting at Harlech until now.

The irony of having lunch with Adam and Gwyn at the Snowdon mansion was not lost on Marlowe. At about noon today, one day after they snuffed three men, the killers may well be dining on a lovely alfresco luncheon of lobster bisque and ginger-salmon arugula salad, with of course iced tea with fresh mint, and warm chocolate chip cookies at a stunning, sprawling estate located on the Main Line. Dining conversation would be chatting about yesterday's unfortunate demise of three rather unsavory characters.

Chapter 41

Heading toward Gwyn's, driving down Acorn Lane past the Snowdon pastures and grounds, Marlowe was anxious to get her questions answered. In addition she wanted to start thinking about what she was going to do if she were truly in the clear. Was she going to join Anglesey if formally invited? Or, positing she would never be caught, was she nonetheless going to turn herself in? Was she going to turn Franny, Malik, Adam, Gwyn, Dominic and James in to the authorities too? What about Jack Danett? She didn't hear anything about him. The guns were at Harlech Gate. He must have been involved.

At this point Marlowe felt comfortable the Anglesey members knew what to do to clean up the Grays Mill mess. How and when they had done this before would be something she would never find out. Nor did she want to know. No question they definitely had experience in these matters. There were other murders. Marlowe was sure of it. What was she going to do in her own situation? She was impatient to hear what Gwyn and Adam had to say. While she would make her decision then, she was leaning toward doing nothing.

Max opened the gate. Marlowe drove slowly in the driveway. She noticed Dominic and James were planting in the pasture where the dapple-grays had been the last time she visited. They'd just installed an oak tree. She could see Dominic steadying the twenty-foot high tree upright while James hammered a stake in the ground to attach a guide wire. A backhoe to dig the hole along with a cherry-red pickup truck with sod on the bed were nearby. They were doing a skillful job. With the sod placed on the disturbed ground the tree would look like it had been planted a few years ago. Such a professional technique. Gwyn's property was incredibly attractive because of attention to such details.

Making the slight turn to park in the courtyard, Marlowe put her window down to wave at Dominic and James as though yesterday never happened. They gave her wide smiles with energetic waves back. Okay, this must be the interaction tenor the day after any Anglesey "business" is taken care of.

Missy waited at the front door for her to show her to the terrace.

"Ms. Llewellyn will be down in just a moment."

"Thank you, Missy. And what's the divine smell if I may ask?"

"Why the chocolate chip cookies, of course. I put both walnuts besides macadamia nuts in this time."

"Missy, you're spoiling me!"

"Just leave the terrace doors open when you go out please. Raspy likes to run in and out."

Marlowe sat on one of the handsome terrace chairs to wait for Gwyn. She chose to sit closer to the doors rather than in the chairs she and Gwyn had sat in before. The last thing Marlowe wanted was for Gwyn to be reminded of their prior conversation on the terrace. From where she was she could still see the men working on the oak. In seconds, tail wagging sixty swipes a minute, Raspy came bounding out of the house, up to Marlowe to place a play bite on her hand.

"Raspy, look at you! Such a good boy. I swear you've grown since the last time I saw you." Raspy was elated to receive such praise besides potentially pets from Marlowe. He sat down, licked her hand and let her give him plentiful rubs behind his ears.

When Gwyn came out Raspy trotted over to greet her. Probably, Marlowe guessed, for the hundredth time that day. Whether it was the hundredth or the tenth, it was obvious Gwyn took great pleasure in his attention. She reached down to pet the puppy, keeping her eyes on her guest. She quickly sat own, leaning toward Marlowe.

"Marlowe, how are you doing? Are you okay?"

"Well when you told me not to worry about anything I didn't until I got home. When I got in the door I had a conversation with John-nie Walker then took a sleeping pill. When I woke up in the evening I looked out the window for the cops. Seeing none I took another two sleeping pills which took me through to the morning. That pretty much sums it up."

"Oh dear, quite a night! Did you go into the office this morning?"

"I did. Regrettably I couldn't take any pills so I had to be me." Marlowe leaned forward, dropping the banter covering her inner turmoil.

"I believe I covered my anxiety and panic, just barely, Gwyn. The drive over here made me feel better. Coming in the driveway seeing Max along with Dominic and James in the pasture doing their normal landscaping work showed me maybe we're all okay. The clincher, I have to say, was Missy."

"Missy? How so?"

"I smelled the cookies!"

"How charming, dear Marlowe. Come here," Gwyn said, getting up, extending her arms.

The two women hugged like old school chums who had not seen each other for ten years. As Gwyn held her she said, "Everything is fine. It's taken care of. You've nothing to worry about."

Marlowe sat back down, quickly wiping away a tear. "I do have some questions though."

"I'm quite sure you do. Rightly so. Let me see if I can provide some details in an effort to explain exactly what happened."

It was all pretty much what Adam had said before they drove to Grays Mill.

"The bottom line," Gwyn finished up, "was Nick was guilty of a whole handful of crimes with the cartel. The FBI would have coerced him into being a witness against the cartel members who we now know are Eduardo and Raul Este. They would have seized Nick's assets including all his homes and the Wynne money. He would have nothing except his freedom. All of that is entirely within the law and what the FBI had to do.

It was Nick's freedom that was the issue of Anglesey. The society was convinced Nick would begin the dogfights in a new area. How else would he believe he could restore his fortune? Had Anglesey let him fly to Scoto, he would have obtained a new identity then flown back to the U.S."

"Great, exactly as I see it. Nick's two men? I recognized them. They were the valets at Nick's party at Rocking Horse Downs."

"They were more than valets. Adam showed you a photograph of Nick at the Lancaster barn."

"Yes."

"There are other photographs, Marlowe. Those two men were in another photograph. They both were part of the operation. That's why they had to go too."

"I had no idea all this time who Nick was. I would never have imagined it," Marlowe said, looking to Gwyn for some sort of explanation of her lifelong relationship with Nick.

"I know. No one else knew either except for those gamblers who went to the fights. They all knew. They're as guilty as he was. They weren't going to rat him out. They liked what he was providing."

"Will you tell me more about Anglesey?"

"I believe Adam explained a few things when he told you about the Knights in Wales and how they came over to America to escape probable persecution."

Marlowe couldn't hide her surprise that Gwyn knew about the conversation with Adam.

"Of course I'm aware you had dinner at Penleigh." Gwyn smiled.

Marlowe sat up a little straighter to study Gwyn for a few seconds. There was something about her face. It looked oddly familiar to her.

"Marlowe, you looked for a second there like you'd seen a ghost. Are you okay?"

"Yes, I'm fine." She laughed from embarrassment at what had just happened.

"Well that's good. Glad you're okay," Gwyn said, grinning.

Again, Marlowe sat up. There it was again. This time she sensed she recognized what she saw. Gwyn's grin wasn't straight, like the rest of her face. Marlowe had never noticed it. She'd seen a grin like that before.

"Gwyn, is Adam any relation to you?"

"The grin?"

"Yes, the grin," Marlowe said, grinning herself.

"I've always felt you were astute, now I'm finding you're a detective. Adam is my son. No one else knows, I'd like to keep it that way please. I've always considered it best for him to make his own way rather than be known as my son."

Marlowe was incredulous. The man she was falling in love with was the son of Judge Llewellyn? Of the woman who's been masterminding the Anglesey Philosophical Society, of the woman whose family pre-dates the Mayflower? This great woman? Marlowe couldn't ponder about that right now, so simply replied of course she wouldn't mention the relationship to anyone.

"Your friend Jayla from your garden club told me you have a house in Wales," Marlowe said.

"Yes, I do. As you've probably guessed, my ancestors were Knights who had migrated there from other parts of Europe. They were masons who found work building Beaumaris Castle. Then only a small group of those knights were prepared to sail off to a new land few had even heard of then, a place that might have been a myth for all they knew. When they felt threatened where else could they go? Unfortunately few survived the seas."

"Enough people arrived here to give us places named Bryn Mawr and Gladwyne and the like."

"Exactly. My family landed around what was to become the Philadelphia area. They eventually moved to around here to what would become Haverford. The native people were not threatened by so few strangers so they got on well. It was those locals who helped the Welsh when they landed in the middle of a harsh winter. They helped build what is now the Beaumaris Club in Gladwyne. The original part of it was where my early family first lived. Even with the Indians' care, more died that first winter. In the end only a few survived. As you said, many names around here are names of places or things in Wales, including 'Snowdon.'"

"What does 'Snowdon' mean, Gwyn?"

"Snowdon is the highest mountain in Wales," explained Gwyn, with a just a hint of pride. "This particular Snowdon property has belonged to my family since the early 1300's. The first house was nothing more than a tiny log cabin. As you can imagine over the centuries each house was torn down to make way for a new, more modern house. All of this ground has always been ours."

"A personal question, Gwyn. If you're a descendant of the Knights, who weren't Welsh, why is your last name clearly a Welsh name, Llewellyn?"

"Interesting question and smart of you, Marlowe. Adam may not have mentioned to you when England's King Edward I decided he was going to put an end to the Welsh rebellions, he killed the Welsh King Llewellyn. Later a daughter of one of the Knights fell in love with one of Llewellyn's sons and they were married. When the small group of Knights with their families made the decision to flee, that couple went along and indeed survived. They are my ancestors."

"Quite a story," Marlowe said, looking at Gwyn like she'd just seen a movie about a prince and princess getting married, it was a happy ending.

"My ancestors also the others who came on the ship continued to maintain the Knights' high standards in their new chosen homeland. They cared for each other, and they cared for the native people who were here. Not strictly religious they believed it was the obligation of every man to protect neighbors. That's what they did. That's what we still do today through Anglesey."

"That principle sounds like what we talked about at the two *Candide* meetings."

"Yes, that's why we chose *Candide* for the discussion. That particular novel would be good to talk with you about. Adam may have already told you we had you at the meeting to see what your reaction would be if we were certain about Nick. We had to know we could rely on you. We knew we could never get Nick to talk to us without you being a part of it. The pistol Adam gave you was for your own protection, though the way things turned out, you did what you had to do. You realized Nick was the horrific man we believed he was."

"Then Anglesey has never been about reading philosophy."

"No, it isn't. The laws in this country normally function properly and well. When they don't, it's usually because of something like Nick's situation where some sort of mitigating circumstances exist. I saw it when I was on the bench, which is one of the reasons I retired. I spent so much valuable time on my cases other criminals were getting way with a wrist slap, witness protection, or some other sort of light sentence. This is where we come in. Not everything comes to our attention, in any event a great deal does."

"Anglesey isn't just a Philadelphia organization."

"Remember when you went to the first Anglesey meeting when you were sworn to secrecy?"

"Yes."

"You will continue to honor the oath?"

"Yes."

"Other societies are located in most of the major U.S. areas. They aren't called 'Anglesey.'" That's just our name here. We're all over. Many members hold key or prominent positions in business, the arts, religion as well as government."

"Like president of the United States?" Marlowe asked, fishing.

"Right, Marlowe. Presidents have been members. You would know many of the members' names. This is an intensely private, broad, organized group of people dedicated to our mission."

Marlowe's reaction was she wasn't at all surprised. The Anglesey members were standouts in every way. The other groups would be the same.

"By the way, before I forget, you'll be getting the money back Nick wired to the Scoto account."

"How? I know you're far reaching. How did you pull that one off?"

"I may have intimated before we are international. We have people around the world who believe in what we do. When we need some information, we ask. Nick opened the Scoto account only about a month ago. Our contact saw the amount Nick said he might want to transfer in. She suspected something was wrong. When the money came in she let her contact in the U.S. know. As we speak Maria is waiting for the transfer of the three million back into Wynne."

"You have a contact at a bank on the little island of Scoto?"

"No, we're good, not that good. No, the Scoto bank is a branch of a large international bank. The exact procedure to get the money back into Wynne is something which will have to remain private."

"I can't believe this organization. This is bigger than anyone could possibly imagine, Gwyn."

"Yes it is. It may further interest you to know one of the accounts you have in my name at Wynne really belongs to the governing body of *all* of the Angleseys in the United States."

"The 'Gwynedd Llewellyn A' account. You have maybe twenty million dollars in that one."

"Now three million more. By the way, did you get a call from *The Philadelphia Magazine*?"

"I did. I almost forgot. How did you know? I'm afraid it has something to do with Grays Mill. I haven't returned the reporter's call."

"No, of course it doesn't." Gwyn laughed. "They're calling you because I told them what a great money manager you are. They want to do a cover story on you for the 'Best and the Brightest of Philadelphia Financial Advisors' for the October issue.

"Gwyn, I don't know how to thank you. That's fabulous. It's taken me so long to build my business. To have an article like that would be so valuable. Thank you so much!"

"And try to be your normal cool, confident self when Annabelle from *Fortune* calls you too."

Rising to give Gwyn a hug Marlowe said, "You know everybody! You've been so nice to me yet I've known you only for three months. I'll not let you down. You know I won't."

"Of that I'm assured."

"Gwyn, another thing. You've shared a great deal with me. Am I a member of Anglesey then?"

"You were recruited by Adam because of the circumstances surrounding Nick. He said he had met you at some concert a few months ago. It was his job to get some background on you. I think an invitation to join Anglesey would be forthcoming. How would you feel about that?"

"I'm not sure to be honest."

"It would be essential for you to be sure. Think about it."

Gwyn turned toward the house. "I think Adam is here. I need to speak to him for a few moments. It won't take long and then we'll have lunch."

Lunch is good!

Chapter 42

"Fine, Gwyn. I guess I'm forced to just sit here looking out over this incredible property."

Marlowe gazed at Dominic and James working on the grounds at a distance. She heard Adam greet Gwyn in the reception hall. As she watched a Monarch butterfly flitting from flower to flower, she half heard them discussing a lawsuit Adam was working on. A chipmunk caught her eye in the branches of a dogwood. She watched as another gently chased it in play. Though she'd been only half listening to Gwyn and Adam's conversation, she noticed now they had dropped their voices. Now Marlowe strained to hear what they were saying.

Something about an old photo of a woman holding a baby. The writing on the reverse side was "Our daughter, isn't the red in her hair like yours?"

"He was her *father*," Adam whispered. "He was trying to show her this."

While Marlowe would have heard this, it didn't register with her, only the chipmunks registered with her.

"Well, Adam, this is a strange thread in the turn of events. As is always best, shred it. Nothing good can come of it."

"I think in this case, all things considered, she's a strong woman, like you, actually. I think she can handle it. She knew what she was doing back there."

"Okay, your call."

"Will do," Adam said as they joined Marlowe on the terrace.

"Hi Adam, come look at these two chipmunks playing! They're having a ball!"

"Looks like they're having a great time. Adorable," Adam said as he sat down beside Marlowe.

Gwyn remained standing. "Marlowe, I, I mean we, need to tell you something. There's no easy way to say this. You need to know."

"Okay, what is it?"

Adam glanced from Marlowe to Gwyn and back to Marlowe.

"Nick was your real father." Handing Marlowe the photograph, he explained, "This is what he was reaching for in his pocket."

She looked at the photo. "This is mom from a long time ago. That might be Skip as a baby. So what does that mean?"

"Turn it over."

Neither Adam nor Gwyn said anything or moved. Marlowe stared at the writing on the reverse. Her natural red highlights, his red hair. He was always there for her, supported her, gave her money, obviously had deeply cared for her all her life. Marlowe took a quick look at Adam, then at Gwyn. Focusing her gaze out toward the gazebo, the wretched memories that had appeared in her mind that afternoon made a momentary appearance.

Getting up looking at Adam and Gwyn, she said, "Thank you for showing this to me. It must have been a hard thing for you to do, I'm glad you did it."

She handed the photo back to Adam. "I did what I had to do."

Chapter 43

After lunch Missy gave both Adam and Marlowe take-home bags of her freshly baked cookies. They said their good byes to Gwyn on the front porch then walked together to their cars in the courtyard.

Adam slowed his pace. Marlowe stopped to look at him. "Marlowe, I'd be honored if you'd have a real dinner with me tonight at Terracotta Rose. I'll not only pick you up, I'll bring you flowers."

Marlowe hadn't contemplated it. She unconsciously assumed Adam would no longer be in her future. She'd been used in what had turned out to be a dangerous and deadly game. Game over. No further use for Marlowe. Now this.

She sighed, "Adam, I'm afraid I ate much too much lunch and to boot had innumerable cookies. I can't imagine being hungry for dinner."

Adam looked disappointed. "Oh, okay. You won't go then?"

Laughing and looking happy, Marlowe responded, "Of course I'll go."

Adam's eyes got bigger and the crooked little grin leapt onto his face. "Terrific! Pick you up at seven."

"You realize I'm going not because it's you asking. Terracotta Rose is one of my most favorite restaurants."

"Marlowe, you're a little liar! Pick you up at seven."

"And Adam? I know you're Gwyn's son."

"I knew you'd figure it out. She's an amazing woman."

"She most certainly is." My goodness maybe there is life after Grays Mill, Anglesey and the other vile stuff. She was about to get in her car when she remembered something. Gwyn was still at the front door. "Gwyn?"

"Yes?"

Marlowe started walking back toward the house. Gwyn met her halfway as Adam was going out the driveway. "Before I go, one last question. It's about the bodies. What happened to them?"

Gwyn looked away. She looked over at Dominic and James. Marlowe followed her gaze.

"They do such a lovely job around the property," Gwyn said. "The landscaping is always perfect, thanks to them. I told you they've been with us for a long time, as had their parents as well as grandparents, even further back."

Though Gwyn ignored her question, Marlowe's good manners prompted her to respond appropriately, "Did their ancestors come on the ship too?"

"Yes, they did."

"I saw them when I drove in. They're doing such a fabulous job with the tree. When they're finished it will look like it's been growing there for years. I saw they had the backhoe. I guess they used it to dig the hole."

"When they plant oak trees they always use a backhoe. The holes need to be big enough to accommodate everything."

"By everything, you mean the root ball and dirt?"

"Yes, that. And the bodies."

Marlowe swung around aghast. "The bodies? What bodies?"

"The bodies."

Stunned, Marlowe asked, "Out in the pasture? Under the beautiful new oak tree? Nick and his two goons?"

"All the guns, too."

"Oh my gosh," Marlow said under her breath looking out at the tree. "Nobody will ever find them, will they?"

"No, they won't."

Just then Dominic and James finished their planting. They waved at Gwyn and Marlowe. Marlowe waved back an anemic wave.

"You said you'd take care of it, and you certainly have."

"That's a part my family has always taken care of since they came over here," said Gwyn as she moved her left arm in a sweep around the property.

Marlowe's gaze followed the direction of Gwyn's arm, unsure of what she was being shown. She looked quizzically back at Gwyn then out over the property. What she saw in addition to the house, other buildings and the driveway was the landscape of grass, shrubs, flowers, trees and fences. Directing her eyes over the property something stood out. Oak trees.

"The oaks. I can see a hundred just from here. They're of varying heights, of varying ages. I bet the one over there is three hundred years old."

"Yes, it is."

"That one has to be older."

"Right."

Gwyn stood watching her young friend.

Marlowe shot a quick look at her. Marlowe saw a smile emerging.

"Are these all from…?"

"You're right. Almost all of the oaks on this property."

Marlowe gazed in silence looking out at the oaks around the property. Seeing the visual of the oaks Marlowe comprehended how vast and powerful Anglesey was. This was no small organization. For all she knew Franny, Malik, Adam, Jack and Gwyn were not the only local members. Judging from her one single involvement with them, Marlowe was wholly convinced Anglesey had only stepped in when no other alternative was available. She wasn't sure how she felt. Was each case as clean cut as Grays Mill was?

"Gwyn, what happened on Grays Mill concerned dogfighting. How often has Anglesey gotten involved with animals?"

"Historically we've been interested in situations centered on human rights. Grays Mill was the first animal incident. However, now we've been educated on the pervasiveness of animal cruelty, my guess is it won't be the last. Other Anglesey groups around the country have been interested in what transpired here. You can draw your own conclusions."

"Another question. My brother Skip isn't a member of Anglesey, is he?"

"No, he isn't involved whatsoever. My guess is he'd be a good candidate however. How would you feel about that?"

Hesitating, thinking about the kind of man her brother was, Marlowe said, "That decision would be Skip's."

"Fair enough."

"One last question. The meeting room at Harlech, the door, the portraits, the map. Any significance to any of them?"

"Astute again, young lady. Let's leave those stories to another time, maybe if you decide you'd like to be a member."

"Okay. Thanks for helping me wade through everything. I'm truly sorry about all of it. I do understand it. I must say, you're an extraordinary woman, remarkable is so many ways."

"I feel the same about you, Marlowe. Enough of this. Enjoy your cookies."

Marlowe got in her car and looked at her watch. She was surprised at how late it was. If she hurried she would be on time for the meeting at three thirty. The last thing she wanted to be was late for the prestigious Edward and Martha Baldridge.

Chapter 44

Marlowe she saw she had a message from Parker. She drove out the Snowdon driveway listening to the message. "I'm trying to find Nick. Have you seen him? I'm more concerned. The FBI called me looking for him. If you know where he is tell him to call me now. He shouldn't talk to the FBI without me. Thanks, Marlowe."

Swallowing hard, Marlowe knew she was not going to respond to Parker. What would she say? Don't worry, Parker, I was able to help Nick. By the way I was able to take care of the FBI for him too.

Marlowe called Ashanti.

"I was scared, Marlowe. I was in that little house or whatever it is too long."

It only now sunk in that if Ashanti hadn't used the knife to extricate herself, she might never have gotten out of there. No one other than Nick knew she was in there, worse, no one else ever went down there. She could have died. No one would have been found until who knows when.

"What happened with Nick? Did you call the police?"

"Shortly after you left we saw a car come down Grays Mill. All I know is it turned out to be FBI. They asked Nick to get in the car. Then they drove out. I have no idea how they even knew we were there. I did

284

hear Nick say something about their wanting some information if he had any about his business lenders. He said he'd call me later. He said to apologize for scaring you. I'm sure he'll call you himself to apologize. He was extremely embarrassed by what he'd done."

"Okay, I guess it wasn't all that bad, even though it did look a little shaky when I left."

"Long story. It was just a huge misunderstanding."

Marlowe felt terrible about lying to her best friend. There was no way Ashanti could ever know the truth. As far as Marlowe was concerned, it was a necessity under the circumstances.

Marlowe arrived at Wynne at 3:25. Marty and the Baldridges met every quarter. Sometimes Marty would ask Marlowe as well as their manager Tammy to join the meeting to provide the client with alternate perspectives for comparison. Marlowe was always happy to oblige. When she entered Tammy's office on time for the meeting, the Baldridges and Marty were already there. Marty leaned back in his chair. He gave Marlowe a quick wink. She found that peculiar since Marty usually looked scared to death around the Baldridges. With $300 million invested at Wynne, this wealthy couple were his best clients by far. Any wrong movement meant the end of Marty's representation. Marlowe took note that her colleague was not sitting at attention per usual. Marty smiling let alone winking was unheard of. She said hello to the attendees as she sat in the last vacant chair waiting to find out what was needed from her. With everything happening, she welcomed financial talk. Fit and trim well into their seventies, the Baldridges had obviously led a healthy lifestyle. Martha had a reputation for being one of the finest paddle tennis players in the Philadelphia area. Edward was dressed in golf shorts and a white PGA Tour polo shirt.

"Marty, thank you for setting up this meeting with Marlowe for us, and Marlowe, Martha and I want to thank you for taking time from your schedule to join us once again."

"Yes, thanks to you both," Martha said, sitting there with her hair in what used to be called a pageboy. In their seventies, the Baldridges has obviously taken care of themselves throughout their lives by eating property and staying in shape. Martha had a reputation as being one of the finest paddle tennis players in the Philadelphia area despite being in her early seventies."

"We're always glad when you have time to stop in to Wynne to review your accounts here," Tammy said by way of officially starting the meeting."

Edward and Martha looked at each other with warm smiles. "We are here today to make two major changes."

Marty, who was situated between the couple, still had a smile on his face that left Marlowe dumbfounded. She couldn't help wondering what was going on.

"Tammy, as you would know, I am still the CEO of JED Pharmaceuticals, headquartered in Philadelphia. I'm sorry to have to tell you I've hired Marty to be the new Chief Financial Officer effective immediately."

Tammy gave the string of pearls hanging over her white blouse a gentle tug. "You certainly couldn't find anyone better than Marty to keep your company safe. I'm disappointed to lose him."

"Well, there's a silver lining," Martha Baldridge offered.

"I can't imagine what it would be," Tammy said. Marlowe could tell Tammy was straining to be cordial.

Edward explained, "You would know JED is a private company. No shares trade on any public stock exchange. We're changing that. We're going to take JED public. Marty is going to handle this for us. He will be working with Wynne. As you know, taking a company public takes large fees. Those fees will be going to Wynne."

Marlowe was stunned JED would be going public, considering there would be a plethora of regulations to abide by. Marty would be overseeing all of it. They would give him all the other financial experts he needed to accomplish this. It was a big deal for the company. What was a much bigger deal was the money the Baldridges would get as by far the major shareholders in the company. While Marlowe knew the holdings as well as the investment strategy of their Wynne accounts, she'd never looked at JED because she didn't need to know any information. JED was a huge company. Marlowe didn't know how many zeros would be behind the number of shares they would receive. She had no doubt the value would be near a billion dollars.

Astonished at this turn of events, Tammy and Marlowe shared a look of shock.

Marlowe was first to speak.

"Congratulations on taking this giant step forward. JED is such a fine company now others buying your stock can be a part of your growth. Marty, I know I speak for our manager as well as myself. You are the man for the job. Congratulations to you too. You've earned it. You can do it. Well done."

"There is a second major change for Wynne," Edward said when Tammy's eyes settled upon him. "Martha and I have discussed this at length, we've consulted Marty as well. If Marlowe is willing, we would like her to manage all of our current accounts as well as the new money coming in when we go public."

All eyes in the room turned to Marlowe. At first she met Edward's quizzical look with a deer-in-headlights stare. When Marty jumped up hugging Marlowe where she sat, she was literally shaken into action. She hugged Marty back and kissed his cheek, then hugged each of the Baldridges with her assurance she would be more than willing. She extended her hand to shake Tammy's. Her manager uncharacteristically pulled her into a hug as well.

The Baldridge money meant large fees for Marlowe. What would she use it for? She certainly wasn't going to go clothes shopping, maybe, however, she should put Ms. Snooty on retainer. That would be helpful. She did have one moneyed word in mind:

"JED"

Chapter 45

When Marlowe entered her office a richer woman by far than she'd been previously, Maria congratulated her.

"I'm already in the process of making the Financial Advisor name change from Marty to you, congrats!"

"It was great of Marty to help the Baldridges make the decision to leave the money here at Wynne with me. I guess we know why he gave me the flowers. JED is getting a class act with Marty."

Maria closed the door behind her. Marlowe sat down at her desk. She put her head on her hands on the desk. She wasn't mentally running the numbers to see what her increased income would be from the existing Marty accounts nor what it might be when JED went public. She was thinking about how she would be able to manage her own clients' accounts also Marty's accounts. It didn't take her long to realize she and Marty had the same investment philosophy so had conferred so often on their accounts there would be a lot of similarities. It wouldn't take much to make the necessary changes to align all the accounts. Despite all the added income coming in, Marlowe knew it was crazy. She wanted to stop analyzing that to get back to what was important to her right now. She decided she'd leave the office early.

It was a little after four by the time she got home. All she wanted to do was unwind, think back over what had happened that day. What was she going to do. She slipped into her sweats and lay down on her bed. Strider hopped up with her.

Was she going to accept the invitation to become a member of Anglesey? She had already decided she was not going to report anything having to do with Grays Mill. She along with the others did what they had to do. She willingly closed the Nick Gavin story.

Despite having intellectually resolved these issues, the gruesome images from Duffield remained vivid in Marlowe's memory. She couldn't imagine the pain and suffering those poor animals had endured. Those images were not going away, Marlowe knew it. Just like with Gwyn and Raspberry, they would be with her.

Could she kill again given life or death circumstances like those surrounding Nick? She didn't know for sure. Given similar circumstances, maybe she could. However her thinking had been evolving. She didn't want to find herself in that position.

The ultimate, central question was what could she do to protect animals. She'd promised herself, she'd promised the dapple after being in the gazebo at Snowden, she was going to try to champion the cause of mistreated animals. She walked the dogs at the Shelter. That was such a small thing. She was mindful of the well-known starfish story, helping one animal at a time. With so many animals at risk that wouldn't be enough.

The problem was Marlowe still had no idea of what to do. It was clear to her no one else did either or they'd be doing it. Of course, the animal rescue organizations were doing tremendous work. They were all overloaded. As she now comprehended, the problem of animal protection was monumental. It was more than most people knew more than any one person could handle. What could *one* person do? Marlowe didn't have the answer to that question. One truth remained. It was part of her DNA. She was still the small town girl who never had gotten used to people telling her she couldn't do something.

Marlowe lay there thinking about what she could do to make a significant, meaningful difference in the lives of animals with no future. She looked to each of the portraits of the distinguished personages of her Advisory Board for inspiration. She closed her eyes allowing her mind to wander in contemplation. Suddenly Strider was on the floor with a single bound, as though he was catapulted off. He tore downstairs.

Certain it was the police or the FBI finally coming to get her, she leapt up. On the other hand, she realized, it could be Nick's cartel thugs coming to shoot her, just as they did Julie, because of course Nick was not making any payments to them. Maybe they sent just one man to get her. Marlowe reached for her Smith and Wesson thirty-eight. She kept it loaded in her bedside table.

She instantly understood that it couldn't be the police or FBI because Gwyn had taken care of all of the details. That left the cartel. She took the gun, racing to the window. Strider was beside himself, barking. He had sprinted down the stairs where he remained growling at the front door. Fearful of what might be outside Marlowe looked out of the front window of her bedroom without moving the sheer curtains.

Through the trees she saw a delivery truck on the street. The gun was in her hand. She was ready. She had five bullets. She might need each one of them if it was the cartel people. She went back to the bedside table to pull out more bullets from their case. She put them in her pocket.

She went downstairs and carefully peered through the side windowpanes at the front door. She saw a man, apparently alone, walking up the flagstone path. He had on a brown jacket along with the same brown pants. He looked like a UPS deliveryman. Marlowe's shoulders slumped under the weight of relief.

She commanded, "Strider, no!" Strider stopped barking. A low growl persisted. He was protecting his charge, just as he had been taught to do. Peeking out again, Marlowe didn't recognize the man. It wasn't her regular UPS driver. He'd had the route long enough so she knew his name, Bobby. It wasn't Bobby walking toward the door. She hid the gun behind the basket arrangement of cut daffodils in the hall.

The man knocked on the door. Marlowe pointed Strider to go to the corner.

"Strider, sit." He stopped growling. He didn't sit in the corner. He sat tensed right beside Marlowe. Backing toward the flowers reaching for the gun, she whispered to herself, "Maybe he knows something I don't." It was behind her back when she opened the door.

"Marlowe Evans?"

Marlowe looked at him. He seemed legitimate. He had a nametag, "Ralph." The UPS truck was parked on the street.

She cocked the gun.

"Yes?"

"I have an over-night envelope for you. Can you sign please? The sender requests a receipt." The man extended his arm to give her the computer signing board.

Marlowe hesitated. With the gun still cocked behind her back asked, "I hurt my hand, can you hold it for me?"

Laughing, the man responded, "What, did your dog bite you?"

No, in any case he's about to bite you where it hurts if you try anything funny. She signed with her left hand. He handed her the envelope. As he started walking down the path toward the street, it seemed to her he was walking fast. Suddenly she realized there might be a little bomb or chemical in the envelope. He got close to his truck. She yelled after him. "Hey, what happened to Larry? This is his route."

"Larry?"

"Yes, this is Larry's route. Is he okay?"

"Oh, you mean Bobby! Yes, he's okay. He's getting married on Saturday. He took a couple of days off."

He'd passed the test. The envelope in her hand felt much less threatening. Marlowe breathed easier.

"You're such a good boy, Strider. You would make your dear Esther proud. I'm proud of you!"

Marlowe went to put the envelope on the desk in the study. She was used to getting deliveries so she just set the envelope down in the middle of the desk. Then she noticed the address had been handwritten. It looked like "Syracuse." She figured it must be from some mailing house in New York telling her if she bought a life insurance policy, they would give her a car.

She opened the envelope. She saw two envelopes in it. "Ha, just as I said. An insurance offer with the return-with-check envelope." She was taken by surprise to see what looked like the insurance offer envelope. It was stark white, with her name, Marlowe Clark Evans, written in beautiful script in navy blue ink.

"Wow, these insurance companies are really trying to look like they're Chubb!" Marlowe opened the envelope. Every muscle in her body jerked to a halt. After a moment she sat down heavily at her desk. Laying the letter down, she drew her hands slowly back to her stomach. She involuntarily held her breath as she stared down at the white paper. She heard nothing, not even Strider's rhythmic breathing. It was a letter. It was in a familiar hand.

"*My dearest Punkin,*"

Marlowe's head moved nearer the letter, her eyes wide open. Her pulse quickened, her nostrils flared. All systems were poised to fight or flee.

"Nick?" Her face flushed. Her heart skipped. "I, I shot you. You're dead," she stammered.

Trying to steady herself, Marlowe stared straight ahead. Her head rocked back then sunk forward. Slowly she calmed enough to concentrate on the words before her.

"*My dearest Punkin,*"

"*When you read this I may be dead. The how or why I do not know. It would be related to my businesses. I want you to know you have been the light of my life. I love you, Marley. I care for you more than you know. To think perhaps about coming to the end, dying, not being able to be there for you pains me beyond words.*"

Marlowe's eyes closed. Many emotions were coursing through her. She had to see the next words.

"*If I die you will hear about what I did. I want you to hear it from me. Because of my dealings with a cartel, the FBI has been watching me. If they decide to arrest me and force me to testify against the cartel, they will strip me of all I own. If the FBI doesn't get me first, the cartel will be after me. I have not paid them interest on the loans they gave me because I have been losing money on some of my properties. To show me they meant business they were the ones who found and shot Julie. I had to pay them back or they would kill me. A few months ago I started*" *another business that would give me a great deal of quick cash. That business is dogfighting."*

Marlowe tensed up again.

"The cartel also knows the FBI is after me. If the FBI gets me, the cartel knows I would testify against them. So my days are numbered unless I go into hiding. I must leave the country to go to a small island off the coast of Mexico. The FBI cannot extradite me from there. The cartel will know I won't be testifying against them. Additionally the cartel will leave me alone because they'll believe I have no money or assets left to give them. My plan is to come back in about two years to somehow start up my real estate businesses under a new identity. However, I cannot take the chance of contacting you in any way. Should the cartel discover who I am when I come back, and if they believed you were still an important part of my life, they would come after you as leverage against me."

Marlowe stopped reading for a moment. Images were churning up in her like darts.

"I'm sorry. I never wanted this to happen. I know your love of animals is so strong. With everything caving in I could barely look you in the eyes when you came to Rocking Horse Downs. I'm so disappointed in myself, I was desperate. I had to have more money. I know you will despise me for the rest of your life, which is hard for me. What is done is done. I can only do what I can do now. I give you the only good thing I have done in my life. It is yours. Someday I hope you will think more kindly of me if you can find it in your heart. This is my good bye to you. We will not speak again."

"Your loving, dreadfully sad, Nick."

Marlowe got up. She wandered aimlessly around the house.

"You'd have done it again though, Nick. The only business you could have engaged in is dogfighting. I did the right thing! I *had* to do it—God help me, I'd do it again."

Marlowe started to cry about what she'd done, about the Nick she'd relied on and loved. The fact the Nick she knew compared to the real Nick were two different people was something that would take her a long time to sort out. Nick was a major part of her life that had just been cut cleanly out with a scalpel.

It was a little chilly that evening. Marlowe clicked on the gas fireplaces in the great room, dining room then finally in the study with Strider at her side. The glow and warmth of the flames always elevated her spirits. She looked at Strider's smiling face. Stroking his head and hoping he would understand how heartsick she was, her eyes rested on the UPS envelope. The other envelope inside. She'd forgotten it.

Looking at the clock, she knew she'd better go upstairs to start to get ready for her dinner with Adam at seven. She took the UPS envelope with her.

Sitting on the edge of her bed, she took out the second envelope. She noticed it was a different kind of envelope, a commercial envelope. She carefully read the return address, "Swiss Consolidated Bank." She took the letter out. She read it.

"Dear Ms. Marlowe Clark Evans,

Mr. Nicholas Gavin provided us with instructions in the event we were notified by him to do so, we were to send the sealed letter addressed to you from Mr. Gavin along with the information below. He provided us with that notification Monday morning. He did however ask us to make one request of you. He said you would understand. He said to tell no one about this account.

We have been directed to supply you with complete access to an account Mr. Gavin set up twenty-seven years ago in his and your name. Later he made deposits and gave us the discretionary power to invest the money for growth. As of Monday this account is solely in your name. We await your instructions as you wish to give them to us.

Current balance in the account: $10,890,643.23, US dollars.

Very truly yours,

Jonathan Wirley

Premier Bank of Switzerland"

Marlowe's eyes widened. "Eleven million. Eleven *million*! This isn't the money that was at Wynne, went to Scoto, then back at Wynne in Gwyn's Anglesey account. Nick said he had no more money, that the only money he had not tied up in his real estate was the money he had in his account with me. Why would he have set up an account with my name on it? He was just a friend of my mother and father. He didn't even have much money then. What am I going to do with it, Strider? I don't need anything, moreover you, you're the most spoiled dog in history. You don't need anything. Well maybe you could use a sister. We'll have to think about that one."

Her mind was racing. I've wanted to do something to safeguard, to help animals. I have this money to use. What can I do? This is my opportunity. I know how to run a business, I understand investments, I have the drive and dedication. To do what?

Marlowe sat deep in reflection, her mind going a mile a minute. Her eyes drifted toward her portraits of the whippet, boxer, bulldog, Weimaraner, Bernie, and setter. She noticed for the first time each of the dogs in the portraits was looking back directly at her as she sat on the bed. Looking at them, one after the other in quick succession, she realized at this moment they were indeed her Advisory Board. They were looking to her, waiting for her to make her decision. Then she knew. It came to her in a flash.

"Of course!" In excitement and delight, her forearms involuntarily crossed her heart. Her hands with fingers outstretched were reaching for the opposite shoulder. Her head slowly rocked back as far as it would go. "Yes. *Yes!*" The corners of her mouth were moving of their own volition up and wider into a joyous grin.

Running downstairs with Strider at her heels, she returned to the study. Then in a stentorian voice as she threw her arms wide as though seeing a long lost friend as she shouted, "I can do it! I *will* do it." As quickly as she had exploded in enthusiasm and exhilaration, she diffused.

Sitting down at her desk, she looked out the window. She said softly, choking up a little, "Finally."

She sat in silent relief. Marlowe had been looking for the one thing that would become the passion in her life. With her client account income plus now the three hundred million Baldridge money income coupled with Nick's money, she could sustain her new plan. She was quiet, controlled, determined, resolved. She got up to look at Strider.

In a measured voice, she announced, "This has been my true epiphany. I know what I will do. Oorah!"

Sitting down, she looked at the clock. Five thirty. She had a half hour to develop this idea before she had to get ready. Marlowe's ideas were flowing fast. She had to spew them out in Word immediately or she would forget them. Her fingers danced on the keyboard. It was not long before she had two pages of notes and ideas. It was all there.

Suddenly she saw the time on her computer. It was six ten. Adam was picking her up at seven. She had to shower, do her hair, at least try to look at least a little pretty. She already knew what she was going to wear. It was a little slinky black and gold dress with the plunging neckline, with, of course, the diamond pendant, the drop diamond earrings, silver slings, with her silver bag.

She quickly got Strider's food out of the refrigerator. She saw the chicken she had gotten to cook over the weekend. Marlowe planned to use it for quick dinners next week for herself. She closed the refrigerator door. That little smile she brought out on devious occasions began to reveal itself. The tension of getting ready in time melted away.

She fed Strider, opened a bottle of pinot noir, poured herself a glass, did a couple of things in the dining room, turned Beyoncé music on, and went upstairs. It was a cool evening. She clicked the bedroom fireplace on.

Hoping she would be ready in time, she began the transformation process.

Chapter 46

Marlowe was putting the finishing touches on her hair when the doorbell rang. Strider sprinted down the stairs three at a time as the advanced guard. It was seven o'clock. Adam was exactly on time. Marlowe took a long look at herself in the mirror. Perfect. She pranced down the stairs. Feeling somewhat bold perhaps rather frisky helped along by the pinot, she glanced left into the dining room, right into the great room, plus in the study to make sure the fireplaces were on. Grabbing the bottle of Johnnie Walker Black from the kitchen, she quickly made her way to the front door then opened it.

Here he is standing right here in all of his athletic sexiness, Marlowe observed. Brown hair lightly tossed to the side, the soft, barely crooked grin, the bright, steady blue eyes. Adam is the most patently handsome man I've ever seen. He's maintained the muscled, toned physique he must have had when he was the quarterback at Penn. Add to that he's insanely brilliant. Here he is standing at *my* doorway.

Strider stood wagging his tail at Adam and licking the hand that didn't have the exquisite spring bouquet in it.

"Good evening, Marlowe. You look beyond gorgeous. Where have you been hiding that dress?"

"Hi, Adam. Oh this? Just some old thing I had in the closet."

She'd truthfully called her new friend at Needless Markup the next day after the dinner with Adam at Penleigh. She was embarrassed to admit to herself she'd gone back. If there were to be another impromptu invitation, she wanted to be prepared. she even asked the saleswoman to overnight it—just in case. What was even worse was the knowledge that if anything at all were to develop with McDreamy, she'd be going back—a lot.

Adam grinned and asked, "Ready to go?"

Looking beyond him, Marlowe saw what apparently was Adam's other car, a dark blue Maserati convertible, in the driveway. She was tempted. She had, however, decided on other plans.

"Well, since I've been out so much and because Strider has been by himself all day, maybe we should stay in."

There, she got it out. The second she did, she was mortified. He's going to say *no*—he made reservations at Terracotta Rose. I should not be doing this. He just asked me out because of the other things that have happened. This is a courtesy date. This is inane, laughable really. You've really screwed up this time, Marlowe. Oh my gosh, did I put my earrings on? This dress is too tight, too *low*. He must be thinking I look desperate, or worse, I'm a hooker! This is going to be embarrassing—I'm embarrassed already, he's going to read it all. He'll say no. *Ouch!*

Adam's beautiful smile of perfect white teeth started to fade away. He just stood outside Marlowe's door looking at her. It seemed to Marlowe like a full century had passed before he looked away then down at the bottle of Johnnie Walker Marlowe now had a death grip on, white knuckles and all. He looked back up to Marlowe's face, which she was sure by now was hopelessly contorted in obvious agony, then over her shoulder to the warm look of Marlowe's great room with the fire glowing. Just as the smile had faded away, the engaging grin reappeared.

Marlowe caught herself. She managed to get a vestige of a smile. Maybe he feels sorry for me. Maybe he doesn't think I'm a hooker. Could the tide be turning? She couldn't tell for sure. She felt just maybe her eyes were at the early stages of converting to twinkling. Arriving unannounced a little adrenalin rush presented itself as she'd felt maybe a thousand years ago with Parker.

"Well, yes, for Strider's sake we should stay in, I agree." His eyes were sparkling.

Becoming giddy, Marlowe said to herself, look at those eyelashes! You don't suppose he has mascara on, do you? You don't suppose he's gay, do you? Oh, for heaven's sake, Marlowe, get a grip! Get control of yourself! Well maybe I don't want to be in control of myself. Well you should be for Pete's sake! Will you grow up?

Adam heard no response from Marlowe. He requested, "May we make an exchange?"

An exchange? What's he talking about? She stared at him, mute yet again. Marlowe, can you speak or is that completely out of your purview?

"I mean the flowers for the Johnnie Walker?"

They both laughed. For Marlowe the ice was broken. She wasn't a hooker, he wasn't gay.

"Want to help make dinner?" Marlowe asked, swapping the bottle for the flowers as she turned to go in toward the kitchen.

"Sure, what are we having? What shall I do?

"How about a couple of glasses of JW? Mine on the rocks, please."

"Excellent start!" Adam said, opening the Johnny Walker while Marlowe got two glasses from the cabinet.

"I have chicken so I was thinking of penne with chicken in a blush sauce with black olives, sautéed onions and capers. Maybe a romaine, tomato, mozzarella salad and Johnnie Walker for dessert."

"Fabulous choices except the dessert."

Marlowe was opening the refrigerator door. She stopped.

"Oh? What would you like instead?"

"JW over vanilla ice cream," Adam said, taking a healthy sip of scotch.

"You're such a teenager! We're not having that."

"Really?"

"Really," she said, with a straight face.

"Why, may I ask?" He looked like he might have asked an inappropriate question.

"Because I only have Rocky Road." Marlowe said, taking her own healthy sip.

"Love your style, Marlowe!" Adam said, clinking his glass with hers.

Marlowe focused on making the chicken and pasta. Adam, not surprisingly to Marlowe, produced a luscious salad. At the dinner table Adam asked, "Marlowe, have you ever considered getting another dog? I mean I think Strider would enjoy a companion to rough house with.

You'd like a second dog too, wouldn't you?"

"I can't believe you're saying that. I was thinking this afternoon about getting another dog." Marlowe looked at Strider, who took the opportunity to speak up with a single bark and a brisk tail wag.

"There's your answer!" said Adam, both chuckling at Strider, whose rapt attention was on this newcomer to the dining room table. He was counting on the distinct possibility existing of getting a piece of that chicken he'd smelled cooking.

"If you got him from the Greater Philadelphia Animal Shelter you could rescue a dog that no one else is going to want. You'd be saving a life."

"Molly!"

"Molly?"

"Molly is a brindle pitty at the Shelter! No one has taken her. I love that dog. Well I love all of them. Molly is special. I've been walking her every time I go down on Sundays. I can get Molly, Adam! I can go bright and early tomorrow morning even before they officially open for adoptions. This is exciting, Adam, thank you for suggesting this! I've been deliberating about getting her. I hadn't really focused on making the decision."

Raising his glass of pinot noir, Adam stood and toasted, "To Molly Evans!"

"To Molly Evans!" echoed Marlowe as she got to her feet. "We better eat or the penne will get cold!"

"Good idea!"

Sitting back down, Adam said, "Let me know when you're going. I'll go with you to help."

"Excellent! I can't wait. I want go first thing tomorrow."

"By the way, Marlowe, changing the subject, I know you heard about the background of Anglesey. Do you have any questions about it?"

"I understand how it functions, what its philosophy is, that there are many Angleseys around the country and internationally and how powerful the group is. I do understand all of that."

"I hope you'll believe me when I say your involvement in the beginning of the Nick situation was unfortunately the only way we could stop him."

"I have to say I didn't like it. I understand you had no alternatives available to you. You had to go to those lengths to stop the madness Nick was perpetrating. You did what you had to do."

"No sour feelings on your part, then?"

"None."

"Then will you accept an invitation to be a member of Anglesey?"

Marlowe looked at him. "You and the Angleseys, wherever they are, work, as you put it, alongside the law?"

"Yes, that's accurate."

"I've been thinking about this. I want to work *within* the law to fight those battles to achieve a community where people understand animals are living beings that deserve respect and nurture. For those who prefer to think differently, I want just punishment."

Adam looked intently at Marlowe. "Such an enormous undertaking. Think about it. Even the Shelter and the other rescues haven't been able to do it."

"While the cruelty agents at the various shelters do everything they can to stop animal cruelty, the workload is overwhelming them. They have too many cases to deal with. Too many people are still getting away with literally murdering animals. It needs to stop. Think of it this way. This is a country girl aphorism: 'don't let the horse out of the barn.' Meaning, once a horse is loose, out of his barn, you have the problem of chasing him down and putting him back in his stall. Wouldn't it be better if the horse never got out of the barn in the first place? Wouldn't it better if we could fix it so cruelty is stopped?"

"You're losing me, Marlowe."

"The American SPCA has expressed the situation succinctly. 'We are their voice.' We humans are the voice of the animals that literally have no understandable voice. I'm about to raise the decibel level of our collective voice so the horse isn't getting out of the barn. Simply put, we need to stop the cruelty."

She leaned forward, moving her empty dinner plate aside. She took a drink of wine.

"We need to do two things. First, we need the laws changed. I want significant sentences for those who commit any kind of cruelty. There are a number of influential, committed people already working on this. We need to help them. Legislators cannot turn their backs on this anymore. We, the public, will force them to confront this. Second, we need to stop animal cruelty."

Adam clearly was fascinated by Marlowe's ideas, her tenacity. "May I ask how you intend on doing this?"

"The Raspberry Initiative."

"The *Raspberry* Initiative? After my mother's dog?"

"One and the same. Raspberry will be the poster dog for this whole operation. 'The Raspberry Initiative, where animals thrive.' Everyone must know the story of Raspberry. You have those photos from the barn in Lancaster? The ones from your connection?"

"Yes, I still have them."

"No one will know whose dog Raspberry was. With Gwyn's consent, that graphic photograph will be cropped so the main thing in the photograph is Raspberry. Alongside that photo will be one of Raspberry before she was stolen. On the left, Raspberry full of life. On the right, Raspberry torn to shreds. Incredibly powerful image. When people all over the city see it, they'll be horrified. That's *exactly* what we want. For marketing? 'The Raspberry Initiative: Hurting animals? We're coming for you.'"

"How does that change anything?"

"This plan will work because almost everyone, more than 99.9 percent, of people don't abuse animals. That leaves the other few people who do. They're the ones we're after. How do we get them?" Marlowe leaned back. She smiled. "It's easy. We mobilize the 99.9 percent."

She went on to say the major reason animal cruelty continues is because most people are not really listening to what's going on in the news. If they've heard of it the story gets buried in their minds just like all of the local news of fires and shootings. Or, in the case of something in their neighborhood, they're afraid to say anything. The plan would be to wake up the ninety nine percent by creating a massive awareness campaign that makes people understand we have an appalling problem. If all these people have it driven home to them that animals just like their pets are being hurt and killed on a daily basis and that they themselves are the ones who have the power to stop it, they'll do it. They'll do it if they know how to do it, if it doesn't take too much time to do it.

"That's where The Raspberry Initiative comes in. The face of TRI will be five carefully selected, widely admired Philadelphia mega stars in their fields like the top athlete, The CEO of one of the largest publicly held companies. These types of people are leaders. The community looks up to them. People will listen and follow them. Standing together the mission of these five is getting the attention of those who are in their spheres of influence."

"I'm thinking about my contacts. I've a couple of friends who might be candidates for these. They must be just the right people."

"I have one too. Marty Highland the new CEO of the new public company JED. We were colleagues at Wynne. He'll stand with us, no problem."

"Adam, that's a great start. TRI itself will have a Board of Advisors performing the real behind the scenes work. My Rolling Hill Gang and my three new money clients will all want to be a part of this. No doubt Earl will be doing something in the muscle side. Not sure about Ashanti with all her work. I'm sure she'll be involved though too.

"They'll come up with groundbreaking, incisive campaign ideas to educate the public. Outrage will grow against anyone who is running a fight or abusing an animal. The story will be all over local newspapers, magazines, blogs, Facebook and Twitter, billboards and anything else we can think of. The first phase, education, is completed."

"The second phase is to provide a short phone number to call, just like the 911 number. Only the call goes to TRI. If an abuser is leaving a dog out without food in the cold, like Strider was, boom, their neighbor will report it to TRI. Dog fighters? Maybe the people who go want to be there. Suppose someone like a wife or girlfriend doesn't like it. They just have to pick up the phone to report it anonymously. TRI investigators will be dispatched immediately. It's the people themselves of Philadelphia including the suburbs who will confront animal abuse and animal fighting in the Philadelphia area. Details need to be ironed out. The important point is, hurt an animal? We're coming for you. We'll work hand in hand and coordinate with the Shelter on this."

"This all does sound like it will work. It's going to take money, lots of it. Where does that come from?"

Marlowe hesitated. She didn't want to divulge the initial source. She would only use some of it as seed money to begin the Initiative. The rest would go into a private endowment for TRI. "I think I can raise it."

"That's a risky bet."

"I'll do it. Think about the massive campaign. Everyone will learn about this effort. Think corporate marketing. How much will large companies give to be associated with something that should never ever have been needed. The PR for them would be huge. Wouldn't a major car company want to give vehicles? Wouldn't a gas company want to provide all of the gas? Wouldn't a phone company want to provide all the necessary telecommunications? And on and on for other companies. On the individual side, wouldn't a lot of people want to man the report phones? They'd be doing something that would have the immediate effect of saving animals' lives."

Adam looked at her face. Marlowe could see he was thinking he had seen that look before. It was at Grays Mill. It was when she confronted Nick. Then, like now, her mind was steeled. Nothing was going to dissuade her from doing what she knew in her heart was the exact fitting course of action.

"Mighty Marlowe," he said softly, looking at her across the table.

Smiling, she looked at him confidently, knowing she had a plan for her animals.

"Here's a question for you. Where are your headquarters going to be?"

"The only thing I've been thinking about is it should be away from the Center City area. The Raspberry Initiative should not interfere in the Shelter operation. We will be alongside, supporting and reinforcing them. We won't be big brother looking over their shoulders."

"Are you thinking like, say, an hour away?" Adam asked.

"That would be perfect."

"I may have something for you then."

"Okay, what are you thinking of?"

"Rocking Horse Downs."

"Nick's place?"

"Being the competent, curious lawyer I am, I checked a few things," Adam said with a grin, "You'll never guess what I found. About five years ago, Nick deeded Rocking Horse Downs to you. He continued to use the property, paid the taxes and all of the upkeep. He knew that if he died for some reason, it would be a gift to you. His daughter Julie didn't live in the area and you were his daughter too. There aren't even any close neighbors there who might wonder where Nick is. Besides, what Nick did with his property is none of their business. What do you think of that? We could make that the headquarters for TRI."

Marlowe didn't know whether to be shocked by the ownership of the farm or Adam's use of the word "we." She was speechless on both counts.

Bringing the conversation to a rapid halt, at that moment Strider barked to go out. Glancing at her watch, Marlowe said, "It's already nine thirty!"

"Okay if I take Strider out for a quick walk?"

"Great. I'll take the dishes into the kitchen."

As Adam and Strider went out the door, Marlowe's cell rang. She picked up quickly.

"A birdy told me you went out to dinner with a certain lawyer. How was it?"

"What? How do you know that? Adam must have told you, the creep."

"And well?"

"I can't talk, someone's here."

"*McDreamy*?"

"Bye, Skip!" Marlowe said, hanging up with a "gotcha-back" smile.

Five minutes later Strider trotted in, invigorated by the cool night air. Adam was behind him, his cheeks flushed.

Meeting them at the door, Marlowe said, "I've been thinking while you two were gone."

"Watch out, Strider, here it comes!"

"I have three questions for you."

"Shoot."

"First, would you like a B and B?

"Certainly, please."

Marlowe handed him the snifter she had already poured and had been holding behind her back.

"Second, do you know a good lawyer who can set TRI up as a non-profit, get the necessary insurance, get an accountant and the other legal beagle stuff? All pro bono, of course."

"You're looking at the sharpest lawyer in Philadelphia, even if I do say so myself. The answer is therefore a confirmed yes."

Marlowe looked at him with a silly grin, not saying anything.

"You said there was a third question."

Marlowe paused. While she explained The Raspberry Initiative, she was lucid. However, the Johnnie Walker and the wine had crept up on her. They may have been the teensy nudge she needed to say, "I, ah, I forgot I left the fireplace on upstairs. Want to go up and check on it with me to make sure it's okay?"

The words were no sooner out of her mouth than she saw Strider trotting up the stairs.

Without hesitation Adam answered, "Well, it looks like Strider's on the case and has it under control. On the other hand, he may need back up. So yes, Marlowe, glad to assist."

She started up the stairs. Adam was behind her. All she could think of was, "God's in his heaven, all's right with the world," like the time many years ago when she'd looked down the long, snow-covered driveway across from her bedroom in Somerbury.

At the top of the stairs, Adam lightly took her arm and turned her around. He said ever so tenderly, "You realize, Marlowe, the only reason I'm staying is so we can be up bright and early to get our Molly tomorrow morning."

There it was again, "our."

"Yes, of course, Adam. To get Molly."

His arms were around her waist. "If we're both getting Molly, if she's our dog, it might be prudent to work out the custody agreement and her legal residence before we get her."

"Well, that would be wise. In that case I have one more question for you."

"Yes?"

"Your house or mine, Adam?"

"Lady's choice, my mighty Marlowe," Adam whispered to her gently as he drew her toward him. "I know we've really only known each other for two weeks. I've already fallen in love with you. Ever since I met you at the concert months ago I've wanted to be with you."

She closed her eyes thinking, I guess that means Molly won't be Molly Evans. She'll be Molly Mansfield, how lovely....

For his part, Strider was already on the bed, looking for a double snuggle.